The Life of Peter and His Teachings

The Making of a Disciple

BOB CONWAY

Unless otherwise noted, Scripture is taken from the HOLY BIBLE, NEW INTERNATIONAL VERSION. Copyright © 1973, 1978, 1984 International Bible Society. Used by permission of Zondervan Bible Publishers.

Scripture quotations marked HCSB have been taken from the Holman Christian Standard Bible®, Copyright © 1999, 2000, 2002, 2003 by Holman Bible Publishers. Used by permission. Holman Christian Standard Bible®, Holman CSB® and HCSB® are federally registered trademarks of Holman Bible Publishers.

Scripture quoted by permission. Quotations designated (NET) are from the NET Bible® copyright © 1996-2006 by Biblical Studies Press, L.L.C. www.bible.org. All rights reserved.

Scripture quotations marked KJV are from 1969 Authorized Version, commonly known as the King James Version.

Scripture quotations marked LXXE are from the English translation of the Septuagint by Sir Lancelot Charles Lee Brenton (1807-1862) originally published in 1851.

Scripture quotations marked YLT have been taken from Young's Literal Translation.

ISBN-13: 978-1500893408
ISBN-10: 1500893404

CONTENTS

ACKNOWLEDGEMENTS

My deepest gratitude is expressed to my loving wife Lois of fifty years, who proof read the manuscript of this commentary. To close the book, I have included her poem, *Gone Fishing*, which she wrote when I was preaching on the miracles of Christ.

I am indebted to countless teachers and commentators of the Bible, who have enhanced my understanding of God's Word in concert with the Holy Spirit's insights.

The painting *Crucifixion* by Antony van Dyck, 1622.

The maps are public domain.

Photographs and charts are by the author.

Cover photograph by the author is of the Sea of Galilee from Capernaum, the hometown of Simon Peter.

PREFACE

This book probes the making of a disciple, in particular the Galilean fisherman Simon Peter, who Christ called to be a fisher of men—the first Christian evangelist. To wavering and inconsistent Peter, Christ Jesus entrusted the keys to the kingdom of heaven. Endowed with power from on high, this apostle became the unswerving pioneer of the church. From Jesus' first words to Simon Peter, *"Come, follow me"* to His final personal instructions to him, *"You must follow me,"* the apostle never failed his calling—even though he often stumbled—he would fulfill the Lord's commands to feed His sheep and care for them.

Simon Peter is one of the most colorful, intriguing and fascinating characters of the Bible. He is a man of paradoxes—bold, forthright, reckless, wavering and coward—a living picture of the doctrines of the sinful nature, the Spirit, and new birth. Except for spiritual insight and the grace of God, psychologists, psychiatrists and psychoanalysts would be hard-pressed to explain Simon Peter, the saint and sinner. The Bible alone answers the riddle of this man.

In the NIV, the names "Peter (Greek), "Simon" (Hebrew) and "Cephas" (Aramaic) occur over 240 times, indicating this disciple's tremendous contribution to the Christian faith. Simon Peter's actions and words before and after his conversion make a fascinating study of the making of a disciple.

A careful study of Scripture shows that Peter's brash and impulsive actions and words before his conversion are changed into brilliant and premeditated principles in his encounters, sermons and writings. The reader will find them recorded in the Gospels, Acts, Galatians and his two letters—First Peter and Second Peter.

Peter's first letter is filled with living hope and a call to holy living in spite of sufferings that precede glory. His second letter is filled with warnings and exhortations for those expecting the Second Coming of Christ. Combined, the two letters encourage a living faith, which is anchored in the certainty of the apostolic testimony and the divine inspiration of prophetic revelation. In light of our glorious future, we are encouraged to live a balanced life and grow in the grace and knowledge of our Lord Jesus Christ.

Upon completion of your study of *The Life and Teachings of Peter: The Making a Disciple* you should be able to:

1. Appreciate the privilege of being a disciple of Christ.

2. Know how to follow Christ in the way that pleases Him.

3. Share the Gospel effectively with others.

4. Explain what it means to be born again as well as other doctrines.

5. Know the steps to holy living, a living faith, and a living hope.

6. Understand the conflict between the Christian's sinful nature and the Spirit.

7. Discern and handle the schemes of the Devil.

8. Grasp the importance of the prophetic Scriptures in light of Christ's Second Coming.

9. Recognize the many reasons why people suffer.

10. Endure in the midst of suffering.

My prayer is that with a prepared mind for action you will be a faithful disciple, growing in the grace and knowledge of our Lord and Savior Jesus Christ.

Robert P. Conway

INTRODUCTION

The Greco-Roman World

To appreciate the life of Peter and his teachings, it is important to understand the conditions in the Greco-Roman World during the first century A.D. It was:

1. A world of plenty
2. A world of many religions
3. A world of many philosophies
4. A world of many crosscurrents
5. A world of peace
6. A world of one common language—Greek along with many other languages and dialects, especially Aramaic in Palestine
7. A world of servitude—over one half were servants (slaves)
8. A world of the privileged few—citizens with full rights
9. A world with one civil law, but allowing for religious laws and practices that did not conflict
10. A world of seeking a philosophical and spiritual foundation for the sake of political stability
11. A world amalgamation versus the Gospel

The Christian faith when it appeared had to compete with other movements offering salvation by:

1. Knowledge (The mystery religions, such as a Proto-Gnostism and Shamanism)
2. Ethics (Stoicism and Epicureanism)
3. Emperor Worship
4. Judaism Beliefs:
    a. One God
    b. One People
    c. One Law
        1. Decalogue
        2. Torah-Pentateuch

3. Prophets and Writings
4. Oral Law—Traditions the Fathers (Rabbis) had adapted the Law to changing conditions, thereby building a protective hedge around the Law.
d. Sects within Judaism:

1. *Pharisees* (about 6,000 "separated ones" along with Teachers of the Law (Scribes)

    a. Hillel School (liberal)
    b. Shammai School (conservative)

2. *Sadducees* (priestly aristocrats aligned with Herod and with the Teachers of the Law (Scribes))

3. *Essenes* (ascetic sect, which aspired to ideal purity and divine communion)

4. *Herodians* (Jewish political party, which supported the Herodian dynasty)

5. *Zealots* (hostile against the Romans and the aristocratic segments of Jewish society)

6. *God-fearers* (about 700,000 Gentile proselytes attracted by the purer faith and higher morality of the Jews so they worshiped Yahweh)

7. *Samaritans* (mixed race that hated Jews and they were hated by Jews. They worshiped Yahweh in the Temple on Mount Gerizim and only accepted the Pentateuch as Scripture)

8. *Aristocrats* (within Judaism, there was an aristocratic religious group, consisting chiefly of the families of the priesthood (Sadducees) and leading Rabbis as well as the Pharisees. Seventy belonged to the Sanhedrin plus the High Priest. However, the majority of the Palestinian Jews

were poor, but free! Some were farmers, shepherds, artisans, businesspersons, and others fishermen. The wealthy were considered blessed by God's favor, and therefore, righteous. Good works merited God's favor in the eyes of most Jews).

Israel's Annual Feasts

FEASTS	Month	Day	Corresponding Months
Passover, Unleavened Bread, First Fruits	Nisan	14-21	March-April
Pentecost (*Firstfruits, Weeks or Harvest*)	Sivan	6	May-June
Trumpets (*Rosh Hashanah—New Year*)	Tishri	1, 2	September-October
Day of Atonement (*Yom Kippur*)	Tishri	10	September-October
Tabernacles (*Booths* or *Ingathering*)	Tishri	15-22	September-October
Dedication (*Lights* or *Hanukkah*)	Kislev	25 (8 days)	November-December
Purim (*Lots*)	Adar	14, 15	February-March

The Synagogue

As a young boy, Simon would have been educated in the synagogue, where he would have learned the OT Scriptures, and Jewish traditions. During or after the Babylonian Exile, the Jews of the Diaspora developed the synagogue. During the Intertestamental period, the synagogues were Jewish community centers and places for Sabbath worship, study and prayer. In addition, the synagogues were educational centers for dispersed Judaism, usually under the guidance of the Pharisaic party, with a group of elders in charge, with one designated as "the ruler of the synagogue." The ruler would select persons to read the Scriptures and otherwise participate in the service. There was no resident priest or rabbi in charge of conducting the services.

By Peter's time, the synagogue was a well-established institution, not to be confused with the one Temple in Jerusalem, which was under the control of the priests. In larger cities, there were many synagogues. Jews of differing nationalistic backgrounds or interests would gravitate to one or another synagogue in accord with their preference (cf. Acts 6:9).

Synagogue at Capernaum

The Temple

The Temple in Jerusalem was the focal point of Jewish worship of Yahweh God. In 20/19 B.C., Herod the Great began a massive refurbishing of the Temple that had been rebuilt and dedicated by Zerubbabel in 516 B.C. It would be completed in A.D. 64. Under the Law, Jewish males were to make three annual pilgrimages to the central sanctuary on the feasts of Passover and Unleavened Bread, Pentecost and Tabernacles.

At the Temple, the rituals of daily or continual burnt offerings were presented to Yahweh God about 9:00 a.m. and every afternoon about 3:00 p.m. The burning of incense by priests chosen by lot along with prayers offered by the people accompanied the offerings. When two silver trumpets were blown, the people prostrated themselves in adoration and silent prayer (cf. Bruce M. Metzger, *The New Testament Its Background, Growth and Content*, 53-60).

The Second Temple played a prominent role in Christ's ministry and early church history. The early Christians assembled at the Temple for worship (Acts 2:46). Here Peter healed a man crippled from birth and preached an objectionable message to the Sanhedrin at Solomon's Colonnade (Acts 3:1-26). Most likely, his message on Pentecost was preached here also.

Model of the Second Temple in Jerusalem

The Land of Palestine

Geographically, Palestine was divided into five areas: Galilee, Perea and Judea along with two areas that were off-limits to the Jews—Decapolis with its ten Gentile cities and Samaria. The southern Jews of Judea looked down on the northern Jews of Galilee. Hence, the boundaries were social barriers as well as political.

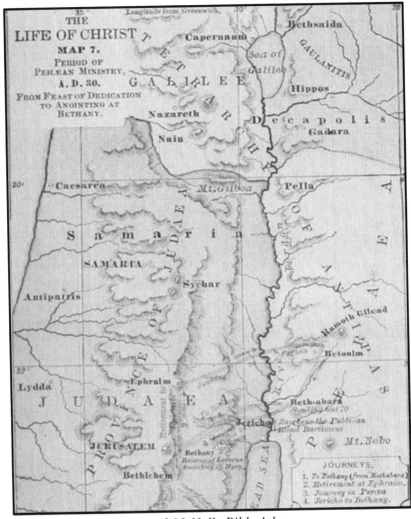

Rand-McNally Bible Atlas

Four major periods and geographical locations of Christ's ministry:

1. First Year of Obscurity — Mostly Around Judea
2. Second Year of Popularity — Greater Galilee
3. Third Year of Opposition — Galilee, Judea, Perea
4. Passion Week — Bethany, Jerusalem

The Two Covenants

Peter was a disciple of Christ under two covenants—the old and the new. Until Pentecost A.D. 33, he was an OT Israelite saint, who did not possess the indwelling power of the Holy Spirit. His obligation was to know the things revealed and follow the Law in the fear of Yahweh God.

> The secret things belong to the LORD our God, but the things revealed belong to us and to our children forever, that we may follow all the words of this law (Deuteronomy 29:29).

> Now all has been heard; here is the conclusion of the matter: Fear God and keep his commandments, for this is the whole duty of man (Ecclesiastes 12:13).

As a new disciple of Christ, the Law would begin to take on a deeper and fuller meaning as Jesus taught him that outward observance was insufficient for godliness since its commands, decrees and precepts were lived from the inside out.

> I will give you a new heart and put a new spirit in you; I will remove from you your heart of stone and give you a heart of flesh. And I will put my Spirit in you and move you to follow my decrees and be careful to keep my laws (Ezekiel 36:26-27).

With the giving of the Holy Spirit, who Jesus identified as the παράκλητος (*Parakletos*, counselor or helper), the disciples would receive power to love Him, obey His commands and be His witnesses to the world (John 14:15-21: Acts 1:8). Therefore, Peter's New Covenant discipleship commenced with his rebirth and renewal by the Holy Spirit.

> But when the kindness and love of God our Savior appeared, he saved us, not because of righteous things we had done, but because of his mercy. He saved us through the washing of rebirth and renewal by the Holy Spirit, whom he poured out on us generously through Jesus Christ our Savior, so that, having been justified by his grace, we might become heirs having the hope of eternal life. This is a trustworthy saying. And

I want you to stress these things, so that those who have trusted in God may be careful to devote themselves to doing what is good. These things are excellent and profitable for everyone (Titus 3:4-8).

A significant change took place in Peter on Pentecost, his shortcomings and failures as an Old Covenant saint would begin to diminish as New Covenant saint. Yes, struggles would continue but now he was capable of overcoming them. The contradictory life he lived before being born again as Simon would give way to Peter. Yet, he would always be Simon Peter.

The Two Natures

With rebirth and renewal, every Christian enters into a battle between the sinful nature (σάρξ *sarx*, flesh) and the Spirit.

> For the sinful nature desires what is contrary to the Spirit, and the Spirit what is contrary to the sinful nature. They are in conflict with each other, so that you do not do what you want (Galatians 5:17; cf. Romans 7:7-25).

The sinful nature can never become Spirit; therefore, the Spirit must overcome the flesh. In chapter 8 of Romans, Paul tells how to live according to the Spirit. Peter tells his readers how to be self-controlled in his first letter.

An examination of the life of Peter before and after conversion reveals the struggles Christians face in their two natures. True spiritual victory comes only by recognizing the enemy within us and preparing to overcome him. Peter recognized his own sinfulness, sought God's grace, confessed his sin, and appropriated the power of the Spirit through the renewal of his mind, prayer and a growing faith.

Peter's Personality

Peter was the most intriguing of the Twelve Apostles. His character comes across very clearly in the Gospels and Acts. On the positive side, Peter was eager, energetic and charming. On the negative side, especially before his conversion, he was impulsive, unstable, fickle, weak, cowardly, rash and inconsistent and had foot-and-mouth disease—speaking without thinking.

Peter was a take-charge guy, a natural born leader with strong convictions and a courageous outgoing personality. However, Peter failed his Master miserably in the hour of crisis, being the only disciple to deny Christ, yet was restored and recommissioned by Jesus after His resurrection.

He was the first Christian evangelist, and for a short time, he became the dauntless leader of the infant Church. He would remain firmly loyal to Christ being martyred for his enduring faith in Him.

He was the spokesman for the Twelve, speaking their thoughts and questions as well as his own. As their spokesman and a member of the inner circle along with James and John, Peter was privileged to witness the raising of Jairus' daughter, the Transfiguration, and our Lord's agony at the Garden of Gethsemane. He himself became a miracle worker, especially during the time portrayed in Acts.

When called by Christ, Peter was married, and later his wife accompanied him in his ministry (Mark 1:29-31; 1 Corinthians 9:5). In A.D. 69, Peter and his wife became martyrs after Emperor Nero burned Rome and accused the Christians of setting the fire. According to tradition, Peter had to watch as his wife was crucified, and afterwards he was crucified upside down because he had pled that he was not worthy to be crucified like his Lord.

Simon Peter was a man with many facets of character. His life can be approached from many angles. For instance, this disciple of Christ was:

1. Naturally impulsive (Matthew 14:28; 17:4; John 21:7)
2. Tenderhearted and affectionate (Matthew 26:75; John 13:9; 21:15-17)
3. Gifted with spiritual insight (John 6:68)
4. Yet sometimes slow to apprehend deeper truths (Matthew 15:15-16)
5. Courageous in his confession of faith in Christ (Acts 4:8-13)

6. Yet guilty of a most cowardly denial (Matthew 16:16; John 6:69; Mark 14:67-71)
7. Self-sacrificing, yet inclined towards self-seeking (Matthew 19:27)
8. Presumptuous (Matthew 16:22; John 13:8; 18:10)
9. Immovable in his convictions (Acts 4:19-20; 5:28-29, 40, 42)

Stages of Peter's Life

Peter's life can be divided into six stages:

1. Birth-29 A.D.   His Galilean childhood until called to leave fishing to become a disciple of Christ.

2. 29-33 A.D.   His training received from Christ for discipleship, apostleship, service and leadership.

3. 33-39 A.D.   His Jerusalem activities recorded in the early chapters of Acts. Peter was the catalyst of the primitive church until James succeeded to leadership. The stoning of Stephen signaled the outbreak of a general persecution against the Christian community at Jerusalem, and the great majority of the disciples fled from the city, scattering throughout Judea and Samaria.

4. 40-47 A.D.   His Palestinian (cities to the northwest of Jerusalem) ministries while he resided at Lydda and Joppa. He opened the doors of the kingdom of heaven to the Jews, the Samaritans and the Gentiles (Matthew 16:19; cf. Acts 2:14-41; 8:14-25; 10:1-48).

5. 48-61 A.D.   His Syrian ministries when Antioch was his center. During this time, he was accompanied by his wife on his evangelistic endeavors (1 Corinthians 9:5). He returned to Jerusalem for the first church council held in A.D. 50.

19

| 6. | 61-69 A.D. | His ministry in Rome, according to uniform church tradition, may have commenced before or shortly after Paul's release from his first imprisonment. In 69 A.D., Peter was martyred by crucifixion, as Christ prophesied. Early church tradition holds that Peter requested to be crucified upside down. |

The chronology of the life of Peter must be harmonized from the Gospels, Acts, Galatians and his two letters. The Gospel of Mark tends to show Peter in a less favorable light than Matthew, Luke and John, which is a true indication that Peter's pride was turned into humility.

According to ancient tradition and Eusebius (3.39), John Mark, whom Peter considered his son (1 Peter 5:13), traveled with him and interpreted his messages into Latin, which was the official language of the Roman Empire. The Septuagint, the Greek translation of the OT, was employed by Peter in his writings.

John Mark according to Papias (c. A.D. 140), who quotes an even earlier source as saying Mark was a close associate of Peter, from whom he received the tradition of things said and done by the Lord. Hence, Mark's Gospel of the life of Christ came about as a result of the preaching of Peter. Therefore, Peter is directly or indirectly accountable for three books of the NT.

PART I: THE LIFE OF PETER

Life of Peter Prior to His Call

Twice the Lord employed Peter's surname Ἰωνᾶς (*Ionas*), which has been translated "son of Jonah" (Matthew 16:17) or "of John" (John 21:15). Each occasion was significant. On the first, Jesus told Peter he was blessed since the Father had revealed His true identity to him. On the second, Jesus restored Peter to fellowship with Him. Thus, we know Peter's family name.

Peter's brother was Andrew and most likely younger. They were fishing partners with the sons of Zebedee, James and John (Luke 5:7, 10). Peter was married. Apparently, Andrew lived with Peter, his wife and mother-in-law (Matthew 8:14-15; Mark 1:16-18, 29; Luke 4:38).

In the eyes of the Sanhedrin, Peter was uneducated and ordinary (Acts 4:13). In today's terms, he had not been to college and had no academic or professional standing.

Peter might have heard about Jesus, who was from nearby Nazareth in Galilee, but paid little or no attention to early reports about Him.

Chronologically, we first encounter Peter on the pages of the Bible when Andrew brought his brother to Jesus.

> The first thing Andrew did was to find his brother Simon and tell him, "We have found the Messiah" (that is, the Christ). And he brought him to Jesus. Jesus looked at him and said, "You are Simon son of John. You will be called Cephas" (which, when translated, is Peter) (John 1:41-42).

Andrew is identified as a disciple of John. The brothers often traveled south to Jerusalem for one of the three required annual feasts—Passover and Unleavened Bread, Pentecost or Tabernacles. During one of these trips, Andrew had attached himself to the ministry of John, but apparently not Peter. Andrew took his brother to meet Jesus at Bethany beyond Jordan, where John the Baptist exercised his ministry.

Every disciple should follow Andrew's example: he sought his brother, told him about the Messiah and brought him to Jesus. If it were not for Andrew, Peter may never have known Christ or become His disciple. Andrew was emphatic, "We have found the Messiah." He was not alone; others were convinced that Jesus was the Anointed One. If we are to convince others, we must be convinced first.

Life of Peter from His Call to Pentecost

Christ's First Call of Peter

Peter received a triple call from the Master. The importance of Simon's first encounter with Christ should not be underestimated. Andrew heard John the Baptist declare that Jesus was "the Lamb of God," and he reasoned that Jesus was the long awaited Anointed One promised in the Scriptures. Bubbling over with the certainty of his discovery, Andrew had to tell his brother. His joy and excitement must have compelled Peter to go with his brother to determine if he was correct.

Thus, we are introduced to two brothers who were expecting the Scriptures to be fulfilled. They were watching, waiting and ready for "the faith and love that spring from the hope" (Colossians 1:5). It would be the dawning of a new life for the two brothers as they arrived in the presence of Jesus.

Before Simon could say a word, Jesus changed his name. From the time that Adam named the animals in Eden, the right to name had been the mark of dominion. As King Nebuchadnezzar changed the names of Daniel, Hananiah, Mishael and Azariah to Belteshazzar, Shadrach, Meshach, and Abednego, Simon's name from this day forward would be Cephas, translated Peter. The change of Simon's name was the first step of discipleship as Christ claimed His lordship over Simon.

"Simon" (σιμων) comes from the Hebrew שמעון (Shim`own) and "Peter" (πετρος Petros) is Greek for the Aramaic Κηφας (Kephas), which is translated "Cephas," meaning "rock" or "stone."

We might be tempted to call this name change the salvation or conversion of Peter, but we would be mistaken since that would occur several years later in a house in Jerusalem. Here Jesus was laying claim to Peter, who He would later call to be one of His disciples.

Peter and Andrew were fishermen by trade and in partnership with Zebedee and his two sons, James and John. Along with Philip, Peter and Andrew were from Bethsaida on the shore of the Sea of Galilee (John 1:44);

however, Peter and Andrew also had a house in Capernaum (Matthew 8:14; Mark 1:29).

The Sea of Galilee

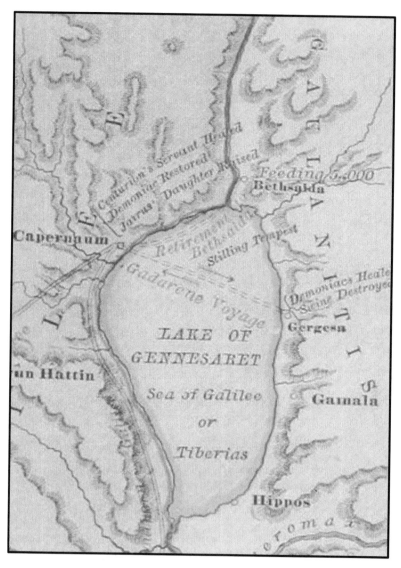

Sea of Galilee or Tiberias

Much of Christ's ministry took place on the shores and in the towns and cities surrounding the Sea of Galilee. Josephus says that some 330 fishing boats operated on the body of water in the first century. Most fishermen worked at night from small wooden boats, using three kinds of nets.

1. Cast Nets designed as a circle about twenty to twenty-five feet across were used by single fishermen. Lead sinkers on the edge

pulled it in down like a falling parachute, trapping fish between the net and the lake bottom (cf. Matthew 4:18).

2. Drop Nets were long and narrow like a fence with weights on the bottom and floats on the top. They were dropped over the side of the boat and pulled in from both sides of the boat turning the net into a U filled with fish.

3. Drag Nets were reinforced with three layers of netting, stretching almost two hundred yards between two boats. As fishermen rowed their boats forward, fish were trapped in the net (cf. John 21:8).

The hard work of fishing, requiring strength and stamina, was very profitable since the dry, salt or pickled fish were transported to distant markets. Even one of the gates of Jerusalem was called the fish gate (2 Chronicles 33:14; Nehemiah 3:3). Therefore, we are not surprised that Peter and Andrew owned a large home in Capernaum. Their partnership with James and John, the sons of Zebedee, was a lucrative enterprise (Luke 5:10). Seven of Christ's disciples were fishermen: Peter, Andrew, Philip, James, John, Thomas and Nathanael. Although not formerly trained by Rabbis, these men were savvy and wealthy business men, who would be trained and taught by the greatest Teacher of all. Jesus would make them His disciples!

It appears from the Gospels that Peter and Andrew did not immediately follow Jesus, who made a trip south and there gained more disciples than John the Baptist. At Jerusalem, Jesus cleared the Temple and Nicodemus visited Him at night. On His return north, he traveled through Samaria with some of His new followers and encountered a Samaritan woman at Jacob's well, resulting in many Samaritans believing in Him. Returning to Galilee, he preached, healed a government official's son and was rejected at Nazareth (John 2:12-4:54; Luke 4:16-30).

Christ's Second Call of Peter

Sometime after Andrew introduced Peter to Christ and His return to Galilee, Jesus called Peter, Andrew, James and John as the first of the Twelve Disciples.

As Jesus was walking beside the Sea of Galilee, he saw two brothers, Simon called Peter and his brother Andrew. They were casting a net into the lake, for they were fishermen. "Come, follow me," Jesus said, "and I will make you fishers of men." At once they left their nets and followed him.

Going on from there, he saw two other brothers, James son of Zebedee and his brother John. They were in a boat with their father Zebedee, preparing their nets. Jesus called them, and immediately they left the boat and their father and followed him (Matthew 4:18-22).

It was the practice of Jewish Rabbis to call disciples (students or learners) to follow them. Prior to this invitation, Jesus had been preaching in Galilee, "Repent, because the kingdom of God has come" (Matthew 4:17 HCSB), which confirmed Andrew's testimony that He was the Messiah. Therefore, the four fishermen's decision to follow Jesus was with eyes wide open—made in anticipation of the kingdom promised by the prophets.

Peter's third call came when Christ appointed the Twelve Disciples as His Apostles, who particularly were commissioned to be sent forth with the Gospel (Mark 3:13-19; Luke 6:12-16).

There is no indication in the Scriptures as to the age of the twelve disciples. It appears that John is the youngest and possibly Peter is the oldest; thus, assuming the role of leadership among them. On the other hand, Peter's brashness and boldness might have made him the natural leader regardless of age. Since Jesus may have been in His mid-thirties (cf. Luke 3:23; John 8:57), when He began His earthly ministry, we can assume that most of the disciples were younger.

When Simon reached the appropriate age, his father would have taught him his trade of fishing, which was big business. The Sea of Galilee had hundreds of species of fish and they were sent to markets throughout the region. To follow Jesus, these fishermen left behind much!

The majority of the Jews in Christ's time were intensely religious, even to the point of being fanatics. For instance, Peter refused several times to take and eat unclean foods when commanded by the Lord, even though Jesus had declared earlier that all foods are clean (cf. Acts 10:9-16; Mark 7:19).

Peter grew up in the district of Galilee (*Galil* in Hebrew means a region or encircled area) surrounded by Gentiles; hence, he would have spoken colloquial Greek, but his native tongue would have been Aramaic. The Galilean Jews spoke Aramaic, which was adopted by the Jews during the Babylonian captivity, and the apostle wrote in Greek, which is among the finest in the NT. Greek was the language of the civil literature in all countries, strongly opposed by the Pharisees, but employed by the Jews of the Diaspora (Dispersion), and used in the court of Herod and Pilate.

When Jesus said, "Come, follow me and I will make you fishers of men," He invited Peter and Andrew to be His disciples. He would teach them how to cast the divine net of the Gospel into the sea of humanity and catch men instead of fish. Their education would take over three years and require them to leave their world behind them. "At once they left their nets and followed Him." With the faith of Abraham, they would set out on a journey with the Messiah that will take them to places unknown.

Why did Jesus select fishermen for His first disciples? The qualities of a good fisherman are required to catch men—evangelize, such as patience to wait for the fish to take the bait, perseverance even when nothing is caught, courage to stay the course even in the midst of storms, an eye for the right moments to cast the line, the right bait for the fish, ability to stay out of sight and the wisdom to know when to move on to another spot. Jesus will take their knowledge and skills and sharpen them for His purpose and glory.

All four fishermen were from Bethsaida, on the west side of the Jordan River in Galilee, and were partners. James and John along with their father Zebedee were preparing nets. They also immediately left their work when called by Jesus. It was going to be the most wonderful opportunity and experience of a lifetime—to rub shoulders and elbows with the Son of God for over three years and to learn the mysteries of the kingdom from Him. They could not have imagined the joys and sorrows that lay before them.

Christ's call to long-term discipleship would be for life. The martyrdom of

James by Herod Agrippa I marked the beginning of a time of severe persecution in the early church (Acts 12:2). For a short time, John was banished by the Emperor to the island of Patmos and died of old age in Ephesus. According to tradition, Andrew was crucified at Patras in Achaea in Greece and Peter was crucified upside down in Rome.

Christ's call of these busy fishermen would have been inconvenient and involved a long-term commitment, investment of time and possessions; for example, their boats would be used by the Lord on several occasions. The call to discipleship comes at a high cost—the giving of one's life to Christ. Three years later, Jesus would teach the large crowds following Him:

If anyone comes to me and does not hate his father and mother, his wife and children, his brothers and sisters—yes, even his own life—he cannot be my disciple. And anyone who does not carry his cross and follow me cannot be my disciple.

Suppose one of you wants to build a tower. Will he not first sit down and estimate the cost to see if he has enough money to complete it? For if he lays the foundation and is not able to finish it, everyone who sees it will ridicule him, saying, 'This fellow began to build and was not able to finish.'

Or suppose a king is about to go to war against another king. Will he not first sit down and consider whether he is able with ten thousand men to oppose the one coming against him with twenty thousand? If he is not able, he will send a delegation while the other is still a long way off and will ask for terms of peace. In the same way, any of you who does not give up everything he has cannot be my disciple (Luke 14:26-33).

Christ's Bolstering Peter's Faith

Peter, Andrew, James and John had stepped out in faith to follow Jesus and become fishers of men. The next events would bolster their faith in Him.

Jesus went throughout Galilee, teaching in their synagogues, preaching

29

the good news of the kingdom, and healing every disease and sickness among the people. News about him spread all over Syria, and people brought to him all who were ill with various diseases, those suffering severe pain, the demon-possessed, those having seizures, and the paralyzed, and he healed them. Large crowds from Galilee, the Decapolis, Jerusalem, Judea and the region across the Jordan followed him (Matthew 4:23-25).

It would be a year of popularity for Christ and His disciples. The four disciples' faith had already been bolstered by several events. Jesus and His disciples had been invited to a wedding. At His mother's urging to do something about the wine being gone, Jesus turned six jars of water into wine.

This, the first of his miraculous signs, Jesus performed at Cana in Galilee. He thus revealed his glory, and his disciples put their faith in him (John 2:11).

They had witnessed Christ's power. It became obvious to the four fishermen that this was no ordinary man or rabbi they were following—His glory had been revealed and they put their faith in Him. They had recognized that He was the Messiah and now it had been confirmed. Interestingly, Moses had turned water into blood as an act of judgment. Jesus turned water into wine symbolic of joy. A new day was truly dawning and the disciples were to be partakers of it. Three and half years later, Jesus will present them with a cup of wine, symbolizing His blood in the New Covenant, which brings the joy of salvation. Christ is the Creator and Sustainer of life—the joy of living!

The second miracle had a personal significance for Peter.

When Jesus came into Peter's house, he saw Peter's mother-in-law lying in bed with a fever. He touched her hand and the fever left her, and she got up and began to wait on him (Matthew 8:14-15; cf. Mark 1:29-30; Luke 4:38).

Having manifested His compassion for Peter's mother-in-law, Jesus proceeded that evening to drive out the spirits of the demon-possessed brought to him and heal all the sick, manifesting His deity in Galilee.

Peter's House at Capernaum Covered by a Dome

The third miracle was a test of Peter, Andrew, James and John's new found faith. Had they recognized the deity of Jesus?

That day when evening came, he said to his disciples, "Let us go over to the other side." Leaving the crowd behind, they took him along, just as he was, in the boat. There were also other boats with him. A furious squall came up, and the waves broke over the boat, so that it was nearly swamped. Jesus was in the stern, sleeping on a cushion. The disciples woke him and said to him, "Teacher, don't you care if we drown?" He got up, rebuked the wind and said to the waves, "Quiet! Be still!" Then the wind died down and it was completely calm. He said to his disciples, "Why are you so afraid [δειλός *deilos*, fearful]? Do you still have no faith?" They were terrified [φοβέωρ μέγας *phobeo megas*, terrified greatly] and asked each other, "Who is this? Even the wind and the waves obey him!" (Mark 4:35-41; Matthew 8:23-27; Luke 8:22-25).

This event was premeditated and planned as the climax to His teaching on

31

the Kingdom of God. The boat was probably a small, open fishing craft, which sailed smoothly on the Sea of Galilee, which lies about 600 feet below sea level, near the northern end of the Jordan River. The snowcapped Mt. Hermon to the north rises to 9,200 feet so that strong northerly winds often plummet down the upper Jordan valley with great force. When the winds meet the warmer air over the Galilee basin, the intensity is increased. Hitting the cliff on the eastern shore, the winds swirl and twist, causing the water to churn violently with little warning.

Exhausted from a long day of teaching, the Creator slept in the stern as the storm howled and winds and waves were about to capsize the vessel. So great was the storm that the professional fishermen believed they were going to be drowned in the raging sea. In absolute desperation, they turned to this Carpenter from Nazareth, who lived twenty miles inland. Could he help? Would Jesus help as they woke Him? The way He helped was beyond their wildest expectations.

> He got up, rebuked the wind and said to the waves, "Quiet! Be still!" Then the wind died down and it was completely calm (Mark 4:39).

Creation responded to its Creator! Two miracles occurred at once as the wind and waves obeyed His powerful word. "Why are you so afraid? Do you still have no faith?"

We might want to scream, "You idiots, how dense can you be?" Of course, they are not different than everyone else who is rejecting Jesus as Lord. They were afraid to have childlike trust—to rely upon the comfort and confidence that should have been derived from the presence, promises, power and love of the Master.

Ironically, fear is like a coin. On one side, cowardly fear will keep a person out of the kingdom, dooming them to Hell.

> But the cowardly, the unbelieving, the vile, the murderers, the sexually immoral, those who practice magic arts, the idolaters and all liars—their

32

place will be in the fiery lake of burning sulfur. This is the second death (Revelation 21:8).

On the other side, fear is the doorway to wisdom and knowing the LORD.

The fear of the LORD is the beginning of wisdom, and knowledge of the Holy One is understanding (Proverbs 9:10).

An inkling, spark to discovery is kindled in their question, "Who is this? Even the wind and the waves obey him!" Their Teacher is greater by far than they had previously imagined. He exercises control not only over sickness and demons but even over wind and waves. The lesson of this day is over—the disciples have experienced for themselves the Power of God's Word.

The fourth miracle to bolster faith would not be as dramatic as the previous one, but would make an everlasting impression on the fishermen.

One day as Jesus was standing by the Lake of Gennesaret, with the people crowding around him and listening to the word of God, he saw at the water's edge two boats, left there by the fishermen, who were washing their nets. He got into one of the boats, the one belonging to Simon, and asked him to put out a little from shore. Then he sat down and taught the people from the boat.

When he had finished speaking, he said to Simon, "Put out into deep water, and let down the nets for a catch." Simon answered, "Master, we've worked hard all night and haven't caught anything. But because you say so, I will let down the nets" (Luke 5:1-5).

Now Carpenter from Nazareth was telling Simon Peter how to fish. He must have thought Jesus knew nothing about fishing. After sunrise, the fish would seek the cool deep waters of the lake and casting nets would yield nothing. Not one net, but all the washed nets. Yet, Simon obeyed the ridiculous command expecting nothing to happen.

When they had done so, they caught such a large number of fish that their nets began to break. So they signaled their partners in the other boat to come and help them, and they came and filled both boats so full that they began to sink (Luke 5:6-10a).

The catch of fish was astonishing, beyond Simon's wildest dreams and fear overwhelmed him.

When Simon Peter saw this, he fell at Jesus' knees and said, "Go away from me, Lord; I am a sinful man!" For he and all his companions were astonished at the catch of fish they had taken, and so were James and John, the sons of Zebedee, Simon's partners (Luke 5:10b).

Peter immediately realized he was in the presence of the Holy One exercising His divine power, and he was convicted with shame over his own sin. Here we find the first two steps of discipleship. First, Simon sees himself to be a sinner, who is not worthy of Christ. Second, he drops the title of "Master," and calls Him, "Lord." There can be no true discipleship until one realizes his own unworthiness and is willing to submit to the One who is worthy. After the stilling of the storm, Simon Peter asked, "What manner of man is this?" He was finding out!

Then Jesus said to Simon, "Don't be afraid; from now on you will catch men." So they pulled their boats up on shore, left everything and followed him (Luke 5:10b-11).

"Don't be afraid" for "the fear of the LORD is the beginning of wisdom and knowledge of the Holy One" (Proverbs 9:10). "From now on you will catch men."

At this juncture in our Lord's ministry, it is easy to discern two responses of those living in Israel to His presentation of Himself as Messiah. One response involved opposition and rejection; the other involved faith, not only in Israel, but in the surrounding nations. It was in this setting Christ chose the Twelve from among the multitude of His disciples in order to commission them as apostles. "Apostle" denotes one sent with authority.

The growing work demanded more organization and training. The Twelve were to be with Him at all times and in all places, companions in His travels, witnesses of all His work, students of His doctrines, fellow-laborers in His practical school of experience, and finally to become in reality as now in name, commissioned apostles of His worldwide campaign for the establishment of His church as witnesses and ambassadors. From this time on their training would occupy a large part of the time and attention of their Teacher.

Simon Peter most likely would have been with Jesus during the following events before being commissioned as one of Twelve Apostles.

Events Prior to Apostleship

Events	Matthew	Mark	Luke	John
Jesus heals a man with leprosy	8:1-4	1:40-45	5:12-16	
Jesus heals a paralyzed man	9:1-8	2:1-12	5:17-26	
Jesus calls Levi (Matthew) and eats with sinners at his house	9:9-13	2:13-17	5:27-32	
Religious leaders ask Jesus about fasting	9:14-17	2:18-22	5:33-39	
Jesus heals a lame man by the pool				5:1-18
Jesus claims to be God's Son and supports His claim				5:19-47
The disciples pick wheat on the Sabbath	12:1-8	2:23-28	6:1-5	
Jesus heals a man's hand on the Sabbath	12:9-14	3:1-6	6:6-11	
Large crowds follow Jesus	12:15-21	3:7-12		

Christ's Third Call of Peter
The Twelve Apostles

After spending the night prayer in to God, Jesus appointed twelve from His disciples to be apostles (Matthew 10:2-4; Mark 3:13-19: Luke 6:12-16).

Peter/Cephas (Simon)	Matthew (Levi)
Andrew	Thomas
James	James the Son of Alphaeus (James the Less)
John	Simon the Zealot (the Canaanaean)
Philip	Judas the brother of James (Thaddaeus)
Bartholomew (Nathanael)	Judas Iscariot (from Kerioth, Judea)

The number twelve (like the twelve sons of Jacob) suggests the nucleus of the new people of God—the Church. With one exception, the apostles were Galileans. This very fact put a stamp upon them from the beginning. All the prejudice that men of Judea held toward this northern community—due to difference in dialect, occupation, attitude toward pagan life and thought, failure to produce a prophet—meant that these disciples as well the Master they served were viewed with suspicion.

Mere numbers meant little to Jesus. What is needed is a devoted, intelligent following. Peter affirmed that the Twelve had made this commitment to Jesus (Luke 18:28).

Having left their various occupations, they were without a means of livelihood. But so was the Master. He had left the carpenter shop behind even as they had left their jobs. His example taught them to be grateful and content with such things as came to them for their daily provisions. They learned to count on the divine preservation of their lives so that future dangers would not shake their courage and faith. The Gospels reveal the ways Christ formally and informally trained the Twelve, who are usually identified as disciples or the Twelve.

Matthew 10:1-42 records that Jesus gave His twelve disciples authority to drive out evil spirits and to heal every disease and sickness along with sending them out with specific instructions concerning:

1. The mission field—the lost sheep of Israel, Matthew 10:5-6
2. The message—preach that the kingdom of heaven is near, 10:7
3. The work—heal the sick, raise the dead, cleanse leprosy, drive out demons, 10:8
4. The equipment—nothing but themselves, 10:9-10
5. The reception—give them your greeting and peace, 10:11-13
6. The rejection—leave them for judgment, 10:14-15
7. The opposition—shrewd as snakes and as innocent as doves, 10:16
8. The animosity—do not worry, the Spirit will speak through you, stand firm to the end and you will be saved, 10:17-23
9. The position—the disciple is not above his Master, 10:24-25
10. The light—fear not the darkness but preach upon the housetops, 10:26-27
11. The courage—fear not them which kill the body and confess Christ before men, 10:28-33
12. The sword—Christ came not to bring peace, but enmity in households, 10:34-36
13. The love for Christ—take up your cross and follow Me even to the point of losing your life so you will find it, 10:37-39
14. The rewards—reward for the smallest service to Christ's disciples, 10:40-42

Harmonies of the Gospels reveal that the Twelve would have been with Jesus for some one hundred fifty recorded events from the time He selected them to be apostles. It is beyond the scope of this work to cover each event that would have impacted Peter's life. Therefore, the reader should refer to the Harmony of the Gospels in the *Life Application Bible* or *A Harmony of the Gospels* by A. T. Robertson in *eSword* for a thorough study of all the events.

Christ's Inner Circle

Peter, James and John were the inner circle of Christ's twelve disciples. These three were the closest to Jesus and were alone with Him during at least four significant occasions.

1. The Raising of Jairus' Daughter, Matthew 19:18-26; Mark 5:35-43; Luke 8:49-56
2. The Transfiguration, Matthew 17:1-8; Mark 9:2-13; Luke 9:28-36
3. The Mount Olivet Discourse, Matthew 24:1-25:46; Mark 13:1-37; Luke 21:5-36
4. Jesus Praying in Gethsemane, Mark 14:32-42; Luke 22:39-41

Turning Point in Christ's Ministry

On his birthday, Herod Antipas beheaded John the Baptist (Matthew 14:1-12). John's disciples buried him and went and told Jesus, who withdrew by boat privately to the other side of the Sea Galilee. There were at least six reasons for His withdrawal.

1. Grieving the death of John the Baptist
2. Jealousy of Herod Antipas (cf. Matthew 14:13 with Mark 6:30)
3. The misguided zeal of followers who sought to force Jesus to accept the throne of Israel prematurely (cf., John 6:15)
4. The hostility of Jewish leaders (cf. Mark 7:1-23)
5. The disciples' need for rest after their grueling tours (cf. Mark 6:31)
6. The opportunity for more personalized training of the disciples

The accusation by the leaders was that Jesus was demon-possessed and the death of John the Baptist brought about a turning point in the life of Christ. Mark 6:31 marks a shift from a predominantly public ministry to a predominantly private one. The crowds, however, followed Him on foot from the towns. When Jesus landed and saw a large crowd, He had compassion on them and healed their sick. He would feed five thousand men besides women and children with five loaves of bread and two fish. There would be twelve basketfuls of leftovers. His miracles were not performed solely for authentication, but out of compassion also.

Christ's Deity Discovered by Peter

On the Sea of Galilee

Another miracle at sea revealing Christ's deity would take place following Christ's feeding of the five thousand besides women and children.

> Immediately Jesus made the disciples get into the boat and go on ahead of him to the other side, while he dismissed the crowd. After he had dismissed them, he went up on a mountainside by himself to pray. When evening came, he was there alone, but the boat was already a considerable distance from land, buffeted by the waves because the wind was against it (Matthew 14:22-24).

As before, the trial of a storm would test the disciples' faith. It was Jesus who sent them onto the sea. He prayed; the wind blew and waves buffed the boat. Did Jesus pray for the storm to arise? Are the disciples being tested like Abraham to see if they fear God (Genesis 22)? What would be their response?

> During the fourth watch of the night [between 3 a.m. and 6 a.m.] Jesus went out to them, walking on the lake. When the disciples saw him walking on the lake, they were terrified. "It's a ghost [φάντασμα *phantasma* phantom, apparition, imagination]," they said, and cried out in fear (Matthew 14:25-26).

Instead of thinking logically and spiritually, they were terrified by either superstition or imagination. They were to be courageous, not afraid. It appears that Peter jumped at the opportunity to display his courage to the others. A shortcoming that would persist until he denied Christ three times.

> But Jesus immediately said to them: "Take courage! It is I. Don't be afraid." "Lord, if it's you," Peter replied, "tell me to come to you on the water." "Come," he said. Then Peter got down out of the boat, walked on the water and came toward Jesus (Matthew 14:27-29).

Impulsive Peter would have drowned in the raging sea if he was seeing or hearing an apparition. Surely, this was not an act of unbelief and rashness

39

in him requiring a miracle for confirmation? He would have never stepped out of the boat fully clothed—swimming in the raging sea would have been impossible. So why did Peter make the request? Was it for the proof of Christ's identity, passion for Him, or protection from Him since the boat was in danger?

He asked two things. First, for the Lord to identify Himself, and second, for Him to perform a miracle—"tell me to come to you on the water." We can imagine what Peter was thinking as he stepped onto the waves—"Guys, look at my faith and courage, I am not afraid!"

Unwittingly, Peter had plunged himself into a test of faith and courage as he stepped out of the boat and began to walk on water, but not for long. While walking on the surface of the water, it appeared to be an act of great faith and courage by the apostle.

> But when he saw the wind, he was afraid and, beginning to sink, cried out, "Lord, save me!" Immediately Jesus reached out his hand and caught him. "You of little faith," he said, "why did you doubt?" (Matthew 14:30-31).

The bubble burst! His faith and courage sank with him into the sea. What might have been a boastful moment turned into an embarrassment with Jesus' rebuke.

We would think that Jesus would have commended Peter for his faith, but not so. He declared Peter to be of little faith and questioned his doubt. The disciple had taken his eyes off Jesus and focused on his perilous situation.

If we yearn for faith and courage in the midst of life's storms, "Let us fix our eyes on Jesus, the author and perfecter of our faith" (Hebrew 12:2). As soon as we take our eyes off the Lord, we will sink into despair and hopelessness.

The lessons are obvious. When our courage and faith begin to sink, we need to cry out, "Lord, save me!" Jesus will reach out his hand and catch us. Peter was sinking and desperately needed saving. Mankind is likewise sinking in sin and desperately needs saving. For some, it takes sinking in hopeless desperation until they will cry out, "Lord, save me!" The appropriate response to being saved is worship.

> And when they climbed into the boat, the wind died down. Then those who were in the boat worshiped him, saying, "Truly you are the Son of God" (Matthew 14:32-33).

For the second time, the disciples experienced the miracle of the stilling of a storm. This time, the Lord said nothing. As quickly as the storm came, it passed. After the first storm, they asked, "What manner of man is this?" They now knew the answer. For the first time, the disciples worshiped Jesus, affirming Him to be "the Son of God." The key verse of Scripture turn into a reality for the disciples.

> The fear of the LORD is the beginning of wisdom, and knowledge of the Holy One is understanding (Proverbs 9:10).

How often do believers ascribe their unpleasant experiences to some sinister power, when in reality they are the manifestations of Christ's loving care? Significantly, Jesus waited until the waves buffeted their boat until He came to them. Help and answers to the storms of life are seldom available at our beckoning, but at the Lord's will.

As days and nights passed in His presence, Peter and the disciples were learning that Jesus has authority over the destinies of all people. He has authority over all the supernatural world, including the evil world under the sway of Satan and his demonic fallen angels, and over the natural world.

A major topic of Peter's first letter is that suffering precedes glory. Through His words and their experiences with Him, Jesus taught His disciples that life is often stormy, painful, threatening and frightening. However no matter how great the trial, test or temptation, it takes place under His watchful eye and He has the authority and power to overcome it and provide a way out of it.

Ultimately, the outcome of the storms of this life are in His hands. Paul assured those with him in the midst of the storm, "So keep up your courage, men, for I have faith in God that it will happen just as he told me" (Acts

41

27:25). From his two dreams, Joseph knew the promises of God concerning his future. He trusted Yahweh when sold into slavery and falsely imprisoned. In his life, God overcame evil for good. Yet, not all storms of life turn out the way we desire. However, we can be assured the Lord knows about them and He allows them for His purposes and plans. Eventually, these disciples would die for their faith in Christ. Yet, this present life is not the end.

In his second letter, Peter assured his readers of their future when he wrote of the home of the righteous in a new heaven and new earth (2 Peter 3:10-13). Faith comes little by little, day by day! Peter learned that faith and discipleship is a growing process as seen in his last recorded words.

But grow in the grace and knowledge of our Lord and Savior Jesus Christ. To him be glory both now and forever! Amen (2 Peter 3:18).

At Capernaum

The next day, the crowd realized that Jesus went to Capernaum; they got into their boats, sought and found Him in the synagogue. When they asked Him, "What must we do to do the works God requires?" Jesus answered, "The work of God is this: to believe in the one he has sent." Then they asked Jesus to give them bread. Instead, He preached a sermon on being the Bread of Life and the necessity of eating His flesh and drinking His blood to have eternal life. On hearing it, many of His disciples said, "This is a hard teaching. Who can accept it?" (John 6:22-65).

From this time many of his disciples turned back and no longer followed him. "You do not want to leave too, do you?" Jesus asked the Twelve. Simon Peter answered him, "Lord, to whom shall we go? You have the words of eternal life. We believe and know that you are the Holy One of God" (John 6:66-69).

Jesus had declared that He must fill their life spiritually as physical nourishment does if they were to have eternal life. Although not fully understanding all the implications of His sermon, Simon Peter, spoke on behalf of the Twelve. They believed Jesus was the Holy One of God and in

Him were the words of eternal life. Peter knows that the words of Jesus are more than mere sounds or dead utterances—they are words of life. There is no other person or source of eternal life except Jesus. As the disciples will learn, imbedded in them is the deeper significance of the Lord's Supper or Holy Communion—His death for their sins and resurrection to new life.

We should expect some of the doctrines of the Bible will be mysterious and difficult to understand; however, they should never be rejected because they are too hard. The Gospel is offensive to human pride and self-sufficiency and there is great danger of apostasy when the Word of God is not taken to heart. The very fact that Jesus spoke of death being the way to life was not acceptable to many of His disciples, including one of the Twelve.

> Then Jesus replied, "Have I not chosen you, the Twelve? Yet one of you is a Devil!" (He meant Judas, the son of Simon Iscariot, who, though one of the Twelve, was later to betray him) (John 6:70-71).

Clearly, Jesus never let the disciples know who would betray him. If Peter would have known it was Judas Iscariot, with his impulsive temperament, he might have killed him at that very moment.

At Caesarea Philippi

As with the previous test of faith on the Sea of Galilee, Jesus performed a miracle of feeding crowds. This time He fed four thousand men besides women and children with seven loaves of bread and a few fish and the disciples gathered seven full baskets instead of twelve. Jesus got into the boat with His disciples to depart for the other side of the sea. However, the disciples forgot to take bread with them. He used their forgetfulness to teach them about their little faith. "Then they understood that he was not telling them to guard against the yeast used in bread, but against the teaching of the Pharisees and Sadducees" (Matthew 16:5-12). At last, they were beginning to possess a degree of spiritual insight.

From time to time, all students are given tests by their teachers to find out how they are progressing; it is examination time for the disciples.

When Jesus came to the region of Caesarea Philippi, he asked his disciples, "Who do people say the Son of Man is?" (Matthew 16:13).

Christ's question contained the answer to His question. Jesus used the title "The Son of Man" for Himself some eighty times in the Gospels. This title was rooted in the Prophet Daniel's vision of His deity.

> In my vision at night I looked, and there before me was one like a son of man, coming with the clouds of heaven. He approached the Ancient of Days and was led into his presence. He was given authority, glory and sovereign power; all peoples, nations and men of every language worshiped him. His dominion is an everlasting dominion that will not pass away, and his kingdom is one that will never be destroyed (Daniel 7:13-14).

Three titles associated with Christ's sonship appear in the Gospels:

1. Son of David, which points to His earthly throne
2. Son of God, which points to His eternity
3. Son of Man, which points to His relationship to the human race

Interestingly, Jesus did not refer directly to Himself by the first two titles. However, He had to become man in order to fulfill all three titles. Through the Son of Man's incarnation, the Second Person of the Trinity was able to fulfill the threefold role of the Kinsman-Redeemer. *First*, the kinsman-redeemer redeemed the land, which his brother had wasted away (Leviticus 25:25). *Second*, he redeemed his brother from his voluntary slavery (Leviticus 25:48). *Third*, he became the avenger of the blood of his brother, who was wrongly slain (Numbers 35:27).

It is very clear that Jesus took this title from Daniel 7:13 and applied it to Himself (cf. Matthew 24:30; 26:64; Mark 13:26).

"Like a son of man" refers to Christ's incarnate nature. He is a true man as well as true God—100% man and 100% God. Through incarnation by virgin birth, He became the seed of the woman without being a son of man. The article ("the") as used in the title by Jesus points to the one Daniel saw in his night vision.

"The one like a son of man" is appointed absolute Lord and Judge by virtue of His propitiatory ministry as God incarnate. He is King of kings and Lord of lords; hence, *The Great Commission* begins by echoing Daniel 7:14.

> Then Jesus came to them and said, "All authority in heaven and on earth has been given to me (Matthew 28:18).

Christ does not usurp authority; He does not take honor for Himself; He receives the kingdom from God the Father—the Ancient of Days (Hebrews 1:1-14; Philippians 2:5-11).

There are four proofs that the one identified as "a Son of Man" is deity in Daniel 7:13-14.

1. He was given what God will not give away—authority, glory and sovereign power.
2. He is worshiped—only God is to be worshiped.
3. He is given an everlasting kingdom—only God's kingdom is everlasting.
4. He is like a son of man—only through incarnation can "one be like a son of man" and not actually be so.

When Jesus called Himself "the Son of Man," every Jew should have known that He was referring to Daniel's prophecy. The Sanhedrin understood that this title denoted His deity; note their reaction.

> Again the high priest asked him, "Are you the Christ, the Son of the Blessed One?" "I am," said Jesus. "And you will see the Son of Man sitting at the right hand of the Mighty One and coming on the clouds of heaven." The high priest tore his clothes. "Why do we need any more witnesses?" he asked. "You have heard the blasphemy. What do you think?" They all condemned him as worthy of death (Mark 14:61-64).

The city of Caesarea Philippi, in northern Galilee was located about thirty miles from the Sea of Galilee on the south slopes of Mt. Hermon, near the primary source of the Jordan River. It was an ancient site of Baal worship.

With the coming of the Greeks, it became a cult center for the god Pan, after which city became known as Paneas. According to pagan mythology Pan was born in a nearby cave. Caesar Augustus gave the town to Herod the Great, who built a temple to Pan in honor of the emperor.

Surrounded by idolatry and political power, what would be the disciples' answer?

They replied, "Some say John the Baptist; others say Elijah; and still others, Jeremiah or one of the prophets."

Christ's question was asked at an appropriate place.

Cave of Pan at Caesarea Philippi

Obviously, they had their ears to the ground. They knew what people were saying about Jesus. Incredibly, some recognized Jesus' miraculous power was unexplainable so they supposed Jesus was a resurrected John the Baptist, Jeremiah or the prophets. Perhaps some saw in Jesus something of the character of John the Baptist, while others saw the fire and intensity of Elijah and still others the lament and grief of Jeremiah.

Even today, people go to great lengths to explain Jesus away. For example, the Muslims recognize Jesus as a great teacher and prophet, but deny His deity. The disciples were not to be persuaded by what people think and say. They had been with Him for two and one-half years; surely they knew the answer!

"But what about you?" he asked. "Who do you say I am?"

Simon Peter answered, "You are the Christ, the Son of the living God" (Matthew 16:14-16).

The apostle hit the nail on the head with his great confession! However, His answer did not come from Daniel's vision or Psalm 2, where the conversation between the First and Second Persons of the Trinity reveals that the Anointed One (Messiah) is the Son of the living God. Amazingly, Jesus said that Simon Peter would not have known his answer without help from above.

Jesus replied, "Blessed are you, Simon son of Jonah, for this was not revealed to you by man, but by my Father in heaven (Matthew 16:17).

This is an extremely important lesson for the disciples to learn from the test. Without spiritual assistance, it is impossible to recognize the Person of the Messiah. Jesus had already taught them, "No one can come to me unless the Father who sent me draws him" (John 6:44). After Pentecost, this drawing will be done by the Holy Spirit through Christ's disciples. The making of a disciple is not simply a human endeavor. In this present age, no one can be a disciple of Christ without recognizing His deity!

Upon their first meeting Jesus, Andrew had enthusiastically proclaimed Jesus to be the Messiah and Nathaniel had called Him "the Son of God" and the "King of Israel" (John 1:41, 49). The truth of His identity was head knowledge that had not penetrated their hearts since they were not finally and completely convinced of His deity. In their presence, Jesus had made many claims about His deity, such as fulfilling the law and prophets (Matthew 5:17), having the authority to forgive sins on the earth (Matthew 9:6), and being the Lord of the Sabbath (Matthew 12:8).

Consequently, faith comes from hearing the message, and the message is heard through the word of Christ (Romans 10:17).

Jesus taught in the *Parable of the Sower, Seed and Soils* (Matthew 13:4-9, 18-23) that the sowing of the message of the kingdom can be snatched away by the evil one, wither away under persecution and trouble, be choked by material possessions or produce fruit, yielding a hundred, sixty or thirty times what is sown. An obvious lesson is that it takes time for the Word of Christ to produce fruit. Jesus has been patiently sowing the Word into the hearts of His disciples and it is taking root in all but one of the Twelve. The evil one will snatch it from Judas Iscariot because his heart is set on material possessions.

Opposition and obstacles to the Gospel of the Kingdom is to be expected. Yet, based on Peter's great confession of faith, Jesus made several blessings or predictions.

> And I tell you that you are Peter, and on this rock I will build my church, and the gates of Hades will not overcome it (Matthew 16:18).

Some have interpreted "this rock" to mean that Peter is the foundation of the Church. This contradicts the apostle own understanding in 1 Peter 2:4-8. Thus, there is a word play in the Greek—"you are Peter (*petos,* a little stone) and on this rock (*petra,* a massive rock) I will build my church." In the Parable of the Wise and Foolish Builders, Jesus is the rock on which the wise man builds his house—life and His words are the foundation (Matthew 7:24-27; Isaiah 28:16; Psalm 118:22).

> Jesus said to them, "Have you never read in the Scriptures: "'The stone the builders rejected has become the capstone; the Lord has done this, and it is marvelous in our eyes'? (Matthew 21:42).

God's Temple—the Church—is built on Christ, not Peter.

> Consequently, you are no longer foreigners and aliens, but fellow citizens with God's people and members of God's household, built on the foundation of the apostles and prophets, with Christ Jesus himself as the chief cornerstone. In him the whole building is joined together

and rises to become a holy temple in the Lord. And in him you too are being built together to become a dwelling in which God lives by his Spirit (Ephesians 2:19-22).

Therefore, the rock is Peter's confession that Jesus is the Messiah and the Son of the Living God; therefore, He built His church on Himself.

At this time, neither Peter nor the others grasped the meaning of "I will build my church (ἐκκλησία, called-out assembly)." This term was applied to the assembly of Greek citizens that helped to govern a city or district (Acts 19:32, 39, 41). The Septuagint translated it as for religious assemblies (Deuteronomy 31:30). Jesus employed *ekklesia* for the assembly that would be called-out of the nations; hence the church.

Prior to Christ's ascension into heaven, the disciples' burning question was "Lord, are you at this time going to restore the kingdom to Israel?" They still did not understand Christ's *Parable of the Tenants*.

> But when the tenants saw the son, they said to each other, 'This is the heir. Come, let's kill him and take his inheritance.' So they took him and threw him out of the vineyard and killed him (Matthew 21:38-39).

> Therefore I tell you that the kingdom of God will be taken away from you [Israel] and given to a people [the church] who will produce its fruit (Matthew 21:43).

Following Peter's confession and His predictions, Jesus would teach in certain terms for the first time of His rejection by Israel.

The next prediction, "the gates of Hades will not overcome it," has been misunderstood and erroneously used by many.

First, Gates are entrances and departure places of cities and towns. Jesus is speaking of entering and departing Hades, not Hell which is presently unoccupied and will be so until the Beast and the False Prophet are thrown alive into it (Revelation 19:20).

Second, Hades is not the lake of fire—Hell. It is Sheol of the OT, the place of the departed spirit and soul. To understand what Jesus is predicting can be discovered at the Cross.

Third, the forces of evil have prevailed in the world against the church throughout history, which is predicted by Christ in the seven letters to the churches of Asia Minor (Revelation 2-3).

Obviously, Christ died two deaths on the Cross. First, He experienced spiritual death during the three hours of darkness, when Jesus cried out in a loud voice, *"Eloi, Eloi, lama sabachthani?"*—which means, "My God, my God, why have you forsaken me?" (Matthew 27:46). He experienced physical death—"And when Jesus had cried out again in a loud voice, he gave up his spirit" (Matthew 27:50). So where did His spirit go? Not to the Father since on resurrection morning, Jesus said to Mary, "Do not hold on to me, for I have not yet returned to the Father" (John 20:17).

> Then he said, "Jesus, remember me when you come into your kingdom." Jesus answered him, "I tell you the truth, today you will be with me in paradise." (Luke 23:42-43).

His spirit did not linger in limbo awaiting the resurrection of His body, it went somewhere and that somewhere is Hades until being reunited with His resurrection body on the third day.

> One day the poor man died and was carried away by the angels to Abraham's side. The rich man also died and was buried. And being in torment in Hades, he looked up and saw Abraham a long way off, with Lazarus at his side (Luke 16:22-23 HCSB).

Abraham's side in Hades is called Paradise. Another difficult passage to interpret is Ephesians 4:7-10, which seems to indicate that with His ascension, Jesus took Paradise (Abraham's side) to heaven with Him.

50

In 2 Corinthians 12:1-4, Paul wrote about being caught up to the third heaven—the Paradise of God and said, "To be absent from the body yet we are confident and satisfied to be out of the body and at home with the Lord" (2 Corinthians 4:8 (HCSB).

The chart below shows the souls and spirits of those in Paradise were taken to heaven at Christ's ascension and the souls, the souls and spirits of NT saints go to heaven at death awaiting the Rapture when the dead in Christ will receive their resurrected bodies and those who are alive will be changed in a twinkling of an eye (1 Thessalonians 4:13-18; 1 Corinthians 15:51-54). This is the hope of every disciple of Christ.

THE HOLDING PLACES OF FALLEN ANGELS AND MANKIND

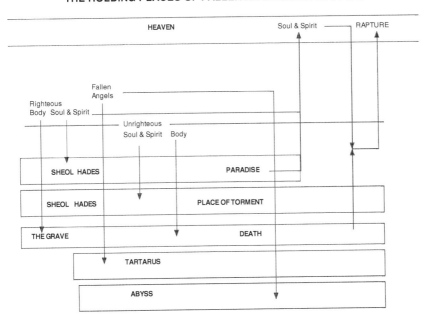

With two more passages from the book of Revelation, we can understand why the gates of Hades will not overcome the church.

> Do not be afraid. I am the First and the Last. I am the Living One; I was dead, and behold I am alive for ever and ever! And I hold the keys of death and Hades (Revelation 1:17-18).

51

The sea gave up the dead that were in it, and death and Hades gave up the dead that were in them, and each person was judged according to what he had done. Then death and Hades were thrown into the lake of fire. The lake of fire is the second death. If anyone's name was not found written in the book of life, he was thrown into the lake of fire (Revelation 20:13-15).

Not one born again believer of Christ's church will ever entered into Hades!

The next prediction given to Peter.

I will give you the keys of the kingdom of heaven; whatever you bind on earth will be bound in heaven, and whatever you loose on earth will be loosed in heaven (Matthew 16:19).

Peter will have the leading role in opening God's kingdom:

1. To the nation of Israel, Acts 2:36-42
2. To the Samaritans, Acts 8:14-17
3. To the Gentiles, Acts 10-11

If Peter's possession of the key is closely tied to his further role of "locking" and "opening," it may have something to do with church leadership and church discipline. In addition, "binding and loosing" can refer to "forbidding or permitting." Certainly, Peter will possess awesome responsibility in the formation of the Church, which Christ later gives to the other disciples in Matthew 18:15-20. In verse 19, the Greek verbs indicate that the church does do not get man's will done on earth, but it obeys God's will on earth.

And whatever you bind on earth [forbid to be done], shall have been already bound . . . in heaven; and whatever you loose on earth [permit to be done], shall already been loosed in heaven (Matthew 18:19, *Expanded Translation* by Kenneth S. Wuest).

Jesus will build His church; yet it will be accomplished through the ministry of His disciples and the Holy Spirit. Though Christ's disciples will face obstacles and persecutions throughout the Church Age, the building of it is certain. Whenever believers are committed to the kingdom and righteousness the Lord builds His church.

Unexpectedly, "He warned his disciples not to tell anyone that he was the Christ" (Matthew 16:20). Why? The Gospel was not complete. Paul sheds some light on His command.

> That power is like the working of his mighty strength, which he exerted in Christ when he raised him from the dead and seated him at his right hand in the heavenly realms, far above all rule and authority, power and dominion, and every title that can be given, not only in the present age but also in the one to come. And God placed all things under his feet and appointed him to be head over everything for the church, which is his body, the fullness of him who fills everything in every way (Ephesians 1:19-23).

It was not yet the time for the church. His death, resurrection and ascension would be the ultimate proof of His identity (cf. Matthew 17:9). When the time came, Jesus would affirm that He is the Messiah and Son of God before the Sanhedrin.

> The high priest said to him, "I charge you under oath by the living God: Tell us if you are the Christ, the Son of God." "Yes, it is as you say," Jesus replied. "But I say to all of you: In the future you will see the Son of Man sitting at the right hand of the Mighty One and coming on the clouds of heaven" (Matthew 26:63-64).

Christ Rebukes Peter

Though Peter would have understood few details about Christ's predictions relating to him, his pride may have soared to the heights. If so, it would soon be brought back to earth. Having declared His Person, Jesus now clearly declares His mission for the first time.

> From that time on Jesus began to explain to his disciples that he must go to Jerusalem and suffer many things at the hands of the elders, chief priests and teachers of the law, and that he must be killed and on the third day be raised to life (Mathew 16:21).

Jesus was on a schedule to fulfill God's set purpose and foreknowledge, which Peter would not grasp until Pentecost (Acts 2:22-24).

It was now apparent that the Twelve were not following Jesus for all the right reasons. Like the crowds, their idea of the Messiah was not spiritual but political. They believed that Jesus was the Davidic King, who would overthrow the Roman rule in Israel and establish the kingdom. Peter's great confession had reinforced this hope only to be crushed by Jesus' explanation.

> Peter took him aside and began to rebuke him. "Never, Lord!" he said. "This shall never happen to you!" Jesus turned and said to Peter, "Get behind me, Satan! You are a stumbling block to me; you do not have in mind the things of God, but the things of men" (Matthew 16:22-23).

It is clear from Peter's rebuke that his perspective of the divine Messiah did not fit his beliefs. Throughout the Church Age, many have been invited to come to Jesus for the wrong reasons, such as promised good health, wealth, and power only to discover the opposite once they trust in Him. It is easy to accept the Lord's blessings, but His testings are not easy to take. Prosperity and health as part of God's plan are welcomed, but hardship and sickness are another story.

Christ rebukes Peter's rebuke! The word "rebuke" refers to an authoritative judgment. Peter is trying to tell the Messiah what to do!

Calling Peter "Satan" (adversary) should have shaken Peter's inner being since Satan can never be a follower of Christ because of his pride; consequently, Satan would never submit to Him.

Origen suggested that Jesus was saying, "Peter, your place is behind me, not in front of me. It is your place to follow me in the way I choose, not to try to lead me in the way you would like me to go." If so, some of the sting of Jesus' rebuke is lessened. Peter might be mistaken and might fail and might sin, but for him there was always the challenge and opportunity to follow instead of trying to lead. Clearly, Peter is being taught two lessons: pride goes before a fall and to be a great leader one must be a follower.

At this moment, however, Peter was a stumbling block to Jesus since he does not have in mind the things of God, but the things of men. One of Peter's many faults was his tendency to argue with the Word of God. Satan agreed with Peter since he used the same approach to tempt Jesus (Matthew 4:8-10). If Jesus listened to Peter and Satan, His mission would end in failure.

Describing Peter and his own arrival at the empty tomb, John wrote, "They still did not understand from Scripture that Jesus had to rise from the dead" (John 20:9). The disciples were not yet thinking like God thinks. Like Peter, they were placing their own will before Christ's. So Jesus used Peter's rebuke as a teaching moment on true discipleship, which entails self-denial, taking up one's cross and following Him.

> Then Jesus said to his disciples, "If anyone would come after me, he must deny himself and take up his cross and follow me. For whoever wants to save his life will lose it, but whoever loses his life for me will find it. What good will it be for a man if he gains the whole world, yet forfeits his soul? Or what can a man give in exchange for his soul? For the Son of Man is going to come in his Father's glory with his angels, and then he will reward each person according to what he has done. I tell you the truth, some who are standing here will not taste death before they see the Son of Man coming in his kingdom (Matthew 16:24-28)

Not grasping Christ's mission, the disciples were seeking worldly gains at the risk of forfeiting their souls. There would be rewards for those who follow Him but not until Christ returns in His Father's glory with His angels.

We tend to look at the Cross and see God's love and sacrifice but in the first century crucifixion on a cross was a horrible means of capital punishment. Taking up one's cross meant enduring shame, embarrassment, reproach, rejection, persecution, and even martyrdom.

The paradox of discipleship is winning by losing. Suffering precedes glory if the disciples are going to continue to follow Him. Self-esteem and self-love are "another gospel" that appeals to man's natural egotism and vanity instead of the Gospel requiring repentance, humbleness and brokenness that calls for one to lose his life in order to save it.

Jesus told them plainly that He would die, rise and come again but it went in one ear and out the other. However, Peter would eventually understand Jesus' threefold teaching of that day: (1) the Messiah must suffer, die and rise; (2) His disciples must be prepared to participate in His suffering, death and resurrection; and (3) His and their suffering must be viewed in the backdrop of ultimate and certain glory.

Christ's Transfiguration Witnessed by Peter

Matthew 17:1-8, Mark 9:2-13 and Luke 9:28-36 record a preview of this certain glory at the transfiguration of Jesus. It was about a week after Peter's confession and rebuke that Jesus led Peter, James and John up a high mountain, which could have been Mount Hermon, a position of grandeur and beauty overlooking Palestine. Mount Hermon stood high above the vicinity of Caesarea Philippi.

The tradition from the time of Jerome identifies the mountain with Tabor in Galilee; however there was a fortress on its summit at this time, making it an unlikely location.

Others think the mountain was Jebel in Upper Galilee, the highest elevation in that entire region, rising four thousand feet above the Mediterranean Sea. It provided a beautiful view in all directions and it was a relatively short distance to Capernaum, which Jesus seemed to have reached soon afterward (Matthew 17:24; Mark 9:28, 33).

As Jesus was praying, the appearance of his face shone like the sun, and His clothes became as bright as a flash of lightning, white as light, whiter than anyone in the world could bleach them.

Two men, Moses and Elijah, appeared in glorious splendor, talking with Jesus. They spoke about his departure, which he was about to bring to fulfillment at Jerusalem (Luke 9:30-31).

Jesus knew His mission; therefore, the two men from heaven might have been sent to encourage Him to impress upon the inner circle God's plan of salvation. On Pentecost, Peter preached that the death of Christ was not by accident but according to the foreordained plan of God.

The transfiguration along with the two men gave the disciples a glimpse and foretaste of Christ's coming kingdom glory, which would fulfill the Scriptures—the law symbolized by Moses and the prophets symbolized by Elijah. All the law and the prophets point to Christ and are fulfilled in Him (Matthew 5:17; Luke 24:27).

The glory seen in the transfigured Christ was the same Shekinah Glory that shone in both the Tabernacle (Exodus 40) and Temple (1 Kings 8). Immanuel was in their midst. Christ's transfiguration and Yahweh God calling to Moses from the cloud (Exodus 24:13-18) as well as Moses' face shining brilliantly after he met with Him (Exodus 34:29-35) serve to identify Jesus as the predicted Prophet to be heard and obeyed.

At Christ's second coming His glory will be revealed to the whole world (Matthew 25:31-32).

Moses died and was buried by God (Deuteronomy 34:5-6) and Elijah was taken alive to heaven in a chariot of fire (2 Kings 2:11). The appearance of the two men assured the disciples that there is glorious, intelligent and useful life beyond the grave. Many years later, Peter wrote of the significance of this event (2 Peter 1:16-21), which will be probed in the study of his second letter.

> Peter said to Jesus, "Rabbi, it is good for us to be here. Let us put up three shelters—one for you, one for Moses and one for Elijah." (He did not know what to say, they were so frightened) (Mark 9:5-6).

Peter's proposal to build three shelters or tabernacles was ill-conceived. Fearful and impulsive Peter may have believed the kingdom had arrived. The King of kings had been crowned with majestic splendor and glory. Mentally, Peter skipped over the Feasts of Passover, Unleavened Bread, Firstfruits, Pentecost, Trumpets and the Day of Atonement to arrive at Tabernacles; therefore, he said, "Let us put up three shelters."

Peter also errs in placing Moses and Elijah on the same level as Jesus. He desired to have the two prophets remain, but like John the Baptist, they belonged to the Old Covenant and they vanished.

> While he was still speaking, a bright cloud enveloped them, and a voice from the cloud said, "This is my Son, whom I love; with him I am well pleased. Listen to him!" (Matthew 17:5).

God the Father's voice from heaven affirmed that Jesus was the long anticipated prophet predicted by Moses.

> The LORD said to me: "What they say is good. I will raise up for them a prophet like you from among their brothers; I will put my words in his mouth, and he will tell them everything I command him. If anyone does not listen to my words that the prophet speaks in my name, I myself will call him to account (Deuteronomy 18:17-19).

> When the disciples heard this, they fell facedown to the ground, terrified. But Jesus came and touched them. "Get up," he said. "Don't be afraid." When they looked up, they saw no one except Jesus. As they were coming down the mountain, Jesus instructed them, "Don't tell anyone what you have seen, until the Son of Man has been raised from the dead." (Matthew 17:6-9).

> The disciples kept this to themselves, and told no one at that time what they had seen (Luke 9:36).

It must have been very difficult for impulsive and brash Peter not to tell anyone about what he witnessed on the mountain, but he listened to Jesus and obeyed the voice from heaven. He was learning the steps to being a faithful disciple.

Peter Fishes for Tax Money

The next significant event involving Peter is recorded only by Matthew, a tax collector.

After Jesus and his disciples arrived in Capernaum, the collectors of the two-drachma tax came to Peter and asked, "Doesn't your teacher pay the temple tax?" "Yes, he does," he replied. When Peter came into the house, Jesus was the first to speak. "What do you think, Simon?" he asked. "From whom do the kings of the earth collect duty and taxes—from their own sons or from others?" "From others," Peter answered. "Then the sons are exempt," Jesus said to him. "But so that we may not offend them, go to the lake and throw out your line. Take the first fish you catch; open its mouth and you will find a four-drachma coin. Take it and give it to them for my tax and yours" (Matthew 17:24-27).

Peter often spoke without thinking. Possibly, he answered in the affirmative because he did not want to dishonor or endanger Christ, or he previously observed Jesus paying the tax. Whatever the case, he had not considered why Christ paid the temple tax. Sometimes right answers are given for the wrong reasons.

Jesus took the opportunity to teach Peter an important lesson. His disciples are to submit to the authorities and powers established by God. God gave Adam and Eve dominion over nature, including the fish of the sea (Genesis 1:26: Psalm 8:6-8). However, man lost this dominion because of rebellion against God. Peter has been learning that Jesus has authority and power over everything, including the fish of the sea. Yet, the Lord does not exploit His lofty position and neither should His disciples—the sons of the King.

At least seven miracles Jesus performed were on Peter's behalf. He healed Peter's mother-in-law (Mark 1:29-34), twice helped him catch fish (Luke 5:1-11; John 21:5-11), enabled him to walk on water (Matthew 14:22-33) and healed Malchus' ear, which Peter cut off (Matthew 26:47-56). And through Peter, He healed a crippled man (Acts 3:1-8), raised Dorcas from the dead (Acts 9:36-41) and He rescued the disciple from prison (Acts 12:11). Certainly, Peter believed what he wrote, "Cast all your anxiety on him because he cares for you" (1 Peter 5:7).

Peter had faith in Christ and His commands; consequently, the disciple's trust and obedience were honored. Through this miracle of the fish and coin, Peter learned an important lesson.

Submit yourselves for the Lord's sake to every authority instituted among men: whether to the king, as the supreme authority, or to governors, who are sent by him to punish those who do wrong and to commend those who do right (1 Peter 2:13-14).

Since Christ Jesus submitted to governing authorities while on earth, so must His disciples. A child of the king does not offend the rulers instituted by God.

Peter's Inappropriate Question

In Luke 8:41-46, a woman who had been subject to bleeding for twelve years touched the edge of Jesus' cloak, and immediately her bleeding stopped. "Who touched me?" Jesus asked.

When everyone in the crowd denied touching Him, Peter said, "Master, the people are crowding and pressing against you." But Jesus said, "Someone touched me; I know that power has gone out from me."

On the surface, Peter statement seems logically. Yet, it was a presumptuous and impulsive questioning of Christ for asking such a thing. Such rationale marked the imperfect stage of the character of Peter and other disciples, who joined in (Mark 5:31). Peter, as usual, took the lead and the others followed. They had interrupted! Jesus was not ignorant of who touched Him; He wanted the woman to acknowledge what she had done.

> Then the woman, seeing that she could not go unnoticed, came trembling and fell at his feet. In the presence of all the people, she told why she had touched him and how she had been instantly healed [ἰάομαι iaomai]. Then he said to her, "Daughter, your faith has healed [σώζω sozo, saved] you. Go in peace" (Luke 8:47-48).

The Greek phrase, "instantly the blood flow stopped," translated "instantly healed (ἰάομαι iaomai)" had to do with the woman's physical condition. The second word translated "healed" is "saved (σώζω sozo) in the Greek and refers to her spiritual condition. She had been healed physically, but not saved spiritually until she fell and his feet and confessed that she touched

Him. Jesus was looking for her confession when He asked, "Who touched me?" Peter had interrupted!

Peter's Appropriate Question

We do not want to be too quick to condemn Peter's inquisitive mind. Although his questioning statement in the previous section was inappropriate, his question at the conclusion of Jesus' *Parable on Watchfulness* is appropriate.

In Luke 12:35-41, Jesus told a parable that His second coming would be without warning as a thief comes at an unknown time and therefore to be watchful. When Jesus finished, Peter asked, "Lord, are you telling this parable to us, or to everyone?"

Jesus answered with the *Parable of the Faithful and Wise Manager* (Luke 12:42-48). Here Jesus is very clear that after a very long time there is a judgment day, a day of reckoning for everyone. Christ is both a generous Rewarder and a stern Judge.

His servants are obligated to use and develop what they have been given. Grace never condones irresponsibility; use it or lose it!

Thus, both parables are for everyone.

> But the one who does not know and does things deserving punishment will be beaten with few blows. From everyone who has been given much, much will be demanded; and from the one who has been entrusted with much, much more will be asked (Luke 12:48).

Peter's Important Question

In Matthew 18, the disciples came to Jesus and asked, "Who is the greatest in the kingdom of heaven?" Jesus answered by explaining that unless they change by humbling themselves and becoming like little children they will

61

not enter into the kingdom of heaven. The disciples are responsible for welcoming and not causing anyone to fall who comes to Him. With the *Parable of the Lost Sheep*, the disciples learn they are responsible for seeking anyone who goes astray. Furthermore, if anyone sins against them, they must exercise His prescribed steps of restoration. This sparks Peter's important question concerning forgiveness.

Then Peter came to Jesus and asked, "Lord, how many times shall I forgive my brother when he sins against me? Up to seven times?" (Matthew 18:21).

We might want to give Peter an "A" for this very important question, but it deserves an "F." It smacked of rabbinism as well as pride. The Rabbis instructed their disciples to forgive a person three times. Peter added four more times for good measure. They treated forgiveness as a commodity that could be weighed, measured, and counted within a defined limit.

Jesus' answer must have startled Peter, "I tell you, not seven times, but seventy-seven times [or up to seventy times seven]." In other words, an unlimited amount of times.

To drive this point home, He told the *Parable of the Unforgiving Servant* (Matthew 18:23-35). This parable is a two-edged sword, showing the importance of humility and the necessity of forgiveness in the kingdom. If Peter was thinking of a shallow kind of forgiveness, Jesus wipes such ideas away. The main point of this parable is once forgiven, but now worse off!

Here, we discover the holiness of God—His compassion and anger. The King's compassion is followed by His anger. In anger his master turned the unforgiving servant over to the jailers to be tortured. The Greek ὀργίζω (*orgizō*) indicates he was "provoked to anger." Human anger terminates, but God's anger is divine, fierce and everlasting. Our anger has an ending point; it is limited. God's anger goes on forever. It is a consuming rage against the unforgiving-wicked-servant. There is no end to the anger of God directed against those in Hell.

Because of Peter's question, the Twelve learned that an important mark of discipleship is forgiveness, which Jesus had already taught them in the Sermon on the Mount.

> For if you forgive men when they sin against you, your heavenly Father will also forgive you. But if you do not forgive men their sins, your Father will not forgive your sins (Matthew 6:14-15).

Peter's Prudent and Proud Question

In Matthew 19:16-30, Mark 10:17-31 and Luke 18:18-30, a rich young ruler came up to Jesus and asked, "Teacher, what good thing must I do to get eternal life?" Jesus exposed the wealthy man's covetousness and told him, "If you want to be perfect, go, sell your possessions and give to the poor, and you will have treasure in heaven. Then come, follow me." The young man went away sad.

> Then Jesus said to his disciples, "I tell you the truth, it is hard for a rich man to enter the kingdom of heaven. Again I tell you, it is easier for a camel to go through the eye of a needle than for a rich man to enter the kingdom of God." When the disciples heard this, they were greatly astonished and asked, "Who then can be saved?" Jesus looked at them and said, "With man this is impossible, but with God all things are possible." Peter answered him, "We have left everything to follow you! What then will there be for us?" (Matthew 19:23-27)

Peter's question is a paradox; it is prudent and proud. The disciples have been following Jesus with mixed motives. They believed that He had the words of eternal life, but they also believed that He would soon establish His kingdom and they would become powerful and rich, like the young rich ruler. Peter is astonished to hear that riches hinder one from entering the kingdom of God. Such thinking goes against everything the Jews believed about wealth. In reality, there is the poverty of riches and the riches of poverty.

Peter's statement, "We have left everything to follow you!" was factual. It smacked of pride, but at the same time it was a wise question. Peter, James, John, Andrew, Philip, Thomas and Nathaniel had left their profitable fishing enterprises; Matthew left his lucrative position as a tax collector; and apparently the other four disciples had left plentiful situations to follow Him. In doing so, the Twelve were seeking a greater monetary reward in this life and after three years they were no longer wealthy. Now they were economically dependent and in a position to serve instead of being served.

> Jesus said to them, "I tell you the truth, at the renewal of all things, when the Son of Man sits on his glorious throne, you who have followed me will also sit on twelve thrones, judging the twelve tribes of Israel. And everyone who has left houses or brothers or sisters or father or mother or children or fields for my sake will receive a hundred times as much and will inherit eternal life. But many who are first will be last, and many who are last will be first (Matthew 19:28-30).

Little did the disciples realize that the renewal of all things—the inauguration of the Millennial Kingdom—would be in the distant future—at least twenty centuries away! Yet, Jesus promised they would sit on twelve thrones, judging the twelve tribes of Israel when He sits on His glorious throne. The apostle Paul would take Judas' place.

Additionally, there will be equality in the kingdom—many who are first will be last, and many who are last will be first, which is the point of the *Parable of the Workers in the Vineyard* (Matthew 20:1-16). When it comes to salvation, there is equality in the kingdom since each receives salvation no matter if they work for twelve hours or one hour.

But this reasoning does not fit the disciples sitting on the twelve thrones, judging the twelve tribes of Israel and other passages when it comes to rewards. In the *Parable of the Ten Minas*, Jesus taught that when He returns He will reward the trustworthy servant with ten cities, another with five cities, and the unfaithful servant will receive nothing (Luke 19:12-27). The apostle Paul taught there are different rewards.

64

For no one can lay any foundation other than the one already laid, which is Jesus Christ. If any man builds on this foundation using gold, silver, costly stones, wood, hay or straw, his work will be shown for what it is, because the Day will bring it to light. It will be revealed with fire, and the fire will test the quality of each man's work. If what he has built survives, he will receive his reward. If it is burned up, he will suffer loss; he himself will be saved, but only as one escaping through the flames (1 Corinthians 3:11-15).

Therefore judge nothing before the appointed time; wait till the Lord comes. He will bring to light what is hidden in darkness and will expose the motives of men's hearts. At that time each will receive his praise from God (1 Corinthians 4:5).

So we make it our goal to please him, whether we are at home in the body or away from it. For we must all appear before the judgment seat of Christ, that each one may receive what is due him for the things done while in the body, whether good or bad (2 Corinthians 5:9-10).

If the disciples seek to be first in the things of this life, they will be last in the kingdom of God; however, if they are last in worldly things, they will be first in the kingdom of God. This was Jesus' point in three of the beatitudes.

Looking at his disciples, he said: "Blessed are you who are poor, for yours is the kingdom of God. Blessed are you who hunger now, for you will be satisfied. Blessed are you who weep now, for you will laugh. Blessed are you when men hate you, when they exclude you and insult you and reject your name as evil, because of the Son of Man. Rejoice in that day and leap for joy, because great is your reward in heaven. For that is how their fathers treated the prophets (Luke 6:20-23)

The making of a disciple involves the exclusion of the praise, glamor and luster of this world for Christ. One must be willing to be last, to be first!

Peter During the Passion Week of Christ

Even though Peter is not directly mentioned in all the events of the week of the Lord's passion, many are included since they are the foundation of the apostle's sermons, speeches and teaching.

The Passion Week

Monday, Nisan 10	The Day of Selecting the Passover Lamb	Christ the King
Tuesday, Nisan 11	The Day of Rejection	Christ the Priest
Wednesday, Nisan 12	The Day of Teaching and Confrontation	Christ the Prophet
Thursday, Nisan 13	The Day of Preparation	Christ the God
Friday, Nisan 14	The Day of Slaying the Passover Lamb	Christ the Lamb
Saturday, Nisan 15	The Day of the Distress	
Sunday, Nisan 16	The Day of the Christ's Resurrection	Christ the Lord

On Monday, Nisan 10, the Passion Week of Jesus began with His entry into Jerusalem riding on a donkey as King. The disciples must have been thrilled at the shouts of the crowds, "Hosanna to the Son of David!" "Blessed is he who comes in the name of the Lord!" "Hosanna in the highest!" The whole city was stirred and asked, "Who is this?" The crowd's response was that He was "the prophet from Nazareth in Galilee." For the disciples, it appeared that it was time for Jesus to restore the kingdom to Israel (Matthew 21:9-11).

Jesus entered the Temple and looked around. What He saw must have grieved and angered Him to the core of His being. He said nothing and did nothing. Since it was late in the day, Jesus and His twelve disciples left the city conflicted over Him and returned to Bethany to lodge for the night. How tragic for the Jews, they unwittingly selected and passed over the Lamb of God, while they searched for Passover lambs that day.

On Tuesday, Nisan 11, early in the morning, as Jesus was on his way back to the city, He was hungry. Seeing a fig tree by the road, He went up to it but found nothing on it except leaves. It is a well-known fact, that in Palestine, the figs appear before the leaves. Then He said to it, "Let no one ever eat out of your fruit into the age," according to the literal reading of the Greek (Matthew 21:18-19).

This cursing is to be connected with the *Parable of the Fig Tree* in Luke 13:6-9. Israel failed to recognize its season of opportunity. Jesus had warned right before He told this parable that "Unless you repent, you too will all perish."

Jesus entered the Temple for the second time to cleanse it (cf. John 2:12-17). As Priest, He cast out all those who were buying and selling in the Temple, and overturned the tables of the moneychangers and seats of those who were selling doves. The religious establishment, who profited from the Temple being a market, had not acquiesced to His authority.

> It is written," he said to them, "My house will be called a house of prayer,' but you are making it a 'den of robbers" (Matthew 21:13).

His claim that the Temple is "My house" more than Christ's cleansing of it prompted the priests, teachers of the law, and leading men among the people to seek how to destroy Him. Yet, they were afraid of Him, for the people hung on His words and were astonished at His teaching.

On this day, Jesus demonstrated that He rejected Israel with two acts of judgment. First, He cursed the fig tree, and second, He cleansed the Temple while quoting from the prophet Jeremiah. His authority not only as the King of Israel was manifested and declared, but His authority as God was manifested in their midst by the miracles that He performed earlier.

He ended the day with a solemn warning of judgment. For the second evening, Jesus and the disciples left the city in conflict. The people were popularizing Him, the religious establishment was rejecting Him, and many leaders were believing in Him but unwilling to confess Him. They returned to Bethany for the night. Jesus never slept In Jerusalem during Passion Week—the city that rejected Him, He rejected it.

On Wednesday, Nisan 12, Christ spoke as Prophet, teaching a lesson about faith in response to Peter's observation and responding to five questions.

1. The Sanhedrin asked an authoritative question
2. The Pharisees and Herodians asked an explosive question
3. The Sadducees asked a dumb question
4. One of the teachers of the law asked an intelligent question
5. The disciples asked a prophetic question

Peter's Observation

In the morning, when returning to Jerusalem from Bethany, the disciples noticed the fig tree withered from the roots and Peter points it out to Jesus, who uses it as an opportunity to teach them a lesson on faith rather than interpreting the event. "Have faith in God," Jesus answered. His point is that the nation of Israel is cursed because it had lost faith in God. It substituted instead an empty system of man-made laws and traditions for the sake of performance, which had an outwardly religious glaze to it but inwardly was unreal and hypocritical. It behooves the disciples to have faith in God if they do not want to wither from the roots also. Notice that Christ employs the triad of faith (Mark 11:22-23), hope (11:24) and love (11:25) in this lesson.

"I tell you the truth, if anyone says to this mountain, 'Go, throw yourself into the sea,' and does not doubt in his heart but believes that what he says will happen, it will be done for him." The mountain symbolizes obstacles as it did in Yahweh's message given to Zechariah for Zerubbabel to encourage Him to build the second temple in Jerusalem.

> So he said to me, "This is the word of the LORD to Zerubbabel: 'Not by might nor by power, but by my Spirit,' says the LORD Almighty. "What are you, O mighty mountain? Before Zerubbabel you will become level ground. Then he will bring out the capstone to shouts of 'God bless it! God bless it!'" (Zechariah 4:6-7).

Christ will build His church beginning with Peter, who holds the keys to the kingdom. He needs to have the faith in God which possesses authority and power to accomplish immeasurably more than he can imagine. Jesus has demonstrated authority and power in His earthly ministry. Now it is about to be challenged.

While in the Temple courts, Jesus taught responded to the official challenge of His authority with the *Parable of the Tenants* (Matthew 21:33-46). With this parable, Christ revealed that He is the capstone or cornerstone of the spiritual temple—the Church. The kingdom would be taken from the nation of Israel and given to a people who would produce fruit—righteousness.

This was an important parable for Peter since on the apostle's confession and his using of the keys of the kingdom of heaven Christ would begin to build His Church! Peter needed to understand that Israel would be set aside as the chosen people of God in the new dispensation of the kingdom.

Christ sandwiched this parable between the *Parable of the Two Sons* (Matthew 21:28-32) and the *Parable of the Wedding Banquet* (Matthew 22:1-14).

It would be absolutely necessary for Peter to understand that for the near and distant future the Kingdom of God would not be the physical kingdom of Israel, but a spiritual kingdom of the Church comprised of people from all nations.

Moreover, these three parables are critical to understanding Romans 8:28-11:36, Paul's discourse on the status of the Church and Israel in this present age.

This was the last time Christ entered the Temple. "Ichabod"—"the glory has departed" can be written over it. The Sanhedrin comprised of chief priests, the teachers of the law, and the elders come to Jesus to challenge His authority; they could not disavow His power. Everything Jesus said and did during the first three days of Passion Week was with authority! On Monday, He rode into Jerusalem on a donkey as Israel's King. On Tuesday, He performed an official act reserved for a Priest; He cleansed the Temple. On Wednesday, He is the Prophet predicted by Moses.

Peter's Eschatological Question

As Jesus and the disciples were leaving the temple, one of them said to Him, "Look, Teacher! What massive stones! What magnificent buildings!" "Do you see all these great buildings?" replied Jesus. "Not one stone here will be left on another; every one will be thrown down." (Matthew 24:1-2; Mark 13:1-2; Luke 21:5-6). After the small group crossed the Kidron Valley, they climbed the mountain.

As Jesus was sitting on the Mount of Olives opposite the temple, Peter, James, John and Andrew asked him privately, "Tell us, when will these things happen? And what will be the sign that they are all about to be fulfilled?" (Mark 13:3-4).

The Temple Mount from the Mount of Olives

The Mount Olivet Discourse unveils the conditions connected with Christ's Second Coming to inaugurate the Millennial Kingdom:

1. The First Half of the Tribulation, Matthew 24:4-14
2. The Middle of the Tribulation, Matthew 24:15-20
3. The Second Half of the Tribulation, Matthew 24:21-26
4. The Signs of His Return, Matthew 24:27-35
5. The Suddenness of His Return, Matthew 24:36-41
6. The Parables of His Return, Matthew 24:42-25:30
7. The Judgment of the Nations, Matthew 25:31-46

The most obvious lessons from the Sermon on the Mount (Matthew 24:4-25:46; Mark 13:1-37; Luke 21:5-36) are to watch, work and wait. Christ promised that He would return to earth and no person knows when this event will occur. For Peter and the other disciples, Jesus' sermon did not resonate until after Christ's ascension to heaven and the endowment of the Holy Spirit.

Jesus the Prophet had predicted the distant future in the Mount Olivet Discourse. So now, to authenticate His predictions, He foretells the immediate future, saying to His disciples, "As you know, the Passover is two days away—and the Son of Man will be handed over to be crucified" (Matthew 26:1-2). On Wednesday, Jesus ended His teaching on a sad note—Friday was coming!

Thursday, Nisan 13, for the Galileans and Pharisees was the Day of Passover since they used the sunrise-to-sunrise reckoning of a day, whereas the Judeans and Sadducees used the sunset-to-sunset reckoning. The priests did not object to the two days since it allowed them to perform the great number of sacrifices. Hence, Jesus and His disciples celebrated the Thursday Passover and He died on the Friday Passover.

Peter Taught Lessons in Humility

Peter's first lesson in humility comes when Jesus sent John and him as servants into the city of Jerusalem to prepare for the Passover meal. They were told to follow a man with a jar on his head, who led them to a large and furnished upper room. Peter and John would have prepared the Passover meal after securing a lamb, sacrificing it at the temple and then roasting it.

Since the two disciples made the necessary preparations, they would have been responsible for fulfilling the tasks of a servant by caring for the following when the guests arrived at the Upper Room:

1. Burning of fragrant incense when the guests arrive
2. Anointing of the guests' head with fragrant oil
3. Washing the dust from the guests' feet
4. Giving the guests a cup of cold water

When evening came, Jesus arrived with the ten disciples at the Upper Room. Jesus knew that His hour had come, that He would depart out of this world to the Father, and that the Devil had already put into the heart of Judas Iscariot to betray Him.

The host was responsible for seating the guests. Therefore, Christ gave to Judas and John the places of honor; Judas received the highest place of honor on Christ's left. This was an evidence of the love and grace of the Lord, who knew Judas' heart before the seats were assigned.

Peter sat in the lowest seat—opposite John on the right wing of the table. Surely, Peter expected either the left or right side of Christ since he helped John to make the preparations for the Passover, but Judas ended up in "his" place. Whether Jesus sat him in lowest place, or Peter marched over and took it; we are not told.

But Peter was about to learn a lesson in humility and service. In the lowest position, it would have fallen upon him to wash the feet of the guests in the absence of a servant; this was not the job of the Host. But Jesus used the opportunity to teach a two-fold lesson of submission.

Christ laid aside His robe, wrapped a towel around His waist and made His way around the table washing each of the disciples' feet. The laying aside of His robe symbolized Christ removing His equality with God to become a man. Wrapping of a towel around the waist was a common mark of a servant, by whom the service of foot-washing was usually performed. Unexpectedly, Jesus illustrated that He came to serve, not to be served.

> Your attitude should be the same as that of Christ Jesus, who, being in very nature God, did not consider equality with God something to be grasped, but made himself nothing, taking the very nature of a servant, being made in human likeness. And being found in appearance as a man, he humbled himself and became obedient to death—even death on a cross! (Philippians 2:5-8).

What a contrast to the attitude of proud, boastful Peter!

"No," said Peter, "you shall never wash my feet." Jesus answered, "Unless I wash you, you have no part with me." "Then, Lord," Simon Peter replied, "not just my feet but my hands and my head as well!" Jesus answered, "A person who has had a bath needs only to wash his feet; his whole body is clean. And you are clean, though not every one of you." For he knew who was going to betray him, and that was why he said not everyone was clean. When he had finished washing their feet, he put on his clothes and returned to his place. "Do you understand what I have done for you?" he asked them. "You call me 'Teacher' and 'Lord,' and rightly so, for that is what I am. Now that I, your Lord and Teacher, have washed your feet, you also should wash one another's feet. I have set you an example that you should do as I have done for you. I tell you the truth, no servant is greater than his master, nor is a messenger greater than the one who sent him. Now that you know these things, you will be blessed if you do them (John 13:8-17).

Not only was Jesus' actions a lesson in humility for Peter and the others, but an important lesson on what Christ expects of His disciples.

The hour of darkness cast its shadows on the hearts of the Twelve. A dispute arose among them as to which of them was considered the greatest. This contention first raised its ugly head while on the journey to Jerusalem when the mother of James and John came to Jesus and asked, "Grant that one of these two sons of mine may sit at your right and the other at your left in your kingdom" (Matthew 20:20-24).

Disappointment must have raced through Jesus' soul. His vivid illustration of feet-washing—of being a servant of all—had not pierced their hearts and minds.

Satan entered Judas Iscariot so Jesus sent him away to do what he would do quickly. The Eleven would enter into servitude for their Master out of love, instead of the covetousness that possessed Judas. So after Judas was gone, Jesus used this occasion of dissension to teach them of love and servitude.

Now is the Son of Man glorified and God is glorified in him. If God is glorified in him, God will glorify the Son in himself, and will glorify him at once. My children, I will be with you only a little longer. You will look for me, and just as I told the Jews, so I tell you now: Where I am going, you cannot come. A new command I give you: Love one another. As I have loved you, so you must love one another. By this all men will know that you are my disciples, if you love one another (John 13:31-35).

The Eleven did love Jesus and would serve Him until death. However, one would discover his love for the Master the hard way. Satan has invaded Judas and he now desires to have Simon Peter. Peter's foot-in-mouth disease overwhelmed the proud, boastful disciple,

Simon Peter asked him, "Lord, where are you going?" Jesus replied, "Where I am going, you cannot follow now, but you will follow later." Peter asked, "Lord, why can't I follow you now? I will lay down my life for you." Then Jesus answered, "Will you really lay down your life for me? I tell you the truth, before the rooster crows, you will disown me three times! (John 13:36-38).

The bad news is that Peter will deny the Lord three times; the good news is that Christ will pray for him and he will be restored.

"Simon, Simon, Satan has asked to sift you as wheat. But I have prayed for you, Simon, that your faith may not fail. And when you have turned back, strengthen your brothers." But he replied, "Lord, I am ready to go with you to prison and to death." Jesus answered, "I tell you, Peter, before the rooster crows today, you will deny three times that you know me" (Luke 22:31-34)

When Peter is restored, his task is to strengthen his brothers, either the other disciples or all believers since Peter has been bequeathed the keys to the kingdom of heaven (Matthew 16:19).

Jesus gave them a perplexing command, which in the short-term will get Peter into trouble at Gethsemane.

"But now if you have a purse, take it, and also a bag; and if you don't have a sword, sell your cloak and buy one. It is written: 'And he was numbered with the transgressors'; and I tell you that this must be fulfilled in me. Yes, what is written about me is reaching its fulfillment." The disciples said, "See, Lord, here are two swords." "That is enough," he replied (Luke 22:36-39).

On the surface, it would appear Jesus is inviting revolution. How should the necessity of buying a sword and the adequacy of possessing two swords be taken: symbolically or literally? Christ's reply that two swords are enough might have to do with the prophecy that He was numbered with the transgressors (Isaiah 53:12). Certainly, He was accused of being a revolutionary by the Jews.

Symbolically, the swords represent hostility and the need for a purse, bag and sandals indicate that the disciples would not be warmly received as they had been in the past. The nation of Israel has rejected Christ; He has cut them off; the darkness hates the light; and they need to be prepared for the hostility they will face.

Before they leave for Gethsemane for the night, Christ institutes the Lord's Supper by teaching them the significance of partaking of the bread and cup, which they are to continue doing in remembrance of Him.

After they ate the bread and drank from the cup, Jesus gave His disciples five essential reasons why He had to leave them and go to the Father:

1. To prepare a place for them
2. To reveal the Father to them
3. To bestow on them power in prayer
4. To send the Holy Spirit
5. To grant His peace

Jesus and the Eleven likely made their way through the streets of Jerusalem to the vicinity of the Temple and from there they would descend the steep Kidron Valley and ascend part way of the Mount of Olives until they came to a garden called Gethsemane, which means an oil press. Undoubtedly, the Eleven thought Judas Iscariot would join the band at the prearranged meeting place.

On the way to the garden of Gethsemane, Jesus taught His disciples, prophesied and prayed.

1. He taught the *Allegory of the Vine and Branches*, John 15:1-17
2. He predicted that the world will hate His disciples, John 15:18-25
3. He predicted the Holy Spirit's work, John 15:26-16:16
4. He predicted that the disciples' grief will be turned to joy, John 16:16-22
5. He predicted answered prayer in His name, John 16:23-28
6. He predicted the scattering of His flock and reaffirms Peter's denials, Matthew 26:31-35; Mark 14:27-31; Luke 22:39-40; John 16:32-33
7. He prayed a high priestly prayer for Himself, His disciples and those who will believe in Him, John 17:1-25

Peter Denies Christ's Predictions

Before they reached Gethsemane, Jesus shocked the disciples with predictions of His death, resurrection and their responses.

"You will all fall away," Jesus told them, "for it is written: "'I will strike the shepherd, and the sheep will be scattered.' But after I have risen, I will go ahead of you into Galilee." Peter declared, "Even if all fall away, I will not." "I tell you the truth," Jesus answered, "today—yes, tonight—before the rooster crows twice you yourself will disown me three times." But Peter insisted emphatically, "Even if I have to die with you, I will never disown you." And all the others said the same (Mark 14:27-31).

Each time Jesus quoted from the OT; the quotes concerned Him. This time He quoted Zechariah 13:7, which predicted the reaction of the disciples to the horrors and trials that were about to commence. First, Peter denied the prophetic Word of God, insisting that he would never fall away even if the others did. When Jesus predicted that he would disown Him three times, Peter rejected that prediction and the others followed his lead.

Peter's self-confident boasting was a spark that kindled a fire that would burn to the depth of his soul. He would not let the kingdom be taken away; he would fight, even die for it, not so, for he was a coward!

Danger was lurking; it was the hour of darkness. How would the boastful disciples respond to it?

Peter Sleeps as Christ Prays

Gethsemane was a garden-like spot, a thick grove with its knotted rooted olive trees affording an ideal hiding place for anyone who wanted to avoid capture. This night Jesus set an outer guard of eight of His followers. Then Jesus went a little father into the deeper shrub and posted the inner guard of His most intimate and trusted friends, Peter, James and John.

> He began to be deeply distressed and troubled. "My soul is overwhelmed with sorrow to the point of death," he said to them. "Stay here and keep watch" (Mark 14:33-34)

Gethsemane manifests the Word made Flesh. Here the humanity of Jesus is shown not to be above temptation. So far from sailing serenely through His trials like some superior being unconcerned with this world, He almost dies with distress.

Why did Jesus pick these three at this time? They would be the leaders; they might have been the weakest; they have been the most loved. But probably because they had put their foot in their mouth! Peter insisted emphatically, "Even if I have to die with you, I will never disown you" (Mark 14:31) and James and John had affirmed their ability to drink of Jesus' cup. Jesus had asked the two disciples, "Can you drink the cup I drink or be baptized with the baptism I am baptized with?" "We can," they answered (Mark 10:38-39). The boisterous self-confidence of the three had now exposed them to the grave peril of failure in the struggle they confront.

They could see the distress on Jesus face; He told them how He felt. At this critical moment, His command was easy—"keep watch." How would these boastful disciples handle it while He prayed a little distance from them?

Then he returned to his disciples and found them sleeping. "Simon," he said to Peter, "are you asleep? Could you not keep watch for one hour? Watch and pray so that you will not fall into temptation. The spirit is willing, but the body [σαρξ *sarx*, flesh, that is the sinful nature] is weak" (Mark 14:37-38)

With a touch of irony, Jesus chews out Simon, probably because he was the most arrogant and confident. How could He protect Jesus to the death if he was sleeping on guard duty? When Jesus addressed the proud disciple as Simon, He is disappointed with Him; he certainly is not living up to his new name of Peter (Πετρος, rock).

"The spirit is willing" is an expression from Psalm 51:12, where it stands in parallel to the Holy Spirit. The disciples illustrate the struggle between the Spirit and the sinful nature:

> For the sinful nature desires what is contrary to the Spirit, and the Spirit what is contrary to the sinful nature. They are in conflict with each other, so that you do not do what you want (Galatians 5:17).

Jesus faced a similar struggle within His sinless nature.

> He fell to the ground and prayed that if possible the hour might pass from him. "Abba, Father," he said, "everything is possible for you. Take this cup from me. Yet not what I will, but what you will." (Mark 14:35-36).

Commentators indicate in some way or other that Jesus was being tempted by Satan in Gethsemane; they are mistaken. At this point in time, Satan is indwelling Judas and he is a created being who does not possess the power of omnipresence. It is Satan's plan to kill Jesus, not to stop Him from dying. Satan wants Jesus dead and out of the way for good.

If Satan is not tempting Jesus, who or what is? His humanity—the flesh— His human nature is not sinful, however. Clearly, Jesus indicates that this temptation arises out of the distress in His soul (cf. Hebrews 2:17-18

Three times Jesus withdrew to wrestle with His own will. The issues were clear. Would He have His own way and save Himself or would He be utterly selfless and sacrifice Himself to save sinful men? The third time the battle ended in total self-giving; total victory—"Father, I shall drink this cup!" It was not an effortless surrender; it was the most exacting battle ever witnessed in the universe, but Peter, James and John slept through it.

> Returning the third time, he said to them, "Are you still sleeping and resting? Enough! The hour has come. Look, the Son of Man is betrayed into the hands of sinners (Mark 14:41).

Peter, James and John had failed to keep watch; Jesus enemies were upon them. Most likely, they would be guilt harassed until the resurrection.

Some things from this event should impress us about Christ:

1. He was a man of sorrows acquainted with grief
2. He faced the hour of darkness alone
3. He yielded Himself to God the Father
4. He craved the support of His disciples but they disappointed Him by sleeping
5. He made consideration for their being tired

When you come to "the garden" alone with Jesus, think of His sorrow, loneliness, yieldedness, disappointment and consideration—He knows how you feel!

The betrayal and arrest of Jesus was devious, sly, and accomplished in the darkness (Matthew 26:47-56; Mark 14:43-52; Luke 22:47-53; John 18:2-12). It was past midnight, the lights from Jerusalem have grown dim and the city is dark. The other disciples had fallen asleep on watch; they sounded no alarm! The mob approached Gethsemane, carrying torches, lanterns, swords and clubs. There would be no escape! The Master knew they were coming before they arrived.

The mob was large—perhaps a thousand people. It was made up of people from all classes: a detachment of soldiers, some officials from the chief priests, Pharisees and elders of the people. They must have expected resistance—for they arrived in considerable force and they were well armed.

Judas was preceding them, showing the way to Jesus. The Master, knowing all that was going to happen to Him, went out of the olive grove to meet them. With a prearranged signal, Judas went at once to Jesus. While kissing Him much, again and again, tenderly according to the Greek text of Matthew 26:49, the betrayer said, "Greetings Rabbi!"

If you are perplexed at Judas betraying Christ with a kiss—so was Jesus, "Judas, are you betraying the Son of Man with a φιλημα (*philema*, a kiss of affection)?" (Luke 22:48). It caught Jesus off guard. Possibly, Judas thought the kiss would fool the other disciples as well as Jesus. Ironically, instead of hiding him, the kisses marked him for all of history as the betrayer of our Lord. The kiss was not necessary, it was already settled that the Good Shepherd would lay down His life for the sheep.

Peter's Rebellious Action

Jesus asked them what they wanted and they replied, "Jesus of Nazareth." He answered, "I am." These words were hardly out of the mouth of Jesus, when Peter placed Christ's protection in jeopardy. Peter boasted too loudly, prayed too little, slept too much, and acted too fast. He carried one of the two swords.

> Then Simon Peter, who had a sword, drew it and struck the high priest's servant, cutting off his right ear. (The servant's name was Malchus.) Jesus commanded Peter, "Put your sword away! Shall I not drink the cup the Father has given me?" (John 18:10-11).

Jesus made it clear to Peter that his action was counter to the will of the Father and rebellious.

> Jesus said to him, "for all who draw the sword will die by the sword. Do you think I cannot call on my Father, and he will at once put at my disposal more than twelve legions of angels? But how then would the Scriptures be fulfilled that say it must happen in this way?" (Matthew 26:52-54).

Jesus quickly cooled the situation by touching Malchus' ear and healing him. Peter was about to learn what the Lord predicts occurs.

Peter Denies Christ Three Times

Then all his disciples fled fulfilling Zechariah's prophecy; however, Peter and John must have hid in the shadows since they followed as Jesus was taken before Annas, who had been High Priest from A.D. 6 to 15, and who still was the power behind the religious establishment in Jerusalem. From Annas, Jesus was taken to the High Priest Caiaphas's house and finally to the Sanhedrin. Between the first and last, Peter denied Jesus three times (Matthew 26:69-75; Mark 14:66-72; Luke 22:55-62; John 18:15-18, 25-27).

The flaw in the rock was exposed! Peter was like an unpolished diamond in the rough. He was a man of great worth, but no one would have recognized his value this night. The fact that Peter and John followed Jesus indicates that they loved Jesus and were concerned about Him. But Peter's love could not stand the test of fear!

Peter arrived at the courtyard of Annas along with another disciple shortly after the others. The other disciple [John] was known by the High Priest so he entered. Peter stood at the door. John came back, spoke to the girl on duty there and brought Peter in.

Jerusalem sits 2,600 feet above sea level and the night air is chilly in the spring so Peter sat down with guards around the fire to see the outcome. Peter is a paradox of courage and cowardice. He could neither stay away nor could he make a courageous witness. Peter is courageous to a point; he is not ready to die for Christ!

It appears that Peter was the strongest of the disciples, yet he fell. It is important to know the steps of his fall so that we may avoid them. There are five great mistakes Peter made.

1. He was overconfident
2. He did not take seriously the Word of Christ
3. He failed to watch and pray
4. He put himself in the place of temptation instead of fleeing

5. He compromised instead of confessing Christ

People tend to fall in the areas of their greatest strengths. Abraham's greatest strength was his faith, and yet his faith failed him when he went down to Egypt and lied about Sarah. Moses' strength was in his meekness, yet he lost his temper, spoke rashly with his lips, struck the rock, and he was not allowed to enter the Promised Land. Peter was a brave man but learned how easy it is to start going in the wrong direction. We are all flawed like Peter and need to heed the Apostle Paul's advice.

So, if you think you are standing firm, be careful that you don't fall! No temptation has seized you except what is common to man. And God is faithful; he will not let you be tempted beyond what you can bear. But when you are tempted, he will also provide a way out so that you can stand up under it (1 Corinthians 10:12-13).

Jesus had provided the way out for Peter, but he did not take it. Judas had betrayed Jesus, now his sights were set on Peter. Peter must have thought back to this night when he wrote:

Be self-controlled and alert. Your enemy the Devil prowls around like a roaring lion looking for someone to devour. Resist him, standing firm in the faith, because you know that your brothers throughout the world are undergoing the same kind of suffering (1 Peter 5:8-9).

Peter could have resisted temptation by fleeing and trusting Christ's Word, but he was much too daring. Once he walked on water until he took his eyes off Jesus. He had courage! Two followed at a distance—John and Peter! Peter probably imagined that no one would pay any attention to him. But he was sadly mistaken.

Peter's First Denial

While Peter was below in the courtyard, one of the servant girls of the High Priest came by. When she saw Peter warming himself, she looked closely at him. "You also were with Jesus of Galilee," she said. The suddenness and boldness of the girl's accusation must have caught Peter off guard. In spite of all his loud and repeated promises, he panicked and he denied it before them all: "I don't know what you're talking about" was a common reply under rabbinical law for a formal denial. For instance, the prosecutor would ask, "Where is my ox?" and the defendant would reply, "I do not know what you are saying."

Peter could face a mob and draw a sword but could not handle the stare and accusation of a servant girl! The term denial (αρνεομαι *arneomai*) implies a previous relationship of obedience and fidelity. It occurs only when there has been a previous acknowledgment and commitment. Denial carries the idea of forsaking or renouncing or rejecting for one's self interest. At this moment, Peter forsook, renounced and rejected his Lord.

Peter's Second Denial

Frustrated and fearful of being identified and apprehended, Peter retreated into the archway that led into the street, where another girl saw him and said to the people there, "This fellow was with Jesus of Nazareth." He denied it again, with an oath: "I don't know the man!" At this point, some early manuscripts add, "the rooster crowed." If it did, it did not awaken Peter's conscience.

Why did the servant girl try to expose Peter? She most likely wanted to make herself important. She wanted these men to know that she knew something that they did not know. The Evil One loves to pounce upon the foolhardy and to sweep boasters off their feet. It only took a servant girl to fell the chief of the Disciples—not an army or a great warrior—just a young girl. Peter is like Elijah, who could stand up against 850 prophets of Baal and Asherah, but who, after he left the mountain top of victory, floundered in fear over what one woman, Jezebel, might do to him.

Peter's Third Denial

About an hour later another standing there went up to Peter and said, "Surely you are one of them, for your accent gives you away, for you are a Galilean." Peter was like a cornered animal; he began to call down curses on himself and he swore to them, "I don't know the man!" Peter did not use profanity; he had called the anathema of God upon his head if what he said was not true. His words placed him under God's curse if he were lying to them and put himself under oath, as in a courtroom, to confirm the veracity of his denial.

Just as he was speaking, the rooster crowed and the guard brought the Lord out of Caiaphas' house. He turned and looked straight at Peter. What did Peter see in the eyes of Jesus? Heartache and disappointment! It was not the Lord's look that broke Peter's heart but the Word of God that penetrated it.

> For the word of God is living and active. Sharper than any double-edged sword, it penetrates even to dividing soul and spirit, joints and marrow; it judges the thoughts and attitudes of the heart (Hebrews 4:12).

Peter remembered the Word the Lord had spoken to him: "Before the rooster crows today, you will disown me three times." The crowing rooster punctuates Peter's denial since the apostle acted like a proud rooster in his prideful, self-sufficiency.

What a tragic picture! Peter, a disciple of Christ, once more gave into his sinful nature. His joy was shattered and despair overwhelmed him. Like Judas, his remorse was in vain; it could not restore fellowship or the feeling of hope. Only confession of his love for Christ could repair the way he felt, which he would learn on the shore of the Sea of Galilee weeks later.

Guilt ridden, Peter went outside and wept bitterly. Was he crying for himself or for Jesus? Or both? It was the bitterest heartache that life can have—grief and shame over the betrayal of love. The hour of darkness encompassed Peter as it had Judas on this night. On the Judean calendar it is already the day we call Good Friday, but for the disciples, and especially Peter, it was Black Friday!

Friday, Nisan 14, by all appearance was devastating for the disciples. Matthew says Judas hanged himself; Acts states, "He fell headlong, his body burst open and all his intestines spilled out." An early church tradition reports that Judas hanged himself from a tree branch over a ravine, and the branch broke, whether before or after he died, Judas fell to a messy end. One of the Twelve was a betrayer and he was dead.

Peter's Absence at Christ's Crucifixion and Resurrection

A few hours later at 9:00 a.m., the One to whom they had committed their lives hung naked on a cross at Golgotha, beaten beyond human recognition, mocked, crowned with thorns, and to add insult to injury, a notice was ordered by Pilate and fastened to the cross, which read in Aramaic, Latin and Greek—"Jesus of Nazareth, the King of the Jews." Ironically, there could be no mistake about it: the Jews murdered their King! On Pentecost, Peter would pierce the hearts of his Jewish audience with the awfulness of this fact and later charge the Sanhedrin with murder.

John followed Jesus the rest of the night and into the morning, watching and observing from a distance. At the foot of the cross, the disciple Jesus loved joined Mary the mother of Jesus to witness the Son of God's crucifixion. However, broken hearted Peter was nowhere to be found—the bold, proud and courageous Peter was a coward—overwhelmed with shame and remorse.

Crucifixion by Antony van Dyck, 1622

Jesus spoke seven sayings on the cross in six hours, which divide into two segments: the first three hours of light and the second three hours of darkness.

There are three outlooks in Christ Jesus' sayings as He looks to:
- A. Others—The Outward Look.
    1. His concern for those who crucified Him
    2. His assurance to the believing thief
    3. His concern for His mother and loved disciple
- B. God—The Upward Look
    4. His separation from the Father
- C. Himself—the Inward Look
    5. His body
    6. His soul
    7. His spirit

At noon, the sky turned black and Christ cried, "My God, My God, why have you forsaken me?" One thousand years before Christ was born, the Holy Spirit inspired David to pen those words at the beginning of Psalm 22—*The Agony and The Ecstasy of the Cross.*

Psalm 22 not only reveals the thoughts behind the seven utterances of Christ on the Cross, but also much more of what the Lamb of God was thinking as He hung there.

The Agony of:	The Ecstasy of:
The Separation, 1	The Answered Prayer, 21b
The Silence, 2	The Hope of Resurrection, 22
The Disappointment, 3-5	The Believer, 23-24
The Disdain, 6-8	The Obedient, 25
The Desperation, 9-11	The Victor, 26
The Terror, 12-13	The Exaltation, 27-29
The Torture, 14-17	The Completion, 30-31
The Desecration, 18	
The Powerlessness, 19-21a	

The Agony and The Ecstasy of The Cross is finished. This is evident from Christ referring once again to the First Person of the Trinity as "Father." The Father had turned His face back upon His Son in whom He is well pleased and the death of spiritual separation is finished. With confidence, Jesus called out with a loud voice, "Father, into your hands I commit my spirit." With that, He bowed his head and gave up His spirit; He breathed His last—separation occurred. Absent from the body, His spirit was present in Paradise.

At that very moment, the Temple curtain tore in two from top to bottom. No doubt many priests witnessed this tearing since Jesus died at the exact time the sacrifice of thousands of Passover lambs had begun. Theologically, this curtain had been a separation, a barrier between God and men because of sin; it was made and hung for this moment.

> Therefore, brothers, since we have confidence to enter the Most Holy Place by the blood of Jesus, by a new and living way opened for us through the curtain, that is, his body, and since we have a great priest over the house of God, let us draw near to God with a sincere heart in full assurance of faith, having our hearts sprinkled to cleanse us from a guilty conscience and having our bodies washed with pure water (Hebrews 10:19-22).

Like the curtain, Christ's body was torn to open the way into the very presence of God. What Jesus told His disciples the night before became a reality at the very moment this curtain tore: "I am the way and the truth and the life. No one comes to the Father except through me" (John 14:6).

The importance of the torn curtain of the Temple:

1. It signified that we all have access to God the Father through Christ.
2. It testified that Jesus Christ is the Son of God.
3. It showed that Jesus' body was torn for our sin.
4. It demonstrated that the redemption price and ransom is paid in full.

5. It manifests that reconciliation between God and man is accomplished.
6. It commenced the destruction of the earthly Temple and its worship.
7. It signified the change of dispensations:

   a. The end of the Levitical High Priesthood and the beginning of Christ's High Priesthood
   b. The end of the Old Covenant and the beginning of the New Covenant
   c. The end of the Ceremonial Law and the beginning of Grace
   d. It marked the end of Judaism and the beginning of the Church

For Peter and the apostles, the torn curtain marked the end of the Old Covenant and the man-made legalistic traditions and rules of Judaism. The first coming of Christ not only would take on an entirely new meaning, but also a new way of life, which they would experience beginning at Pentecost.

The earth shook and the rocks split after the Temple curtain was torn.

> The tombs also were opened and many bodies of the saints who had gone to their rest were raised. And they came out of the tombs after His resurrection, entered the holy city, and appeared to many (Matthew 27:52-53 HCSB).

The darkness was over—the Light had come to a lost world! Yet, dark despair filled the hearts of Peter and the other ten disciples since they neither listened nor believed Jesus' predictions concerning His death and resurrection.

As evening approached, a rich man, Joseph of Arimathea, went to Pilate and asked for Jesus' body and Pilate ordered that it be given to him.

Joseph and Nicodemus took the body and wrapped it, with the spices, in strips of linen. At the place where Jesus was crucified, there was a garden, and in the garden a new rock-hewn tomb that belonged to Joseph, in which no one had ever been laid. Because it was the Jewish Day of Preparation and since the tomb was nearby, they laid Jesus there. Joseph rolled a large stone against the entrance of the tomb and prophecy was fulfilled.

> He was assigned a grave with the wicked, and with the rich in his death, though he had done no violence, nor was any deceit in his mouth (Isaiah 53:9).

Friday was the most tragic day in history; it was the day man murdered God's Son. Yet, we call it "Good Friday" because the Savior of the world died for our sins.

Saturday, Nisan 15 was anything but good. It was the darkest day in history for Christ's body lay in the tomb. It was the Sabbath—the day of rest, therefore, we would expect the Gospels to be silent regarding any activity on this day and so they are.

Saturday must have been the darkest day the disciples had ever experienced—a dreary, interminable day of shattered hopes, broken dreams, desolated spirits, and wounded, frightened hearts. This was a day in which the future was grim and foreboding. All their brightest hopes had collapsed around them; all their choicest dreams had perished with the death of Jesus. Every act on that day must have been torture with every fiber within them crying out, "What's the use? Why go on?" How ironic! The disciples did not understand Jesus but his enemies did.

> The chief priests and the Pharisees went to Pilate. "Sir," they said, "we remember that while he was still alive that deceiver said, 'After three days I will rise again.' So give the order for the tomb to be made secure until the third day. Otherwise, his disciples may come and steal the body and tell the people that he has been raised from the dead. This last deception will be worse than the first." "Take a guard," Pilate answered. "Go, make the tomb as secure as you know how." So they went and made the tomb secure by putting a seal on the stone and posting the guard (Matthew 27:62-66).

Sunday, Nisan 15, Resurrection Day. The long, dark shadow cast over those who loved Jesus would be erased; for neither death nor Hades could keep its prey! For Jesus took hold of their keys and unlocked their gates.

> I am the Living One; I was dead, and behold I am alive for ever and ever! And I hold the keys of death and Hades (Revelation 1:18).

The hour of darkness was turned to brightness with the rising of the Son of Righteousness! Sunday would not only dawn on a new day but a new era and day of rest for God's people.

Resurrection Morning

Each of the Gospels have slightly different accounts of resurrection morning (Matthew 28:10; Mark 16:1-8; Luke 24:1-11; John 20:1-18). I have merged the four Gospel accounts into one showing how this amazing event might have unfolded.

> After the Sabbath, while it was still dark, Mary Magdalene and Mary the mother of James and Salome set off for the tomb. There was a violent earthquake, for an angel of the Lord came down from heaven and, going to the tomb, rolled back the stone and sat on it. His appearance was like lightning, and his clothes were white as snow. The guards were so afraid of him that they shook and became like dead men.

> As the new day began to dawn on the first day of the week, the three women came to the Tomb. They had not come to look for the resurrection of Christ; they came out of great love and devotion, bringing spices to anoint Jesus' body. The women asked each other, "Who will roll the stone away from the entrance of the tomb?" While they were wondering about this, suddenly two men in clothes that gleamed like lightning stood beside them and they found the stone rolled away from the tomb.

> As they entered the tomb, they saw a young man dressed in a white robe sitting on the right side, and they were alarmed. They did not find the body of the Lord Jesus. In their fright, the women bowed down with their faces to the ground, but the men said to them, "Why do you look

for the living among the dead? "Don't be alarmed," he said. "You are looking for Jesus the Nazarene, who was crucified. Why do you seek the living One among the dead? He has risen! He is not here. See the place where they laid him. He is not here; he has risen! Remember how he told you, while he was still with you in Galilee: 'The Son of Man must be delivered into the hands of sinful men, be crucified and on the third day be raised again.'" Then they remembered his words.

"He is not here; he has risen, just as he said. Come and see the place where he lay. Then go quickly and tell his disciples: 'He has risen from the dead and is going ahead of you into Galilee. There you will see him.' Now I have told you."

Trembling and bewildered, gripped with fear and great joy, the women went out and fled from the tomb. They said nothing to anyone, because they were afraid and ran to report it to His disciples. Mary Magdalene came running to Simon Peter and the other disciple, the one Jesus loved, and said, "They have taken the Lord out of the tomb, and we don't know where they have put him!"

So Peter and the other disciple [John] started for the tomb. Both were running, but the other disciple outran Peter and reached the tomb first. He bent over and looked in at the strips of linen lying there but did not go in. Then Simon Peter, who was behind him, arrived and went into the tomb. He saw the strips of linen lying there, as well as the burial cloth that had been around Jesus' head. The cloth was folded up by itself, separate from the linen. Finally the other disciple, who had reached the tomb first, also went inside. He saw and believed. (They still did not understand from Scripture that Jesus had to rise from the dead.) Then the disciples went back to their homes.

But Mary Magdalene [apparently returning with the other women] stood outside the tomb crying. As she wept, she bent over to look into the tomb and saw two angels in white, seated where Jesus' body had been, one at the head and the other at the foot. They asked her, "Woman, why are you crying?" "They have taken my Lord away," she said, "and I don't know where they have put him."

At this, she turned round and saw Jesus standing there, but she did not realize that it was Jesus. "Woman," he said, "why are you crying? Who is it you are looking for?" Thinking he was the gardener, she said, "Sir, if you have carried him away, tell me where you have put him, and I will get him." Jesus said to her, "Mary." She turned towards him and cried out in Aramaic, "Rabboni!" (which means Teacher). Jesus said, "Do not hold on to me, for I have not yet returned to the Father. Go instead to my brothers and tell them, 'I am returning to my Father and your Father, to my God and your God.'" Mary Magdalene went to the disciples with the news: "I have seen the Lord!" And she told them that he had said these things to her.

Suddenly Jesus met [the other women]. "Greetings," he said. They came to him, clasped his feet and worshiped him. Then Jesus said to them, "Do not be afraid. Go and tell my brothers to go to Galilee; there they will see me." When they came back from the tomb, they told all these things to the Eleven and to all the others. But they did not believe the women, because their words seemed to them like nonsense.

It would be quite troubling to find four accounts that tell the same story the same way. Eyewitness accounts reported through others that totally agree down to the exact details would have been fabricated. Besides, no person fabricating such a fantastic story would have ever chosen women to be the first witness of such a stupendous event. Women were on the bottom of the social scale in first century Palestine. The Jewish attitude toward women was "sooner let the words of the Law be burnt than delivered to women." Additionally, women were not permitted to give legal testimony in a Jewish court.

The Greatest News God ever gave was given to lowly shepherds at Christ's birth and now to these women, who delivered it to men. Why? Because their love lasted through the hour of darkness. The barriers were broken down at the empty tomb. To this day, the two greatest emancipators of women are Jesus Christ and the apostle Paul.

Peter Sees the Empty Tomb

Seeing the empty tomb, Mary Magdalene ran to Simon Peter and John, and said, "They have taken the Lord out of the tomb, and we don't know where they have put him!" John outran Peter, arriving first at the empty tomb, saw and believed what Mary said, but neither connected what they saw with any prophecies of Christ's resurrection so they went to their homes (John 20:1-10). It is clear from Luke's Gospel that Peter was still in the dark.

> Peter, however, got up and ran to the tomb. Bending over, he saw the strips of linen lying by themselves, and he went away, wondering to himself what had happened (Luke 24:12).

Obviously, they needed help to understand the Scriptures. This fact is brought out as Jesus joined two of the disciples traveling on the road to the village of Emmaus that day and explained, beginning with Moses and all the prophets, how Christ had to suffer being crucified and rise from the dead. At their strong urging, Jesus went into the village, sat at the table, took bread, gave thanks, broke it and began to give it to them. Then their eyes were opened, they recognized Him and said to each other how their hearts burned within them when He opened the Scriptures (Luke 24:13-32).

Peter Sees the Risen Christ

> They got up and returned at once to Jerusalem. There they found the Eleven and those with them, assembled together and saying, "It is true! The Lord has risen and has appeared to Simon." Then the two told what had happened on the way, and how Jesus was recognized by them when he broke the bread (Luke 24:33-35; cf. 1 Corinthians 15:3-5).

We are not told how they knew that Jesus appeared to Simon Peter. If he was there with the others, they may have confirmed Peter's testimony, which the others were not believing. Possibly, Jesus thought it necessary to appear to Simon to ease the pain of his denials. However, full restoration would not occur for several weeks.

93

As the two recounted how Jesus disappeared right before their eyes, the group might have thought they had seen a spirit instead of a bodily resurrection. We can speculate, given Thomas' reluctance to believe, that about this time the doubter could not take this kind of foolish talk any longer and left the room.

> While they were still talking about this, Jesus himself stood among them and said to them, "Peace be with you." They were startled and frightened, thinking they saw a ghost. He said to them, "Why are you troubled, and why do doubts rise in your minds? Look at my hands and my feet. It is I myself! Touch me and see; a ghost does not have flesh and bones, as you see I have."

> When he had said this, he showed them his hands and feet. And while they still did not believe it because of joy and amazement, he asked them, "Do you have anything here to eat?" They gave him a piece of broiled fish, and he took it and ate it in their presence. He said to them, "This is what I told you while I was still with you: Everything must be fulfilled that is written about me in the Law of Moses, the Prophets and the Psalms." Then he opened their minds so they could understand the Scriptures (Luke 24:36-45).

Peter learned an important lesson that day, which he would never forget.

> And we have the word of the prophets made more certain, and you will do well to pay attention to it, as to a light shining in a dark place, until the day dawns and the morning star rises in your hearts (2 Peter 1:19).

He had seen the Transfiguration and Christ in His risen body, but it was the opening and understanding of the Scriptures that proved to be the evidence that demanded a verdict of belief and so it would be through the centuries.

Jesus preached the Word to His disciples. Paul devotes chapter ten of Romans to the basic truth that the making of a disciple begins with the preaching of the Word.

That if you confess with your mouth, "Jesus is Lord," and believe in your heart that God raised him from the dead, you will be saved. For it is with your heart that you believe and are justified, and it is with your mouth that you confess and are saved (Romans 10:9-10).

Earlier Jesus had said to His disciples, "After I have risen, I will go ahead of you into Galilee" (Matthew 26:32) and then He told the women as they hurried away from the empty tomb, "Go and tell my brothers to go to Galilee; there they will see me" (Matthew 28:8-10). After Jesus' appearances on resurrection day, the disciples obeyed His command.

Then the eleven disciples went to Galilee, to the mountain where Jesus had told them to go. When they saw him, they worshiped him; but some doubted. Then Jesus came to them and said, "All authority in heaven and on earth has been given to me. Therefore go and make disciples of all nations, baptizing them in the name of the Father and of the Son and of the Holy Spirit, and teaching them to obey everything I have commanded you. And surely I am with you always, to the very end of the age" (Matthew 28:16-20).

Peter Goes Fishing

In the familiar surroundings of the Sea of Galilee, Jesus made a special post-resurrection appearance to seven of the eleven disciples.

Afterward Jesus appeared again to his disciples, by the Sea of Tiberias. It happened this way: Simon Peter, Thomas (called Didymus), Nathanael from Cana in Galilee, the sons of Zebedee, and two other disciples were together. "I'm going out to fish," Simon Peter told them, and they said, "We'll go with you." So they went out and got into the boat, but that night they caught nothing (John 21:1-3).

Again, Peter has seen the risen Christ and though having been called to be a fisher of men, he takes the lead, and the seven disciples go fishing for fish. Peter possibly felt that he disqualified himself for ministry by his denials of Christ or simply had not yet comprehended his calling. Therefore, Jesus would duplicate the experience that the disciples had several years earlier which led to their call to follow Christ full time.

Early in the morning, Jesus stood on the shore, but the disciples did not realize that it was Jesus. He called out to them, "Friends, haven't you any fish?" "No," they answered. He said, "Throw your net on the right side of the boat and you will find some." When they did, they were unable to haul the net in because of the large number of fish.

Peter's Impulsive Actions

Then the disciple whom Jesus loved said to Peter, "It is the Lord!" As soon as Simon Peter heard him say, "It is the Lord," he wrapped his outer garment around him (for he had taken it off) and jumped into the water. The other disciples followed in the boat, towing the net full of fish, for they were not far from shore, about a hundred yards. When they landed, they saw a fire of burning coals there with fish on it, and some bread (John 21:4-9).

In his excitement of seeing the Lord, Peter forgot the deep nagging pain of having denied Jesus three times and made his way to the shore. Filled with extraordinary physical strength, Peter responds to Christ's command.

Jesus said to them, "Bring some of the fish you have just caught." Simon Peter climbed aboard and dragged the net ashore. It was full of large fish, 153, but even with so many the net was not torn. Jesus said to them, "Come and have breakfast." None of the disciples dared ask him, "Who are you?" They knew it was the Lord. Jesus came, took the bread and gave it to them, and did the same with the fish. This was now the third time Jesus appeared to his disciples after he was raised from the dead (John 21:10-14).

From what follows, Peter did not grasp the importance of Jesus' invitation to "come and have breakfast." Eating a meal with the host for centuries signified fellowship and friendship with him. This invitation would be given by Christ to the unsaved members of the church of Laodicea.

Here I am! I stand at the door and knock. If anyone hears my voice and opens the door, I will come in and eat with him, and he with me (Revelation 3:20)

Without friendship and fellowship with the Lord, one cannot be His disciple. On this morning, Jesus demonstrated that He cares for His disciples by abundantly supplying for their needs and feeding them. The uncooked fish could be sold for a large profit. Besides the miraculous catch of fish at the commencement of their discipleship, the fish and bread should have reminded them of His miraculous feeding of the five and four thousand besides women.

Peter Reinstated by Christ

There are two fires mentioned in the NT. The first was in the courtyard of the High Priest, when Peter denied Christ with calling a curse down upon himself (Mark 14:54, 66-72). Now he is looking at a fire again, and no doubt guilt overwhelmed him. Satan desired to have Peter and was still trying to hold to him.

"Simon, Simon, Satan has asked to sift you as wheat. But I have prayed for you, Simon, that your faith may not fail. And when you have turned back, strengthen your brothers" (Luke 22:31-32).

Peter's impulsive actions and recognition of the Lord showed that his faith was intact. It was now time to turn him back so he could do what Jesus called him to do.

Hence, Peter was about to learn a lesson in love and forgiveness. Jesus did not say, "You blew it; I am going to give the keys of the kingdom to someone else. I hoped that you would be my first evangelist. If you get your priorities straight, in a year or so, I will see if I can use you." When they had finished eating, He actually said, "Peter, I can manage with you, provided I am sure of one thing."

"Simon son of John, do you truly love me more than these?" "Yes, Lord," he said, "you know that I love you." Jesus said, "Feed my lambs." Again Jesus said, "Simon son of John, do you truly love me?" He answered, "Yes, Lord, you know that I love you." Jesus said, "Take

97

care of my sheep." The third time he said to him, "Simon son of John, do you love me?" Peter was hurt because Jesus asked him the third time, "Do you love me?" He said, "Lord, you know all things; you know that I love you." Jesus said, "Feed my sheep (John 21:15-17).

In asking Peter if he loved him, Jesus twice used the word ἀγαπάω (*agapao*, to love dearly) and Peter replied with φιλέω (*phileo*, fond of, like, brotherly love). The third time Jesus graciously met Peter at his level and used φιλέω (*phileo*) to ask the disciple if he loved Him and Peter responded with the same word.

With Jesus' questioning of Peter's love, He expands his call to discipleship beyond an evangelist (fisher of men) to feeding and caring (shepherd) of Christ's flock. Peter would come to see himself as shepherd under the Chief Shepherd (cf. 1 Peter 5:4).

Peter was called to make disciples and strengthen his brothers, which carries four responsibilities.

1. Fisher of men—Evangelism
2. Feeding Christ's lambs—teaching the immature believers
3. Taking care of Christ's sheep—pastoring the flock (cf. Psalm 23)
4. Feeding Christ's sheep—teaching the mature believers

To these four responsibilities, a fifth is added—that of prophet as Peter wrote two letters forthtelling the Word of God and foretelling the future. Thus, Peter was an apostle, prophet, evangelist and pastor-teacher.

The Apostle Paul described the disciple making process of the early church.

It was he [Christ] who gave some to be apostles, some to be prophets, some to be evangelists, and some to be pastors and teachers, to prepare God's people for works of service, so that the body of Christ may be built up until we all reach unity in the faith and in the knowledge of the Son of God and become mature, attaining to the whole measure of the fullness of Christ. Then we will no longer be infants, tossed back and forth by the waves, and blown here and there by every wind of teaching and by the cunning and craftiness of men in their deceitful scheming. Instead, speaking the truth in love, we will in all things grow up into him who is the Head, that is, Christ (Ephesians 4:11-15).

With the death of the Apostle John around A.D. 100, the office of apostles and the need for prophets ceased with their having laid the foundation of God's household—the Church, with Christ Himself being the Chief Cornerstone (Ephesians 2:19-20). However, the offices of evangelists and pastor-teachers would continue throughout the church age.

In our day, there has been a decline in both evangelists and pastor-teachers. Preaching and teaching of the Word of God has fallen on hard times. Many pastors major on caring at the expense of feeding Christ's lambs and sheep. Short sermonettes are fed to the flock with the pastor's time being consumed by other matters. Too many pastors rather than standing on the authority of the Scriptures are swayed by society, resulting in lame and sickly lambs. Peter's two letters stand as a polemic against this practice.

Clearly, Peter understood to make disciples and strengthen his brothers required the preparation of minds for action through God's Word (cf. 1 Peter 1:13) and that he was to model the LORD as the Shepherd of His flock (cf. Psalm 23).

Peter's Destiny Predicted by Christ

Jesus accepted Peter's affirmation of friendship love, but the time would come when the disciple would prove he dearly loved Jesus.

> I tell you the truth, when you were younger you dressed yourself and went where you wanted; but when you are old you will stretch out your hands, and someone else will dress you and lead you where you do not want to go." Jesus said this to indicate the kind of death by which Peter would glorify God. Then he said to him, "Follow me!" (John 21:18-19).

The LORD told King Hezekiah that he had fifteen years to live and the king unwisely squandered those years in pride (2 Kings 20:6; Isaiah 38:5). Unlike Hezekiah, Peter humbled himself, serving the Lord the rest of his life. Jesus predicted four things concerning Peter's destiny.

1. He would be able to serve Him without restriction while younger
2. He would grow old
3. He would be bound as a common criminal
4. He would be crucified

Peter Wants to Know John's Destiny

Jesus repeated His earlier command, "Follow Me!" and now insisted, "You must follow Me." The command had not registered, Peter wanted know more than he should know.

> Peter turned and saw that the disciple whom Jesus loved was following them. (This was the one who had leaned back against Jesus at the supper and had said, "Lord, who is going to betray you?") When Peter saw him, he asked, "Lord, what about him?" Jesus answered, "If I want him to remain alive until I return, what is that to you? You must follow me." Because of this, the rumor spread among the brothers that this disciple would not die. But Jesus did not say that he would not die; he only said, "If I want him to remain alive until I return, what is that to you?" (John 21:20-23).

It would have been natural for Peter to want to know about his younger friend, but he would not be told. Ironically, John would reach old age, dying a natural death around A.D. 100. However, John did not know that would be the case. Only Peter was guaranteed a long life.

Peter is not to be concerned with the task that Jesus gave to John or anyone else. His obligation is "You must follow me." Every disciple of Christ has been called and saved for a specific purpose.

For it is by grace you have been saved, through faith--and this not from yourselves, it is the gift of God—not by works, so that no one can boast. For we are God's workmanship, created in Christ Jesus to do good works, which God prepared in advance for us to do (Ephesians 2:8-10).

Understanding the Nature of the Kingdom

A short time after the breakfast on the shore of the Sea of Galilee, the disciples returned to Jerusalem since Pentecost was approaching. Again, the Lord appeared to His disciples at meal time and ate with them.

> On one occasion, while he was eating with them, he gave them this command: "Do not leave Jerusalem, but wait for the gift my Father promised, which you have heard me speak about. For John baptized with water, but in a few days you will be baptized with the Holy Spirit" (Acts 1:4-5).

Jesus confirmed that the prediction given by John the Baptist some four years earlier and that He had made in the Upper Room discourse was about to be fulfilled. The best way to understand the Greek βαπτίζω (*baptizo*, baptize) when employed with the Person of the Holy Spirit is "to be identified with" or "overwhelmed."

> And he took bread, gave thanks and broke it, and gave it to them, saying, "This is my body given for you; do this in remembrance of me." In the same way, after the supper he took the cup, saying, "This cup is the new covenant in my blood, which is poured out for you (Luke 22:19-20).

The gift of the Holy Spirit would create out of the disciples a spiritual union called by Paul "one body"—the body of Christ (1 Corinthians 12:13).

Peter had been given the keys of the kingdom; yet he did not understand what they meant. Along with the others, he was seeking a temporal kingdom with Christ as its King.

> So when they met together, they asked him, "Lord, are you at this time going to restore the kingdom to Israel?" (Acts 1:6).

101

The Jews looked for the Messiah to establish a kingdom of temporal rule promised by the prophets, such as predicted by Isaiah.

> For to us a child is born, to us a son is given, and the government will be on his shoulders. And he will be called Wonderful Counselor, Mighty God, Everlasting Father, Prince of Peace. Of the increase of his government and peace there will be no end. He will reign on David's throne and over his kingdom, establishing and upholding it with justice and righteousness from that time on and forever. The zeal of the LORD Almighty will accomplish this (Isaiah 9:6-7).

There was nothing wrong with their understanding of the promise, just the timing!

> He said to them: "It is not for you to know the times or dates the Father has set by his own authority. But you will receive power when the Holy Spirit comes on you; and you will be my witnesses in Jerusalem, and in all Judea and Samaria, and to the ends of the earth" (Acts 1:7-8).

Christ did not say that there would be no temporal kingdom. He merely said that the time of establishment would not now be revealed to them. Instead, there would be a spiritual kingdom of God, which Paul defined.

> For the kingdom of God is not a matter of eating and drinking, but of righteousness, peace and joy in the Holy Spirit, because anyone who serves Christ in this way is pleasing to God and approved by men (Romans 14:17-18).

The Father would place the disciples in the New Covenant through Christ's blood of the New Covenant as Jesus promised when He instituted the Lord's Supper.

> I will give you a new heart and put a new spirit in you; I will remove from you your heart of stone and give you a heart of flesh. And I will put my Spirit in you and move you to follow my decrees and be careful to keep my laws (Ezekiel 36:26-27).

Discipleship would take on a new meaning with the gift of the Holy Spirit.

Each disciple would become a new creation in Christ—a partaker of the divine nature.

Near the end of his life, Peter wrote about the power the disciples' possessed and all who become Jesus' disciples.

> His divine power has given us everything we need for life and godliness through our knowledge of him who called us by his own glory and goodness. Through these he has given us his very great and precious promises, so that through them you may participate in the divine nature and escape the corruption in the world caused by evil desires (2 Peter 1:3-4).

Therefore, the disciples would not be on their own. The indwelling Spirit would endow them with power for the new task of building Christ's Church. It would be Peter's task to employ first the keys of the kingdom of heaven in Jerusalem, Judea, Samaria, and to the ends of the earth through the power of the Spirit, with the others joining him as Christ's witnesses. Why witnesses? In the Upper Room Discourse, Jesus said how the Spirit would work through their witness of Him.

> When he [the Holy Spirit] comes, he will convict the world of guilt in regard to sin and righteousness and judgment: in regard to sin, because men do not believe in me; in regard to righteousness, because I am going to the Father, where you can see me no longer; and in regard to judgment, because the prince of this world now stands condemned (John 16:8-11).

They could not save people, only God can do that! Christ's disciples would be His instruments of salvation proclaiming the Good News.

Peter Witnessed the Ascension of Christ

Christ's ascension to heaven took place on the Mount of Olives, east of Jerusalem, across the Kidron Valley and near the village of Bethany.

> When he had led them out to the vicinity of Bethany, he lifted up his hands and blessed them. While he was blessing them, he left them and

was taken up into heaven (Luke 24:50-51).

Luke provides more details of the ascension in Acts.

> After he said this, he was taken up before their very eyes, and a cloud hid him from their sight. They were looking intently up into the sky as he was going, when suddenly two men dressed in white stood beside them. "Men of Galilee," they said, "why do you stand here looking into the sky? This same Jesus, who has been taken from you into heaven, will come back in the same way you have seen him go into heaven" (Acts 1:9-11).

Mount of Olives from Across the Kidron Valley towards Bethany

The cloud might have been the Shekinah Glory that rested on the Tabernacle in the days of Moses (Exodus 40:34). Some have speculated that the two men were Enoch and Elijah, who left the earth without dying. They are more commonly understood to be angels, who were described as "men" (Luke 24:4) and a "young man" (Mark 16:5) at the empty tomb.

The disciples wanted to know if the Lord was going to restore the kingdom at this time and basically Christ told them not now you have a job to do. Nevertheless, the two men affirmed that Jesus would return to earth the same way He went to heaven.

> On that day his feet will stand on the Mount of Olives, east of Jerusalem, and the Mount of Olives will be split in two from east to west, forming a great valley, with half of the mountain moving north and half moving south (Zechariah 14:4).

Christ will return in wrath to establish His kingdom—something the Jews and disciples were anticipating. However, there was another event prefigured; something they did not anticipate. In 586 B.C., the Shekinah Glory left the Temple and ascended into heaven from the Mount of Olives prior to the destruction of the Temple and Jerusalem (see Ezekiel 10:3-4, 18-19; 11:22-23).

> O Jerusalem, Jerusalem, you who kill the prophets and stone those sent to you, how often I have longed to gather your children together, as a hen gathers her chicks under her wings, but you were not willing! Look, your house is left to you desolate. I tell you, you will not see me again until you say, "Blessed is he who comes in the name of the Lord" (Luke 13:34-35).

The ascension of Christ into heaven forecasted the end of the Temple and Jerusalem in A.D. 70. The disciples did not understand the meaning of the ascension and prophetic Scriptures until Peter preached on Pentecost.

In his Gospel, Luke recorded a brief statement of what happened following Christ's ascension in his Gospel and a more detailed account in Acts. They worshiped Jesus and returned to Jerusalem with great joy. The Eleven stayed in an upstairs room, joined together in prayer and were continually at the temple, praising God. The number of believers grew to about one hundred and twenty (Luke 24:52-53; Acts 1:12-15).

Peter's Blunder

Jesus had given specific instructions that they were to wait in Jerusalem until they received the gift of the Holy Spirit. Impulsive Peter did not listen carefully to Christ's instructions and obey them. Well and good, they were waiting in Jerusalem, but Peter could not wait for the Holy Spirit without taking action to replace Judas Iscariot, who had killed himself (Acts 1:16-26).

On the surface, we might think that Peter was acting properly.

1. He knew the Scriptures had to be fulfilled concerning the betrayer which the Holy Spirit spoke through David (Psalm 69:25).
2. He knew that the book of Psalms predicted that the betrayer's leadership would be taken by another (Psalm 109:8).
3. He established the criteria for replacing the betrayer.
4. He had the group propose two men to replace the betrayer.
5. He had them pray.
6. He had them cast lots and the lot fell on Matthias.
7. He added Matthias to the eleven apostles.

Significantly, no effort was made to replace the Apostle James when he died by martyrdom (Acts 12:2). The criteria established by Peter for apostleship did not correspond to the way the Twelve were called. Their calling came directly from Christ after He prayed all night to the Father. They were commissioned and given authority by Him. The using of lots was a lack of reliance on the Holy Spirit. Matthias is never heard of again!

But there is another that will be on center stage along with Peter. Christ Himself called Saul of Tarsus, also known Paul, to be an apostle before the Gentiles and Jews, as the replacement of Judas (Acts 9:1-19).

Paul begins nine letters calling himself an apostle. For example, "Paul, an apostle—sent not from men nor by man, but by Jesus Christ and God the Father, who raised him from the dead" (Galatians 1:1). Matthias was chosen by men, not by the Father and Son.

Impulsive Peter had blundered, having put his foot in his mouth once again. However, things are about to change for Peter.

Life of Peter from Pentecost

Peter Baptized by the Holy Spirit

When the day of Pentecost had arrived, they were all together in one place. Suddenly a sound like that of a violent rushing wind came from heaven, and it filled the whole house where they were staying. And tongues, like flames of fire that were divided, appeared to them and rested on each one of them. Then they were all filled with the Holy Spirit and began to speak in different languages, as the Spirit gave them ability for speech (Acts 2:1-4 HCSB).

On Pentecost 1446 B.C., Yahweh God spoke the Ten Commandments and the nation of Israel was born. On Pentecost A.D. 33, the Father and the Son sent the Holy Spirit and the Church was born and the recipients spoke in different languages.

They were baptized (cf. Acts 11:15-17) and filled with the Holy Spirit. Filling with the Spirit is mentioned in the NT as a recurring experience for Christians (cf. Acts 4:8, 31; Ephesians 5:8), but believers are baptized only once by the Spirit at the moment of salvation (see Titus 3:4-8).

In Romans 6:1-14, Paul explains baptism. All believers die with Christ and rise with Christ to new life. Therefore, they are untied with Him in death and live with Him in life.

The gift of the Holy Spirit would not be kept a secret.

There were Jews living in Jerusalem, devout men from every nation under heaven. When this sound occurred, the multitude came together and was confused because each one heard them speaking in his own language (Acts 2:5-6 HCSB).

The miracle of speaking languages was not in the words spoken but the words heard and understood.

And they were astounded and amazed, saying, "Look, aren't all these who are speaking Galileans? How is it that we hear, each of us, in our own native language? Parthians, Medes, Elamites; those who live in Mesopotamia, in Judea and Cappadocia, Pontus and Asia, Phrygia and Pamphylia, Egypt and the parts of Libya near Cyrene; visitors from Rome, both Jews and proselytes, Cretans and Arabs—we hear them speaking in our own languages the magnificent acts of God." And they were all astounded and perplexed, saying to one another, "What could this be?" But some sneered and said, "They're full of new wine!" (Acts 2:7-13 HCSB).

Perhaps those who sneered were unable to understand since they had confirmed their condemnation with their rejection of the Messiah. They were the hard soil that Jesus spoke about in the *Parable of the Sower, Soils and Seed*. The Evil One snatched away the Word as it was sown in their hearts (Matthew 13:18-19).

Peter Unlocks the Kingdom for the Jews

It is obvious from Peter's sermon on this day that he spoke either Aramaic or Greek with a Galilean accent, and those who understood heard the sermon in their own language and dialect.

So those who accepted his message were baptized, and that day about 3,000 people were added to them (Acts 2:41 HCSB).

This was the last proof of the day that the gift of the Holy Spirit had been sent by the Father and Son. Here "baptized" refers to being identified with Christ with the gift of the Holy Spirit, not water baptism, which is an outward testimony of the inward change.

With his sermon on Pentecost A.D. 33, Peter began using the keys that Christ had bestowed on him at Caesarea Philippi.

I will give you the keys of the kingdom of heaven; whatever you bind on earth will be bound in heaven, and whatever you loose on earth will be loosed in heaven" (Matthew 16:19).

See the section *The Teaching of Peter* for the exposition of his Pentecost Sermon.

Peter Heals the Crippled Beggar

In Acts 3:1-10, Peter and John met a man who was lame from his mother's womb at the temple gate called Beautiful. When he saw Peter and John about to enter the temple complex, he asked for help. They asked the man to look intently at them. Peter said, "I have neither silver nor gold, but what I have, I give to you: In the name of Jesus Christ the Nazarene, get up and walk!"

> Then, taking him by the right hand he raised him up, and at once his feet and ankles became strong. So he jumped up, stood, and started to walk, and he entered the temple complex with them—walking, leaping, and praising God. All the people saw him walking and praising God, and they recognized that he was the one who used to sit and beg at the Beautiful Gate of the temple complex. So they were filled with awe and astonishment at what had happened to him (Acts 3:1-10 HCSB).

Peter Preaches at Solomon's Colonnade

This healing resulted in a crowd gathering at Solomon's Colonnade at the Temple. There Peter delivered another sermon, which will be covered later.

> Now as they were speaking to the people, the priests, the commander of the temple guard, and the Sadducees confronted them, because they were provoked that they were teaching the people and proclaiming in the person of Jesus the resurrection from the dead. So they seized them and put them in custody until the next day, since it was already evening. But many of those who heard the message believed, and the number of the men came to about 5,000 (Acts 4:1-4 HCSB).

This number is similar to the feeding of the five thousand men, besides women and children. In both cases, the word ἀνήρ (*aner*) is translated "men," distinguishing males from boys, while excluding women and children. Therefore, it is impossible to know how many people were becoming believers in Christ.

With his two sermons in Jerusalem, Peter has unlocked the Gospel with the keys of the kingdom of heaven to the Jews. Christ had begun to build His Church through the apostle's confession that He is the Son of the Living God accompanied by the Holy Spirit's conviction of righteousness, sin and judgment (John 16:8-11).

Peter Preaches to the Sanhedrin

The next day, their rulers, elders, and scribes assembled in Jerusalem with Annas the high priest, Caiaphas, John and Alexander, and all the members of the high-priestly family. After they had Peter and John stand before them, they asked the question: "By what power or in what name have you done this?" (Acts 4:5-7 HCSB).

These leaders of Israel had rejected his message the previous day because he preached of the resurrection, but a deeper reason lay in the content of his message.

The Sanhedrin's question prompts Peter, filled with the Holy Spirit, to preach his third sermon in Jerusalem, which was rejected. This sermon will be covered later.

Befuddled by the boldness of Peter and John, they were amazed that these men had no rabbinical teaching, except having been with Jesus. They could not deny the man who had been healed standing there, and they had nothing to say in response to Peter's sermon. After privately conferring among themselves, they called for the apostles and ordered them not to preach or teach at all in the name of Jesus.

But Peter and John answered them, "Whether it's right in the sight of God for us to listen to you rather than to God, you decide; for we are unable to stop speaking about what we have seen and heard." After threatening them further, they released them. They found no way to punish them, because the people were all giving glory to God over what had been done; for the man was over 40 years old on whom this sign of healing had been performed (Acts 4:19-22 HCSB).

On their release, Peter and John went back and reported to their people what had happen and what was said. They raised their voices together in prayer

110

quoting from a messianic psalm, spoken by the Holy Spirit through David.

Why do the nations rage and the peoples plot in vain? The kings of the earth take their stand and the rulers gather together against the Lord and against his Anointed One (Acts 4:25-26; Psalm 2:1-2).

They applied these verses to Herod and Pontius Pilate as well as the Sanhedrin.

"Now, Lord, consider their threats and enable your servants to speak your word with great boldness. Stretch out your hand to heal and perform miraculous signs and wonders through the name of your holy servant Jesus" (Acts 4:29-30).

Not every prayer receives an immediate answer, but in this case God strengthens the faith of the believers by answering the first petition.

After they prayed, the place where they were meeting was shaken. And they were all filled with the Holy Spirit and spoke the word of God boldly (Acts 4:31).

The shaking of the meeting place as the wind filled the room at Pentecost was an outward sign that their prayer had been heard and of their filling by the Spirit. These believers did not pray for the removal of the prospect of persecution or make life easier. In fact, their answered prayer would change the climate from bad to worse as they became involved in the very activity they requested.

With great power the apostles continued to testify to the resurrection of the Lord Jesus, and much grace was upon them all (Acts 4:33).

Day after day, in the temple courts and from house to house, they never stopped teaching and proclaiming the good news that Jesus is the Christ (Acts 5:42).

Under Peter's leadership the Jerusalem church continued daily to grow in numbers as people were being saved, and even unbelievers were praising God (Acts 2:47; 4:21). The believers were of one heart and shared everything they had and there were no needy persons among them. From

111

time to time, those who owned lands or houses sold them and brought the money and put it at the apostles' feet (Acts 4:32-37).

Peter Pronounces Judgment on the Lying Couple

Sadly, the beautiful picture of harmony and fellowship was marred by a couple's deceitfulness.

> Now a man named Ananias, together with his wife Sapphira, also sold a piece of property. With his wife's full knowledge he kept back part of the money for himself, but brought the rest and put it at the apostles' feet (Acts 5:1-2).

At the conquest of Jericho, Achan deceitfully "kept back," taking and hiding what was devoted to God. Israel was defeated at Ai because of his sin. Consequently, Achan was exposed for his deceitfulness and along with his family was stoned to death (Joshua 7:1-26). God demanded purity in the nation for Israel to be successful in their mission of taking the Promised Land.

Ananias and Sapphira would contaminate the church if God did not deal with them through Peter. Like Achan's, their sin involved greed and lying. They were under no obligation to sell their property or bring any amount to the apostles, who would use the funds to care for the needy.

> Then Peter said, "Ananias, how is it that Satan has so filled your heart that you have lied to the Holy Spirit and have kept for yourself some of the money you received for the land? Didn't it belong to you before it was sold? And after it was sold, wasn't the money at your disposal? What made you think of doing such a thing? You have not lied to men but to God" (Acts 5:3-4).

Immediately, Peter perceived the spiritual conflict between the Holy Spirit, who led the couple to sell the property and Satan, who convinced them to withhold a portion but act as they were giving the entire amount. Jesus called the Devil "a liar and the father of lies" (John 8:44). As the Spirit filled the believers to speak boldly for God (Acts 4:31), Satan had filled

Ananias with deceitfulness to lie.

> Be self-controlled and alert. Your enemy the Devil prowls around like a roaring lion looking for someone to devour. Resist him, standing firm in the faith, because you know that your brothers throughout the world are undergoing the same kind of sufferings (1 Peter 5:8-9).

Christians are not exempt from attacks by Satan. The best way to defeat the schemes of the Devil is by putting on the whole amour of God and praying (Ephesians 6:11-18).

Peter either recognized supernaturally or by temporal means Ananias' deception. He attributed lying to the Holy Spirit as lying to God, thereby affirming the deity of the Holy Spirit. This couple was saved since they lied to the Holy Spirit so God inflicted the ultimate discipline of physical death.

> When Ananias heard this, he fell down and died. And great fear seized all who heard what had happened. Then the young men came forward, wrapped up his body, and carried him out and buried him (Acts 5:5-6).

Usually, burial was carried out on the day of death and probably three hours intervened before Sapphira appeared before the apostles and repeated the lie of her husband when Peter asked, "Tell me is this the price you and Ananias got for the land?" "Yes" she said, "that is the price."

> Peter said to her, "How could you agree to test the Spirit of the Lord? Look! The feet of the men who buried your husband are at the door, and they will carry you out also." At that moment she fell down at his feet and died. Then the young men came in and, finding her dead, carried her out and buried her beside her husband. Great fear seized the whole church and all who heard about these events (Acts 5:9-11).

Peter links the Spirit with the Lord, referring to Christ Jesus. Thus, the couple lied to the Triune God. Peter did not strike her dead or call on God to do so. Obviously, he was led by the Spirit to question Sapphira and not warn her of what happened to her husband.

Many things happened in the early days of the church as examples and

113

guides that do not necessarily recur throughout the history of the church, such as healing the sick, raising the dead, speaking in languages, which were intended as signs for unbelievers and authentication of prophecy until the completion of the NT.

When Christ's disciples have a healthy fear of God, they recognize that He is holy and righteous, resulting in the church being pure and spotless. When there is no fear of the LORD, the church is plagued by sin. What happened to this couple manifests God's attitude toward sin in the church. This event is a profound lesson for every Christian.

> The fear of the LORD is the beginning of wisdom, and knowledge of the Holy One is understanding (Proverbs 9:10).

> Now all has been heard; here is the conclusion of the matter: Fear God and keep his commandments, for this is the whole duty of man. For God will bring every deed into judgment, including every hidden thing, whether it is good or evil (Ecclesiastes 12:13-14).

In the case of Ananias and Sapphira, the hidden thing was revealed as evil and they paid with their lives for lying to the Father, Son and Holy Spirit. Peter was the Trinity's instrument in exposing the evil. Another important lesson was taught that day; church leaders should never participate in covering up sin, but always expose it.

Peter's Shadow

Unbelievers had respect for the followers of Jesus, but feared the deadly potential of joining the church if they were unsaved or not willing to live a holy life.

> The apostles performed many miraculous signs and wonders among the people. And all the believers used to meet together in Solomon's Colonnade. No one else dared join them, even though they were highly regarded by the people. Nevertheless, more and more men and women believed in the Lord and were added to their number. As a result, people brought the sick into the streets and laid them on beds and mats so that

at least Peter's shadow might fall on some of them as he passed by. Crowds gathered also from the towns around Jerusalem, bringing their sick and those tormented by evil spirits, and all of them were healed (Acts 5:12-16).

Luke has lost count of the believers; however, he now adds that women are being saved. Coming in contact with Peter's shadow for healing appears to be a superstitious act. Luke does not say whether God healed those who came in contact with it. It is possible He did. It could have been like the woman touching the garment of Jesus and power flowing from Him or God's miracle performed through Paul

> God did extraordinary miracles through Paul, so that even handkerchiefs and aprons that had touched him were taken to the sick, and their illnesses were cured and the evil spirits left them (Acts 19:11-12).

Obviously, it was neither Peter nor Paul but the power of the Spirit that performed the healing in response to the people's faith. This outpouring of healing was an answer to the prayer in Acts 4:29-30.

Peter and the Apostles Persecuted

Acts 5:17-42 records the arrest, scourging and trial of the Apostles at the hands of the Sanhedrin, the Jewish ruling council. They were consumed with jealousy and the spreading of Christianity placed in jeopardy their power and popularity. Therefore, they arrested the apostles who were increasing in popularity and power day by day. They arrested them and placed them in the public jail.

God sent an angel during the night to open the prison doors for the apostles and instructed them to return to the Temple and continue to speak the full message of life to the people. Ironically, the Sanhedrin was composed mostly of Sadducees, who denied the existence of angels. In the morning, the Sanhedrin sent for the apostles, whom the officers found missing. Hearing that they were at the Temple, soldiers were sent to rearrest the apostles, who were preaching in clear violation of the council's command (Acts 4:18, 21). The soldiers did not use force since they feared the people would stone them. Caiaphas the high priest questioned them about disobeying the Sanhedrin's strict orders.

> Peter and the other apostles replied: "We must obey God rather than men! The God of our fathers raised Jesus from the dead—whom you had killed by hanging him on a tree. God exalted him to his own right hand as Prince and Savior that he might give repentance and forgiveness of sins to Israel (Acts 5:29-31).

The Sadducees did not believe in resurrection. Furious at his charging them with murder as well as claiming Jesus was resurrected, they wanted to put the apostles to death. Gamaliel, the highly respected Rabbi, who taught Paul, intervened. He argued that if their movement was merely another human movement, it would fade away in time as countless others had. On the other hand, if this new doctrine were of God, the Sanhedrin would not want to oppose it. The soundness of Gamaliel's argument can be questioned since many false movements continue to exist after centuries. However, his logic worked and the apostles were released after being flogged.

The text does not say whether Peter and John received with the maximum lashes. Jewish law allowed for a maximum of thirty-nine lashes or fewer (cf. 2 Corinthians 11:24), which was one less than the forty lashes prescribed in the Mosaic Law.

> If the guilty man deserves to be beaten, the judge shall make him lie down and have him flogged in his presence with the number of lashes his crime deserves, but he must not give him more than forty lashes. If he is flogged more than that, your brother will be degraded in your eyes (Deuteronomy 25:2-3).

In the eyes of the Sanhedrin, Peter and John had committed wrong doing worthy of being flogged. Certainly, the response of the apostles to the flogging was unexpected by the Sanhedrin since they ordered them not to speak in the name of Jesus, and let them go.

The apostles left the Sanhedrin, rejoicing because they had been counted worthy of suffering disgrace for the Name. Day after day, in the temple courts and from house to house, they never stopped teaching and proclaiming the good news that Jesus is the Christ (Acts 5:41-42).

In his letters, Peter connected rejoicing with "suffering for Christ;" for example:

Dear friends, do not be surprised at the painful trial you are suffering, as though something strange were happening to you. But rejoice that you participate in the sufferings of Christ, so that you may be overjoyed when his glory is revealed (1 Peter 4:12-13; cf. 2:18–21; 3:8–17).

From this day forward, joy and suffering would mark many believers indwelt by the Holy Spirit.

You became imitators of us and of the Lord; in spite of severe suffering, you welcomed the message with the joy given by the Holy Spirit (1 Thessalonians 1:6).

Not only so, but we also rejoice in our sufferings, because we know that suffering produces perseverance; perseverance, character; and character, hope. And hope does not disappoint us, because God has poured out his love into our hearts by the Holy Spirit, whom he has given us (Romans 5:3-5).

Jesus had taught the disciples that they could expect this day and how to respond to it.

Blessed are you when people insult you, persecute you and falsely say all kinds of evil against you because of me. Rejoice and be glad, because great is your reward in heaven, for in the same way they persecuted the prophets who were before you (Matthew 5:11-12).

Today, many Christians are suffering physically and being killed at the hands of Muslims in the Middle East and Africa. Others are being imprisoned and persecuted in China. The acceptance of Christianity in

Europe and the United States is rapidly waning. Suffering for Christ will follow the birth pains preceding His Second Coming.

> Then you will be handed over to be persecuted and put to death, and you will be hated by all nations because of me (Matthew 24:9).

For a brief time, Peter steps off center stage in Luke's account of the early church after the appointment of seven men who were full of the Holy Spirit and wisdom for distributing bread to the widows. This delegation allowed the apostles to give their attention to prayer and the ministry of the Word. Luke focuses on two of the men, Stephen and Phillip.

Stephen was dragged away and stoned as he was preaching a lengthy sermon to the Sanhedrin. On that day a great persecution broke out against the church at Jerusalem and the Jewish believers were scattered, preached the Word wherever they went.

Peter Unlocks the Kingdom for the Samaritans

The popularity of the new Jewish movement was over; it was time to open the door to the despised Samaritans, who were of mixed blood lines and they deviated from accepted Judaism. Philip went down to a city in Samaria and proclaimed Christ there and performed miraculous signs.

> When the apostles in Jerusalem heard that Samaria had accepted the word of God, they sent Peter and John to them. When they arrived, they prayed for them that they might receive the Holy Spirit, because the Holy Spirit had not yet come upon any of them; they had simply been baptized into the name of the Lord Jesus. Then Peter and John placed their hands on them, and they received the Holy Spirit (Acts 8:14-17).

The Samaritans were genuine believers in the sense of John the Baptist's ministry. They "believed Philip," "received the Word of God," and "were baptized [with water]." However, they had not received the Holy Spirit. The Father and the Son withheld the Spirit.

First, the Samaritans were to be shown that salvation was of the Jews (cf.

John 4:22). Second, the Jews needed to know that the Samaritans were confirmed as full members of the Church. Third, the Gospel was moving beyond Jerusalem as predicted by Christ (Acts 1:8).

The imperfect tense (ελαμβανον *elambanon*, were receiving) indicates that the Spirit was received in succession, rather than simultaneously; so as Peter and John laid hands on them individually they were baptized in Christ. There is no mentioned that the Samaritan believers spoke and were heard in a different language, as was the case on Pentecost (Acts 10:44-46).

Three additional times hands were laid on the believers in the NT. Paul received the Holy Spirit when Ananias laid his hands on him (Acts 9:17). The church laid hands on Barnabas and Paul before sending them on the first missionary journey (Acts 13:1-3). Through a prophetic message, a gift was given to Timothy when the body of elders laid their hands on him (1 Timothy 4:14). There is no mention of laying on hands of the seven men full of the Holy Spirit, who were chosen to care for the widows. Certainly, there was no laying on of hands at Pentecost.

Peter Rebukes Simon the Sorcerer

Simon, who practiced sorcery, was known as the Great Power, and he was much like boastful Peter before his conversion. Simon boasted that he was someone great and the people believed he had divine power. Simon believed and was baptized and followed Philip everywhere, astonished by the great signs and miracles he saw (Acts 8: 9-13).

When Simon saw that the Samaritans received the Spirit at the laying on of hands, he offered Peter and John money for this ability. Ironically, Judas sold the Lord for money and Simon wanted to buy the Spirit for money. God's gift is not for sale! Peter rebuked and cursed Simon for trying to exploit sacred things for money or prestige.

> May your money perish with you, because you thought you could buy the gift of God with money! You have no part or share in this ministry, because your heart is not right before God (Acts 8:20-21).

Obviously, Peter recognized that Simon was unscrupulous, ambitious, mistaken and a blasphemer. His rebuke was intended to shake boastful Simon to the depths of his soul since Peter did not leave him hanging by a thread over Hell without a ray of hope.

> Repent of this wickedness and pray to the Lord. Perhaps he will forgive you for having such a thought in your heart. For I see that you are full of bitterness and captive to sin." Then Simon answered, "Pray to the Lord for me so that nothing you have said may happen to me" (Acts 8:22-24).

Simon was not asking Peter to make confession for him but to remove the curse that he placed on him. A century later, Justin Martyr, who lived in Samaria, said Simon became a Gnostic. "Simony," the buying and selling of religious rights and practices, became prevalent in later centuries.

Peter and John returned to Jerusalem, preaching in many Samaritan cities on the way (Acts 8:25).

Peter Meets Paul

In Acts 9:1-25, Luke introduces a young man named Saul of Tarsus who was a chief persecutor of the church. On a journey from Jerusalem to Damascus, Saul encountered the Lord and was blinded, taken to Ananias, who placed his hands on him and Saul received his sight and the Holy Spirit.

Through Ananias the Lord told Saul that he was called to be His apostle to the Gentiles and Jews, and even kings. Immediately, Saul went from persecutor to preacher to the one persecuted. After many days, the Jews conspired to kill him and he was saved by being lowered in a basket through an opening in the Damascus wall. Without indicating the time, Luke reports that Saul went to Jerusalem; however, this visit took place three years after his conversion according to Paul.

> When he came to Jerusalem, he tried to join the disciples, but they were all afraid of him, not believing that he really was a disciple. But

Barnabas took him and brought him to the apostles (Acts 9:26-27).

Then after three years, I went up to Jerusalem to get acquainted with Peter and stayed with him fifteen days. I saw none of the other apostles—only James, the Lord's brother (Galatians 1:18-19).

By this time the church was suffering great persecution in Jerusalem. Paul does not mention the Jerusalem church but discloses that the churches in Judea did not know him personally (Galatians 1:22).

After three years, Paul is grounded in his faith and able to share with James, who grew up with Jesus, and Peter, who had been trained by Jesus to unlock the Gospel to Jews, Samaritans and Gentiles. What did these three pillars (Galatians 2:9) of the church discuss? Imagine the personal insights about Jesus they shared. To have been a "fly on the wall" and listen to them clarify doctrines and theology would have been sensational!

We are not told how many times Peter and Paul crossed paths after this encounter. Luke records that both apostles attended the Jerusalem Council of A.D. 50. Later, Paul rebuked Peter for his withdrawing from Gentile believers and leading others astray. Outside of those two events, they are never mentioned together in the NT. Peter and Apollos appear to have been at Corinth since divided assemblies where claiming to follow all three of them (cf. 1 Corinthians 1:12; 3:22). However, Paul may have departed the city before their arrival.

James the brother of Jesus had become the pastor of the church at Jerusalem and Peter was free to travel and evangelize as well as inspect the new churches in Palestine. It is possible Peter retraced Philip's circuit.

Peter Heals Aeneas at Lydda

The disciples were called to be Christ's witnesses in Jerusalem, Judea and Samaria, and to the ends of the earth and while going they were to make disciples.

As Peter traveled about the country, he went to visit the saints in Lydda (modern Lod) on the Plain of Sharon.

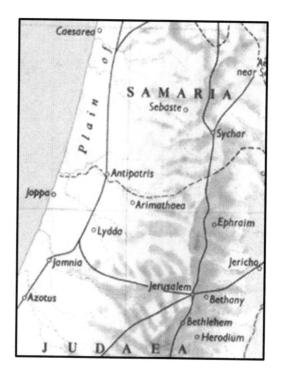

There he found a man named Aeneas, a paralytic who had been bedridden for eight years. "Aeneas," Peter said to him, "Jesus Christ heals you. Get up and take care of your mat." Immediately Aeneas got up. All those who lived in Lydda and Sharon saw him and turned to the Lord (Acts 9:33-35).

It was Jesus Christ who healed the man through Peter. When Peter told him, "Get up and take care of your mat," he was basically repeating what he heard Jesus say to another paralytic years before (Mark 2:11). Discipleship involves following the Lord's examples. Peter gave all the credit to Jesus Christ for healing the paralytic Aeneas. The miracle led to an extremely favorable response to the Gospel.

Peter Raises Dorcas at Joppa

Joppa (modern Jaffa) was on the Mediterranean coast about ten miles from Lydda. Dorcas (translated from Tabitha in Aramaic for "gazelle"), a female disciple of Christ, who was known for her practical Christianity lived there. She devoted her talents as a seamstress to the benefit of others, especially needy widows.

Providing for the needy is one way a disciple honors Christ. The Red Cross would never have come into existence if it were not for Jesus. Its symbol is the blood-red cross of Christ. Countless orphanages and hospitals are the result of the efforts of faithful disciples demonstrating the love of Christ.

When Dorcas died the believers, in amazing act of faith, sent for Peter to come at once. Upon his arrival, he was taken to an upstairs room and he sent the crying widows out of the room.

> Then he got down on his knees and prayed. Turning toward the dead woman, he said, "Tabitha, get up." She opened her eyes, and seeing Peter she sat up. He took her by the hand and helped her to her feet. Then he called the believers and the widows and presented her to them alive. This became known all over Joppa, and many people believed in the Lord (Acts 9:39-42).

Following Christ's example with the raising of Jairus daughter (Mark 5:35-43), Peter removed the spectators, addressed the deceased in Aramaic, and reached out his hand to help.

We can surmise that by prayer and the Spirit, Peter knew the Lord would raise this woman since he confidently commanded her to get up.

Astoundingly, "Peter stayed in Joppa for some time with a tanner named Simon" (Acts 9:43), whose work was an unclean business. The Jews felt abhorrence for people who work with the skins of dead animals, but such barriers were beginning to crumble for Peter. His new found outlook toward certain people primed Peter for the third phase of using the keys of the kingdom of heaven. The apostle's attitude toward Gentiles was that they were "unclean dogs." But within a few days, the apostle would unlock the door for the Gentiles to come into the Church. He would learn and teach that disciples accept all kinds of people, no matter what their background.

Peter Unlocks the Kingdom to the Gentiles

Luke devotes two chapters (Acts 10-12) to Peter and the conversion of Cornelius and his household. The significance of this event cannot be overstated as Peter unlocks the kingdom of heaven to the Gentiles. The unimaginable occurred; the Church became both Jew and Gentile.

Cornelius was a God-fearing centurion of the Italian Regiment stationed at Caesarea, who prayed and cared for the poor. An angel of God told him to send men to Joppa and bring back Simon Peter.

About noon the following day, Peter went to the roof to pray and became hungry. He fell into a trance and saw heaven opened and something like a sheet filled with all kinds of four-footed animals (clean and unclean) as well as reptiles of the earth and birds of the air. Then a voice told him, "Get up, Peter, Kill and eat."

"Surely not, Lord!" Peter replied. "I have never eaten anything impure or unclean." The voice spoke to him a second time, "Do not call anything impure that God has made clean." This happened three times, and immediately the sheet was taken back to heaven (Acts 10:14-16).

Jesus had already declared all foods clean (Mark 7:19), but Peter was perplexed by the meaning of the vision that called for him to violate the Mosaic Law, which forbade the Israelites to eat unclean foods.
The unclean laws were to keep the Israelites from entering into alliances with other nations, since the eating of a meal together was significant in ratifying covenants. The law of clean and unclean foods was a barrier that separated Jews and Gentiles, which would now be broken down in Christ. All that remained was for Peter to share the Gospel with Gentiles and bring them into the Church. By instructing Peter to go with the men, the Holy Spirit helped Peter to arrive at this profound truth.

When Peter arrived at Caesarea, Cornelius fell at his feet in reverence, but Peter made him get up, saying, "I am only a man myself." Peter entered the Gentile's house and talked with him, which was a breach of Judaism. There he found a large gathering of people. Cornelius recounted the circumstances surrounding his sending for him.

> So I sent for you immediately, and it was good of you to come. Now we are all here in the presence of God to listen to everything the Lord has commanded you to tell us (Acts 10:33).

Peter had a prepared and ready audience to preach the Gospel, which will be looked at in Peter's teachings.

> While Peter was still speaking these words, the Holy Spirit came down on all those who heard the message. The circumcised believers who had come with Peter were astounded, because the gift of the Holy Spirit had been poured out on the Gentiles also. For they heard them speaking in other languages and declaring the greatness of God.

> Then Peter responded, "Can anyone withhold water and prevent these from being baptized, who have received the Holy Spirit just as we have?" And he commanded them to be baptized in the name of Jesus Christ. Then they asked him to stay for a few days (Acts 10:44-48 HCSB).

Eight important facts should be noted:

1. There was no invitation
2. There was no public confession
3. There was no praying for the Holy Spirit
4. There was no laying on of hands
5. There was the baptizing by the Holy Spirit
6. There was other languages heard
7. There was no command to be circumcised
8. There was a command to be baptized with water

Peter's Explanation to the Jerusalem Church

News traveled fast! The idea of Gentiles being baptized was startling to the church at Jerusalem; even Samaritans had some Jewish blood in them and

125

their males would have been circumcised. Gentile God-fearers were monotheistic, believing in Yahweh, but the males were uncircumcised.

On his arrival in Jerusalem, Peter discovered that he was being criticized. Faced with this pivotal moment in history, Peter recounted everything that had occurred to the apostles and brethren. Indeed, he had entered a Gentile residence, and ate with the uncircumcised; however, it was not his idea but God's from the beginning to the end.

> As I began to speak, the Holy Spirit came down on them, just as on us at the beginning. Then I remembered the word of the Lord, how He said, 'John baptized with water, but you will be baptized with the Holy Spirit.' Therefore, if God gave them the same gift that He also gave to us when we believed on the Lord Jesus Christ, how could I possibly hinder God?"

> When they heard this they became silent. Then they glorified God, saying, "So God has granted repentance resulting in life to even the Gentiles!" (Acts 11:15-18 HCSB).

Mission accomplished! Having the keys of the Kingdom of Heaven, Peter had unlocked the Gospel to Jews, Samaritans and Gentiles—Christ was building His Church! The Good News for all people was about to breakout at Antioch of Syria, the third largest city of the Roman Empire, and spread to the ends of the earth through Paul and his partners.

Peter Rescued by an Angel

It was about this time that King Herod arrested some who belonged to the church, intending to persecute them. He had James, the brother of John, put to death with the sword (Acts 12:1-2).

The first of the apostles had died for his faith in Christ; now King Herod set his sights on Peter, the founder of the church at Jerusalem, who may have been the only one left in Jerusalem. James death pleased the Jewish leaders so the king had Peter arrested but since it was the Feast of Passover and Unleavened Bread he was not inclined to kill the apostle immediately. He took extra precautions by placing four squads of four soldiers each to guard Peter during three-hour watches at the prison. However, on the night before his trial, the church called a prayer meeting and an angel of the Lord came to Peter's rescue who was sleeping between two soldiers. Thinking he saw a vision, he followed the angel out of the prison, passed the two other sets of guards and walked the length of the street (Acts 12:3-10).

> Then Peter came to himself and said, "Now I know without a doubt that the Lord sent his angel and rescued me from Herod's clutches and from everything the Jewish people were anticipating" (Acts 12:11).

Peter went to the prayer meeting at Mary's house and knocked on the outer entrance, and a servant girl named Rhoda came to answer the door. When she recognized Peter's voice, she was so overjoyed she ran back without opening it and exclaimed, "Peter is at the door!" "You're out of your mind," they told her. She insisted it was Peter, but they said, "It must be his angel." In spite of such little faith, God had answered their prayers. After knocking more, they opened the door and saw him. He described how he got out of prison and told them to tell James and the brothers about what happened, and he left for another place (Acts 12:11-17).

> In the morning, there was no small commotion among the soldiers as to what had become of Peter. After Herod had a thorough search made for him and did not find him, he cross-examined the guards and ordered that they be executed (Acts 12:18-19).

The apostle James was not spared from the sword of King Herod, but Peter was delivered by God. On the surface, it appears that Jesus wasted a great deal of time with James, who was a member of His inner circle. For reasons known only to Him, God determined that James' ministry on earth was finished and Peter's would continue. No matter how important a Christian appears to be needed, there is no guarantee of the future; the one exception being Peter since Jesus predicted how he would die at an old age.

God works providentially as well as supernaturally. Many places in the Bible, we see a situation changing without a miracle, such as the events of the book of Esther and the life of Joseph.

Shaken by the arrest of Peter, these early disciples took the situation to the Lord in prayer. To wait on God in prayer is a disciple's greatest resource. God works according to His purposes, to which we align ourselves if we pray "in Jesus' name" and say "Amen," which means, "so be it."

Peter Speaks at the Jerusalem Council

In Acts 15:1-35, men came to Syrian Antioch from Judea and began teaching that Gentiles could not be saved if they were not circumcised and did not meet other demands of the Mosaic Law. The Antioch church sent a delegation of Paul, Barnabas and others to discuss this matter with the leaders at Jerusalem. The outcome of Christianity was at stake.

There were three sessions. The first session (Acts 15:4-5) was held by the general membership of the church, apostles and elders. Paul and Barnabas reported everything God had done through them and the party of the Pharisees insisted that the Gentiles must be circumcised. The second session (Acts 15:6) was a private meeting of the apostles and elders. The third session (Acts 15:7-29) was with the entire church. There were three speeches—the first by Peter, the second by Barnabas and Paul, and the third by James.

> After much discussion, Peter got up and addressed them: "Brothers, you know that some time ago God made a choice among you that the Gentiles might hear from my lips the message of the gospel and believe. God, who knows the heart, showed that he accepted them by giving the Holy Spirit to them, just as he did to us. He made no distinction between us and them, for he purified their hearts by faith. Now then, why do you try to test God by putting on the necks of the disciples a yoke that neither we nor our fathers have been able to bear? No! We believe it is through the grace of our Lord Jesus that we are saved, just as they are" (Acts 15:7-11).

Peter's speech builds on Cornelius and his household receiving the Holy Spirit and being saved. He asserted that God chose him to preach to the Gentiles and that they were trying to test God since both the Jews and Gentiles were saved through grace, not by the Law! Peter's logic silenced the opposition to hear Barnabas and Paul, who recounted the signs and wonders of God among the Gentiles. After they finished speaking, James spoke on Amos 9:11-12 and recommended that the Gentiles abstain from (1) idolatry, (2) immorality, (3) eating of strangled flesh, and (4) eating of blood in any form. His words were accepted by the First Church Council and were put in a letter for the Gentile believers in Antioch, Syria and Cilicia. The door of salvation was opened wide for Gentiles.

Peter Rebuked by Paul

At this point, Peter drops out of Luke's account of the early church. The next time we see Peter

> When Peter came to Antioch, I opposed him to his face, because he was clearly in the wrong. Before certain men came from James, he used to eat with the Gentiles. But when they arrived, he began to draw back and separate himself from the Gentiles because he was afraid of those who belonged to the circumcision group. The other Jews joined him in his hypocrisy, so that by their hypocrisy even Barnabas was led astray. When I saw that they were not acting in line with the truth of the gospel, I said to Peter in front of them all, "You are a Jew, yet you live like a Gentile and not like a Jew. How is it, then, that you force Gentiles to follow Jewish customs? (Galatians 2:11-14).

Obviously, Peter is a diamond in the rough with some sharps edges that need to be made smooth. The making of a disciple is a progression that lasts a lifetime. Sometimes the best of believers need someone to help them see their shortcomings and faults. "As iron sharpens iron, so one man sharpens another" (Proverbs 27:17).

In this case, Peter's hypocrisy led the Jewish believers and even Barnabas astray. Both unbelievers and believers should know hypocrisy when they see it; unfortunately many do not. To know the truth and not do it is sin; therefore, Paul is quick to rebuke this evil.

> But now in Christ Jesus you who once were far away have been brought near through the blood of Christ. For he himself is our peace, who has

made the two one and has destroyed the barrier, the dividing wall of hostility, by abolishing in his flesh the law with its commandments and regulations. His purpose was to create in himself one new man out of the two, thus making peace, and in this one body to reconcile both of them to God through the cross, by which he put to death their hostility (Ephesians 2:13-16).

Christ broke down the dividing wall between Jews and Gentiles and Peter was erecting it again. What Peter unlocked with the keys of the kingdom of heaven, he was relocking. The unity of the Church was at stake so Paul reprimanded the erring apostle.

All believers are partakers of the divine nature and brothers in Christ. Therefore, a church ceases to be Christian if it separates believers into classes, such as Jew or Gentile, rich or poor, black or white, and male or female. Undoubtedly, Peter learned this basic truth and continued to growing in the grace and knowledge of our Lord and Savior Jesus Christ.

Peter's Wife

The Apostle Paul laid down the principles of marriage in chapter seven of First Corinthians. He preferred singleness over being married. However, he did not condemn marriage for his fellow workers in Christ.

Don't we have the right to take a believing wife along with us, as do the other apostles and the Lord's brothers and Cephas? (1 Corinthians 9:5).

Perhaps Paul singled out Cephas (Peter) by name because of his prominence, the use of his name in the divisions in the Corinthian church (1 Corinthians 1:12) and it was well known that he was married (Matthew 8:14). Of the brothers of Jesus born to Joseph and Mary after His birth, James is mentioned since he was the head of the church at Jerusalem. Clearly, all the other disciples were either married or had the right to be married.

Twice Jesus sent His disciples out two-by-two so we should not be surprised that they took their wives with them. Since their wives were believers in

Christ, they were not only disciples but also partners in their husband's ministry and most likely attributed to it in many wonderful ways.

In the context, Paul is saying that the church is to pay Christian workers enough in order that their wives do not have to work so they can have more time to be with their husbands in the ministry.

PART II: THE TEACHING OF PETER

Peter's Sermons and Speeches

Having surveyed the making of a disciple from the Life of Peter, now we will turn to the teachings of the apostle, which come from sermons, speeches and the two letters he wrote. If anyone ever understood discipleship, it was Peter. He not only knew the principles of discipleship, but lived and taught them. Christ made him a disciple, and in turn Peter made others disciples.

On Pentecost A.D. 33, Peter began to carrying out the Great Commission as he made disciples with the first evangelistic sermon preached.

Peter's Sermon on Pentecost
Acts 2:14-42

Luke does not tell us where Peter gave this sermon. Since it was 9:00 a.m., the time for the morning prayers, we can safely assume the first New Covenant saints had gone to the Temple. With his natural temperament, now empowered by the Holy Spirit—bold, forward, and passionate; Peter stood up to defend the apostles of Christ and the Lord Himself from detrimental charges.

Not intimidated by ridicule or opposition and empowered by the Holy Spirit, it was now the time for preaching the Gospel to the massive crowd that had been assembled by curiosity of the disciples' miraculous speaking in languages.

The Jews, who did not understand these languages, mocked; but Peter declared, to everyone assembled, in their own tongue and according to their own prophecies, the true character of that which was taking place.

The apostle raised his voice and demanded the attention of the large crowd. He spoke in his Galilean dialect of Aramaic, but each person heard him in his or her own language and dialect. This sermon would have been delivered in the outer court of the Temple.

132

With his mind filled by the Holy Spirit, Peter was no longer fumbling to understand the Scriptures and the teachings of Jesus. In less than a quarter of an hour, the apostle delivered a masterpiece sermon.

Peter began somewhat negatively by arguing that the apostles could not be drunk on wine since it was nine in the morning, which gives insight into the practice of the day since Jews did not drink anything before 9:00 a.m. on the Sabbath or a feast day. He quickly moves to the positive with the explanation of the phenomena that was taking place.

The theme or proposition is the climax of Peter's sermon.

> Therefore let all Israel be assured of this: God has made this Jesus, whom you crucified, both Lord and Christ (Acts 2:36).

No message could have been more unwelcome to the Jews, who had rejected His Messianic claims and crucified Him. Peter, therefore, does not announce his theme until he has covered every possible Jewish objection.

The Outline of Peter's Sermon:

    A. Explanation of the Holy Spirit, 2:14-21
    B. Evidence of Christ's Lordship, 2:22-36
        1. Christ's Life on Earth, 22
        2. Christ's Death, Resurrection and Ascension, 23-28
        3. Christ's Reign as Lord on David's Throne, 29-36

His sermon contains three specific designations:

1. Fellow Jews and all of you who live in Jerusalem (Acts 2:14)
2. Men of Israel (Acts 2:22)
3. Brothers (Acts 2:29)

With three quotations from the Greek Septuagint, Peter employs prophetic evidence for the outpouring of the Holy Spirit and Christ's Lordship.

1. Joel 2:28-32
2. Psalm 16:8-11
3. Psalm 110:1

Both Peter's preaching and his first letter are filled with quotes from the OT Scriptures. Those who preach the Word of God should study the preaching of the early church. Clearly, Peter placed all his emphasis on fulfillment without attempting to exegete the details of biblical prophecy. Most likely, his audience had some understanding of these prophecies.

Peter provided five proofs that Christ Jesus was alive:

1. His Person and life demanded that He was raised from the dead, 2:22-24
2. His resurrection was predicted in Psalm 16:8-11, 2:25-31
3. His resurrection was witnessed by the disciples, 2:32
4. His sending of the Holy Spirit proved He was alive, 2:33
5. His resurrection was predicted in Psalm 110:1, 2:34-35

Though Peter quotes a prophecy in its entirety, he does not claim it has been fulfilled entirely. His point is that the last days have commenced with the giving of the Holy Spirit. He alters "afterward" to "in the last days" of Joel's prophecy, indicating the beginning of God's redemptive program, which covers three periods:

1. The pouring out of the Holy Spirit from Pentecost forward (2:17-18 or 2:17)
2. The wonders and signs on earth during the Tribulation Period (2:19-20a or 2:18-20a)
3. The great and remarkable Day of the Lord, when Christ comes to reign (2:20b-21; cf. 2:29-31)

Significantly, on Pentecost 1446 B.C., the Law was given to the people of the new nation of Israel at Mt Sinai (Exodus 19-20). On Pentecost A.D. 33, the Holy Spirit was given to the Church—the people of the New Covenant—so they could live the Law.

> For I will take you out of the nations; I will gather you from all the countries and bring you back into your own land. I will sprinkle clean

134

water on you, and you will be clean; I will cleanse you from all your impurities and from all your idols. I will give you a new heart and put a new spirit in you; I will remove from you your heart of stone and give you a heart of flesh. And I will put my Spirit in you and move you to follow my decrees and be careful to keep my laws (Ezekiel 36:24-27).

In verses 22-24, Peter mentions "God" four times to (1) emphasize God's role in Christ's earthly ministry (2) His mistreatment by the Jews and Gentiles, and (3) His victory over death.

1. "Jesus of Nazareth was a man accredited by God to you by miracles, wonders and signs, which God did among you through him, as you yourselves know." Many were witnesses of Christ's miracles, while others had heard reports of them. Throughout His ministry, the people had been faced with a choice—these miracles were from either God or Satan.

2. "This man was handed over to you by God's set purpose and foreknowledge; and you, with the help of wicked men [by the hand of the lawless], put him to death by nailing him to the cross." Here "foreknowledge" is προγνωσις (*prognosis*), denoting forethought or prearrangement in the Greek. The events surrounding Christ's crucifixion were planned and orchestrated by God. "Wicked men" or "the lawless" refers to the Gentiles and "you" refers to the Jews. Those involved were responsible for their own actions; they were guilty before God. However, under the axiom of corporate solidarity, everyone is guilty since Christ died for all the world.

3. "But God raised him from the dead, freeing him from the agony of death, because it was impossible for death to keep its hold on him." "Agony" (ωδιν *odin*) is frequently used to describe pains associated with giving birth (cf. Revelation 12:2); hence, there is irony here in the mixed metaphor. Faced with the reality of Jesus' resurrection, fear of the Lord's judgment should have overwhelmed the enemies of Christ; clearly, this was the purpose of Peter's climax.

In verses 25-35, Peter's evidence of Christ's resurrection and ascension to heaven comes from David in Psalm 16:8-11 and Psalm 110:1. Both quotations are connected by the phrase "at my right hand" and the introductory statement, "David said about him," which indicates that David was not speaking of himself, but of the Messiah. Obviously, this psalm could not be speaking of David since his body was still buried in Jerusalem.

Peter used Psalm 16:8-11 to show that the Messiah would be someone who was resurrected and subsequently be exalted to the right hand of God with His ascension to heaven.

Important doctrines contained in these two quotations are often blurred in English translations. Here the Greek term Αδης (*hades*) is translated "grave" in the NIV and "hell" in KJV. The Hebrew word for this place is שׁאוּל (*sheol*). Sheol or Hades is the place of the departed spirit and soul. In Luke 16:19-31, Jesus describes this place as having two sides. One is "Abraham's side" and other is "this place of torment"—the two places are separated by a great chasm that cannot be crossed. Jesus referred to Abraham's side as Paradise, when He said to the man beside him on the cross, "I tell you the truth, today you will be with me in paradise" (Luke 23:43).

In 2 Corinthians 12:3-4, Paul wrote of his being caught up to Paradise. On the morning of His resurrection, Jesus told Mary not to touch Him for He had not yet ascended to His Father (John 20:17).

Many believe that Ephesians 4:8-10 refers to Christ taking Abraham's side of Hades to heaven with Him when He ascended. Through His crucifixion and resurrection, Christ conquered Satan and death. In triumph, He returned to God with the OT saints, who had entered this world as captives of Satan (cf. Colossians 2:15; 1 Peter 3:18-20).

After Christ ascended into heaven, He also gave gifts to men, which refers to the giving of the Holy Spirit on Pentecost.

At the end of the second century, Roman Christians developed an early form of the Apostles' Creed, which can be found in Peter's sermon on Pentecost and his two letters. There are many translations and versions of the creed; the following one is from the Church of England's *Common Book*, dated 2000.

The Apostles' Creed

I believe in God, the Father almighty,
    creator of heaven and earth.
I believe in Jesus Christ, his only Son, our Lord,
    who was conceived by the Holy Spirit,
    born of the Virgin Mary,
    suffered under Pontius Pilate,
    was crucified, died, and was buried;
    he descended to the dead [Hades].
    On the third day he rose again;
    he ascended into heaven,
    he is seated at the right hand of the Father,
    and he will come to judge the living and the dead.
I believe in the Holy Spirit,
    the holy catholic [universal] Church,
    the communion of saints,
    the forgiveness of sins,
    the resurrection of the body,
    and the life everlasting.
    Amen.

Note that the change of "Hades" to "dead" and that "catholic" means "universal."

The Apostle John wrote in the Apocalypse:

When I saw him, I fell at his feet as though dead. Then he placed his right hand on me and said: "Do not be afraid. I am the First and the Last. I am the Living One; I was dead, and behold I am alive for ever and ever! And I hold the keys of death and Hades (Revelation 1:17-18).

The sea gave up the dead that were in it, and death and Hades gave up the dead that were in them, and each person was judged according to what he had done. Then death and Hades were thrown into the lake of fire. The lake of fire is the second death. If anyone's name was not found written in the book of life, he was thrown into the lake of fire (Revelation 20:13-15).

Death refers to the place of the physical body and Hades refers to the place of the soul and spirit. Body, soul and spirit of the unsaved will be reunited in the second resurrection and cast into the lake of fire, which is Hell!

Therefore, verse 27 of the HCSB accurately translates and communicates what happened to Christ's soul at the moment He gave up His spirit when His body died on the Cross—as well as the reuniting of His soul and body at His resurrection on the first day of the week.

Because You will not leave my soul in Hades, or allow Your Holy One to see decay.

Looking forward to the fulfillment of the Davidic Covenant (2 Samuel 7:11-16), Peter points to the day when Christ will reign on David's throne; and his proof is His resurrection and ascension.

Brothers, I can confidently speak to you about the patriarch David: he is both dead and buried, and his tomb is with us to this day. Since he was a prophet, he knew that God had sworn an oath to him to seat one of his descendants on his throne. Seeing this in advance, he spoke concerning the resurrection of the Messiah:

He was not left in Hades, and His flesh did not experience decay (Acts 2:29-31 HCSB).

The presence of the Holy Spirit offers logical evidence of Christ's resurrection according to verses 33-36. Since Jesus sent the Holy Spirit, He must be alive and ascended to heaven. Thus, Peter interpreted Psalm 110:1 just as Jesus had done in Matthew 22:41-45.

Peter's sermon ends with the Lordship of Christ.

> Therefore let all Israel be assured of this: God has made this Jesus, whom you crucified, both Lord and Christ (Acts 2:36).

If you want Jesus as your Savior, He must be your Lord!

> That if you confess with your mouth, "Jesus is Lord," and believe in your heart that God raised him from the dead, you will be saved. For it is with your heart that you believe and are justified, and it is with your mouth that you confess and are saved (Romans 10:9-10).

Obviously, Peter's sermon awakened the fear of the LORD in the hearts of some listeners.

> For David did not ascend to heaven, and yet he said, "The Lord said to my Lord: 'Sit at my right hand until I make your enemies a footstool for your feet'" (Acts 2:34-35).

Jesus of Nazareth, whom they had crucified but is risen and ascended, and is coming back and it will not go well for His enemies. Today, the Gospel is often watered down so that it does not strike people's hearts with the fear of God. There is no fear of judgment, no guilt. Yet, the outcome of Peter's sermon (2:37-42) manifests the firstfruits of the Holy Spirit's work.

> When he comes, he will convict the world of guilt in regard to sin and righteousness and judgment: in regard to sin, because men do not believe in me; in regard to righteousness, because I am going to the Father, where you can see me no longer and in regard to judgment, because the prince of this world now stands condemned (John 16:8-11).

Peter did not have to give an invitation; the hearts of the people were pierced when they heard his message—they asked the apostles, "Brothers, what must we do?"

Peter had already laid down one of the necessary responses for being saved and now he adds two more.

1. "And everyone who calls on the name of the Lord [Yahweh] will be saved." Within Joel's prophecy are a new people of God, comprised of Jew and Gentile. The nation of Israel has been set aside for the Church that was born on this day.

2. "Repent" (μετανοεω *metanoeo*), which means to change the mind and here includes all aspects of conversion including faith. Repentance involves turning from self and one's own ways to Christ and His ways.

3. "Be baptized, every one of you, in the name of Jesus Christ for the forgiveness of your sins. And you will receive the gift of the Holy Spirit," which is to "be baptized" (βαπτιζω *baptizo*). Here this term means to be identified with Christ and placed in Him through the indwelling presence of the Holy Spirit.

Today, few presentations of the Gospel contain all of Peter's instructions for obtaining salvation, and thereby lack the power of the Spirit to convict the minds and hearts of those who listen.

The most amazing miracle of Pentecost was not the filling the whole house with the sound like a blowing of a violent wind from heaven or the tongues of fire that separated and rested on 120 gathered in one place or a crowd hearing the Galilean words of Peter in many languages.

The most amazing miracle was the transformation of about 3,000 lives having been indwelt by the Holy Spirit when they heard the Word of God preached. Those who believed and repented were saved through the washing of rebirth and renewal by the Spirit poured out on them. They had received the gift of God.

Salvation in Christ by God's grace that began on Pentecost comes cascading down the centuries until today.

Peter's Sermon at Solomon's Colonnade
Acts 3:11-26

Peter performed the miracle of healing the lame man at the Beautiful Gate of the Temple, first to relieve the man's physical infirmity, second to save his soul, and third as an opportunity to present Christ and offer forgiveness to the nation of Israel.

Peter addressed the people gathered at Solomon's Colonnade as "Men of Israel" as he did in 2:14 and 22. To capture their attention, he asked two questions, "Why does this surprise you? Why do you stare at us as if by our own power or godliness we had made this man walk?" As on Pentecost, the apostle accused his Jewish audience of disowning and killing Jesus, whom Peter identified to be:

1. The Glorified Servant of the God of Abraham, Isaac and Jacob
2. The Disowned Holy and Righteous One
3. The Author of Life
4. The Risen One from the Dead
5. The Messiah of God
6. The Prophet like Moses
7. The One who will Return from Heaven

The Outline of Peter's Sermon:

A. Peter's Questions, 3:12
B. Peter's Declaration, 3:13a
C. People's Guilt, 3:13b-15
D. Power of Faith in Jesus' Name, 3:16-17
E. Prophecies of Christ's Sufferings, 3:18
F. Prophecies of Christ's Return, 3:19-24
G. People's Opportunity, 3:25-26

The theme of Peter's sermon at Solomon's Colonnade is suffering precedes glory as seen through the healing of the lame man and Christ's death, resurrection, ascension and coming again. Therefore, Peter turned their attention to Jesus, whom he gave the credit for the healing of the lame man.

> By faith in the name of Jesus, this man whom you see and know was made strong. It is Jesus' name and the faith that comes through him that has given this complete healing to him, as you can all see (Acts 3:16).

As on Pentecost, Peter told the people they were responsible for the awful crime of killing the Messiah, yet they had acted in ignorance to fulfill the plan and purpose of God revealed by all the prophets. Since they and their leaders acted in ignorance, God was willing to forgive them. Forgiveness was offered, but they had to respond. This was their second opportunity to be saved.

> Repent, then, and turn to God, so that your sins may be wiped out, that times of refreshing may come from the Lord, and that he may send the Christ, who has been appointed for you—even Jesus. He must remain in heaven until the time comes for God to restore everything, as he promised long ago through his holy prophets (Acts 3:19-20).

The OT prophets predicted Israel's future kingdom under the Messiah. God's program is to bless all people through Abraham's seed—the nation of Israel, and ultimately the Messiah (Genesis 12:1-3). Israel's sins must be wiped out prior to the times of refreshing—the establishment of the kingdom of heaven under the reign of the Messiah Jesus. Hence, the kingdom is postponed until Israel no longer disowns the Messiah. The times of refreshing will come after all Israel is saved (Zechariah 12:10-13:1; Romans 11:26) and Christ's kingdom fills the whole earth (Daniel 2:44-45).

Again, Peter turned to the prophetic word; this time to press the point that his audience will be cut off if they do not listen to everything the Messiah—a prophet like Moses—told them. Most likely, "cut off" means from the assembly of the righteous (Psalms 1:5; cf. Deuteronomy 18:19). He continued referring to the prophetic message, "Indeed, all the prophets from Samuel on, as many as have spoken, have foretold these days"—that is "the time of the new order" ushered in by the Messiah (Hebrews 9:10).

Peter concluded his sermon by confirming his audience's unique position as heirs of the prophets and of God's covenant with Abraham. God's raising of His Servant will result in all peoples of the earth being blessed, though He was sent to Israel first. If they turn from their wicked ways (repent), they will be blessed. Yet, imbedded in his conclusion is the truth that salvation in Christ will be offered to the Gentiles. This fact was inspired by the Holy Spirit in Peter's sermon, but was one that the apostle would be slow to grasp.

To understand the Jews attitudes toward the Gentiles, read the book of Jonah, where the prophet would rather die than share God's compassion and mercy with Gentiles!

In every century, Christ's disciples have had to overcome their prejudices toward people of different ethnic origins and backgrounds. During the Crusades, Christians killed Jews as well as Arabs in the name of Christ, instead of evangelizing them. Praise the Lord for the white Christians who took the Gospel to the red, black and yellow people of the world.

Peter's Speech to the Sanhedrin
Acts 4:1-24

At Solomon's Colonnade, Peter's message was very objectionable to the Jewish leaders, especially the Sadducees, who accepted only the Pentateuch as Scripture and denied the resurrection of the dead. Traditionally, the priests and High Priests came from the Sadducees, who were leaders of the Jews at this time, and the last thing they wanted was a couple of Jewish men declaring the resurrection, which threatened their position, influence and wealth.

The Jewish leaders had demanded the execution of Christ as a blasphemer, and now they were disturbed by Peter and John proclaiming in Jesus the resurrection of the dead as well as by the thousands who believed in Him. They detained Peter and John overnight in jail because Jewish law did not permit trials at night. The two apostles faced a hearing the next day and the Sanhedrin (Jewish Supreme Court, Senate, and Council) began to question them: "By what power or what name did you do this?"

The theme of Peter's speech is that salvation is found in no one else but Jesus Christ, whom they had crucified.

Outline of Peter's Sermon:

    A. Peter and John's Kindness Towards the Cripple, 4:8-9
    B. Rulers and Elder's Crucifixion of Jesus Christ, 10a
    C. God's Resurrection of Jesus Christ, 10b
    D. Rulers, Elders and People's Rejection of the Stone, 11
    E. Salvation is found only in Jesus Christ, 12

Peter's speech is short but powerful since his answer to the Sanhedrin came from being filled with the Holy Spirit. The Greek πληθω (*pletho*) is used for describing the filling of anything from a sponge to a boat (Matthew 27:48; Luke 5:7). Luke uses this common term eight times to describe how the Holy Spirit influences a person to speak or preach for God.

There is a touch of sarcasm in Peter's words, "If we are being called to account today for an act of kindness shown to a cripple," made before his proclamation—"then know this, you and all people of Israel."

For the third time, Peter has charged the Jewish leaders of killing the Messiah. Speaking in tongues was Peter's proof of Christ's resurrection on Pentecost and now the healing of the lame man was his evidence. Unquestionably, the crucifixion and resurrection of Jesus Christ is the heart of the Gospel that Peter proclaimed. The apostle had learned from the Master's teaching and example.

> Jesus entered the temple courts, and, while he was teaching, the chief priests and the elders of the people came to him. "By what authority are you doing these things?" they asked. "And who gave you this authority?" (Matthew 21:23).

Jesus answered with the *Parable of the Vineyard* (Matthew 21:42), teaching that the rejected son of the vineyard owner is likened to the rejected stone that became the chief cornerstone (Psalm 118:22). In death, the Messiah was the rejected stone by these leaders, and in resurrection, He became the chief cornerstone or capstone for all who would align their life to Him and His teaching. Now, Peter answered these Jewish leaders, quoting Psalm 118:22 as proof that Jesus is the Messiah; he identified Him as "the chief cornerstone" (cf. 1 Peter 2:7 Romans 9:33; Isaiah 28:16). Just as Peter observed Jesus, the Sanhedrin had observed Peter and John. .Here is an important lesson; there is always someone listening to us, and watching us!

The name of Jesus Christ was the center of contention (4:7, 10, 12) and ever will be. Therefore, Peter insisted that salvation for Jew and Gentile alike is exclusively through the name of Jesus Christ (cf. John 14:6; Acts 10:43; 1 Timothy 2:5). That Christianity is exclusive does not play well in our pluralistic world, where tolerance is a chief virtue. Many assume that all religions are similar and lead to a fantastic destiny. There was no compromise or adjustment of the Gospel by Peter—a significant point in his second letter.

145

Peter's Sermon to Cornelius and His Household
Acts 10:34-43

Chapters 10-11 of Acts are two of the most important chapters of the Bible. They record Peter using "the keys of the kingdom" to open the door to Gentiles. To Peter's credit, he obeyed the Spirit's command to go with three men who had arrived from Cornelius. He acknowledged his own Jewish prejudice before the many gathered at Cornelius' house (Acts 10:28-29).

On hearing Cornelius' explanation (10:30-33), the message of the vision was understood by Peter and he began to preach the Good News (10:34-38). Both the preacher and congregation were prepared for the message.

Peter realized that "God is not one who is a respecter of persons," that is, "God is not one to show partiality," a truth that appears in various books of the NT (cf. Romans 2:11; Ephesians 2:11-22; Colossians 3:25; James 2:1; 1 Peter 1:17).

This was the lesson of the vision of the clean and unclean animals and birds. Peter would have choked on his own words four days earlier. Now he swept away centuries of Jewish prejudice. Next to the incarnation of Christ, Pentecost, and the conversion of Saul, stands these words of Peter to the Gentile world—the Good News is for everyone who believes!

The theme of Peter's sermon to Cornelius and his household was God does not show favoritism since He accepts those who fear Him from every nation.

Before the Holy Spirit interrupts, Peter made two points in his sermon:

- A. God does not show favoritism, 10:34-35
- B. God sent His message of Good News to Israel, 10:36-43
  - 1. Peter was a witness of the ministry of Jesus Christ, 36-39
  - 2. Peter was a witness of the crucifixion and resurrection of Jesus Christ, 40-41
  - 3. Peter was a witness appointed to testify of Jesus Christ, 42-43

The key verse of the Bible is "the fear of the LORD is the beginning of wisdom, and knowledge of the Holy One is understanding" (Proverbs 9:10). Since Cornelius was a God-fearer, he was acceptable to God because he believed only in Yahweh and did righteous things. In fact, such people exist in every nation. However, the new dispensation of the New Covenant had commenced; therefore, such qualities could not save a person—one needed to be born of the Spirit (cf. John 3:3).

No longer can a person fear God and work righteousness to be accepted by God. Otherwise, there would have been no need for God to send Peter to Cornelius or Christ into the world. Peter has established already that "salvation is found in no one else, for there is no other name under heaven given to men by which we must be saved" (Acts 4:12). Clearly, acceptance with God does not depend on the fact of being descended from Abraham, or of possessing external privileges, but on the state of the heart—everyone who believes in Christ will receive a new heart and forgiveness of sins.

"The good news of peace" refers to reconciliation between God and man through Jesus Christ (cf. Romans 5:1). Even though Jesus Christ was sent to Israel, Peter proclaimed, "He is Lord of all," which is the theological key of his speech and events that follow.

The word "Lord" implies Christ's divinity as well as His role as Mediator, Judge and Ruler over all nations. Jesus' favorite title for Himself was "the Son of Man" (81 times), which comes from Daniel 7:13-14, where He is said to be coming in the clouds to establish His everlasting dominion and kingdom. Jesus used this imagery of Himself (cf. Matthew 24:30; 26:64; Mark 13:26).

In Christ's First Advent, He did not come to condemn or judge sin but expose it and save the sinner (John 3:16-21; 8:12-18). However, during His Second Advent, Christ will be the answer to Asaph's prayer, "Rise up, God, judge the earth, for all the nations belong to You" (Psalms 82:8 HCSB),

Here Peter used the human title "Jesus of Nazareth" since He is the One appointed (ορίζω *horizon*, declared, determined, ordained) by God to be the Judge of the living and dead because of His taking on the likeness of men. Jesus received all authority and power from God to be Judge (cf. Matthew 28:18; John 5:22; Philippians 2:5-11).

Undoubtedly, Peter viewed salvation in terms of the Second Coming of Christ, when He would be the Judge of the living and the dead. Within Peter's teaching and preaching, the Second Coming is as important as the death and resurrection of Christ.

The assertion "you know" indicates that his audience had heard the reports of what happened throughout all Judea concerning Jesus Christ. Hence, Peter offered proof of Christ's deity. He referred to God anointing Him with the Holy Spirit and mighty power for doing good and for healing all who were tyrannically oppressed by the Devil. "He went around doing good" epitomizes the life of Jesus, who left us an example to follow. Peter referred to the baptism that John preached to mark the distinction between the OT economy and the beginning of the NT economy.

As an eyewitness, Peter affirmed Christ's death, resurrection and proclaimed His second coming; He is the One appointed by God to be the Judge of the living and dead. As with his preceding messages, Peter referred to the prophetic word—"all the prophets testify of Him." This is the Gospel for Peter and Paul.

> For what I received I passed on to you as of first importance: that Christ died for our sins according to the Scriptures, that he was buried, that he was raised on the third day according to the Scriptures, and that he appeared to Peter, and then to the Twelve (1 Corinthians 15:3-5).

Additionally, Peter proclaimed the forgiveness of sins, which is greatly emphasized in Acts. In his Pentecost sermon, he claimed that the messianic promises are fulfilled by the gift of the Spirit along with the forgiveness of sins (Acts 2:38). In Paul's speeches, the climax is the forgiveness of sins (cf. Acts 13:38; 26:18).

Peter's message was different from on Pentecost, which was addressed to Jews. There are no OT quotations, calls for repentance or for receiving the gift of the Spirit. Peter may have been leading up to the words, "Repent and be baptized," but he never said them. The Word of God did its work in the hearts of the Gentiles—Peter was interrupted by the coming of the Holy Spirit on all those who heard the message. The Jewish believers were astonished, because the gift of the Holy Spirit had been poured out on the Gentiles also.

The outcome of Peter's preaching was the Gentile Pentecost. The Gentiles received the Holy Spirit in exactly the same manner that Jews did at the Jerusalem Pentecost as was evidenced by their speaking in tongues. It should be noted that the speaking in tongues by the Gentiles were for those who did not believe (cf. 1 Corinthians 14:22; Acts 10:44-45; 11:15). Here the giving of the Holy Spirit in a similar manner was intended to convince the Jews to accept Gentiles into the Church.

At first, Peter and his Jewish companions from Joppa were astonished. Then, Peter commanded the Gentiles, who had been baptized by the Spirit, to be baptized with water in the name of Jesus Christ and it was done as indicated by aorist verbs and infinitives. These Gentiles did not pass through the rituals of Judaism to enter the Church. Then Peter did an unthinkable thing—the aorist tenses indicate that he stayed with the Gentiles for a few days!

The news spread like wildfire—Gentiles had welcomed God's message and Peter had visited uncircumcised men and ate with them. Peter defended himself to the apostles and brothers, giving an orderly sequence of the events leading up to the outpouring of the Spirit (Acts 11:4-17). Significantly, Peter does not refer to their willingness to be baptized with water. Instead, he quotes, "John baptized with water, but you will be baptized with the Holy Spirit" (11:16). In other words, it was not an act of man, but an act of God that identified the Gentiles with Christ. Peter had turned the keys of the kingdom for the last time—Gentiles were part of the Church.

Peter's Speech to the First Church Council
Acts 15:7-11

After much debate, Peter stood up and spoke to the Jerusalem council about what had occurred with him regarding the Gentiles in the past and their own failure to keep the Law in the past.

Peter's speech has five main points:

1. God chose him to preach the gospel to the Gentiles
2. God testified to them by giving the Holy Spirit just as He did with the Jews
3. God cleansed their hearts by faith just as He did with the Jews
4. God is tested when the impossible yoke of the Law is placed on the disciples
5. God saves by grace just as He does with the Jews

The importance of Peter's speech is that he affirmed that God saves Jews and Gentiles the same way; neither can obtain salvation through their own merit and efforts—salvation is by grace. The Jews had not received the Holy Spirit by keeping the Law, but by believing God's Word. Though the Law is holy, righteous and good (Romans 7:12), it cannot purify the sinner's heart, impart the gift of the Holy Spirit or give eternal life. Such is the work of the Holy Spirit, who is God's gift (Acts 2:38; 10:45; Romans 8:1-4).

The outcome of Peter's speech was that the whole assembly became silent and was prepared to hear the speeches of Paul, Barnabas and James, who demonstrated how Peter's report agreed with the prophets.

The Jerusalem Council arrived at a *doctrinal decision* that Gentiles are not required to be circumcised and a *practical decision* that Gentiles should abstain from idols, sexual immorality, eating anything that has been strangled, and with blood because Moses is read aloud in the Synagogues.

PART III: THE LETTERS OF PETER

First Peter: Suffering Precedes Glory

INTRODUCTION

WRITER AND DATE: The writer is "Peter, an apostle of Jesus Christ," (1:1) along "with the help of Silas" [δια σιλουανου through Silvanus]" (5:12), indicating the bearer of the letter or a secretary, who polished up the language of the letter. Silas was the intimate friend and companion of Paul, and had labored much with him in the regions where the churches were situated to which this letter was addressed. In what manner Silas became acquainted with Peter, or why he was now with him in Babylon is unknown. The writer was a witness to the sufferings of Christ (5:1).

This letter was written in the summer A.D. 64, probably from Rome, where according to early church tradition Peter labored and where he was martyred in A.D. 68 by Nero. Almost certainly, "Babylon" was a cryptic designation for Rome, the great capital of the pagan world (5:12). The first explicit quote of Peter writing this letter comes from Irenaeus, and thereafter it is routinely accepted that the apostle wrote it. Liberal scholars have questioned Peter's authorship since the Greek is of a literally high level, which one would not expect from an "uneducated and untrained" person.

RECIPIENTS: This is a circular letter addressed to definite readers: "To God's elect, strangers in the world, scattered [διασπορά *diaspora*] throughout Pontus, Galatia, Cappadocia, Asia and Bithynia." These five provinces of the Roman Empire stretched across the northern and western half of Asia Minor (modern Turkey). The five provinces are a combination of urban and rural areas, with both Hellenized areas and regions strongly rooted in native cultures.

James, the first letter of the NT, was addressed to "the twelve tribes in the Diaspora," when the majority of believers were Jews. With the article, "the Diaspora" is a technical term first used of Israel—"thou shalt be a dispersion (*diaspora*) in all the kingdoms of the earth" (Deuteronomy 28:25 LXXE).

151

Peter did not use the article with *diaspora* because by the time of this letter the churches in this part of the world would have been mostly Gentile. On the other hand, Peter's heavy use of OT scriptures indicates a Jewish-Christian presence among the addressees. Interestingly, the writer of Hebrews refers to OT saints as "strangers on the earth" (Hebrews 11:13). This terminology indicates the people of God are strangers among the pagan communities and their real home is heaven.

Additionally, Peter indicated that he did not evangelize his readers (1:12). These believers directly or indirectly owed their origin to Paul. Luke stated that Paul's work at Ephesus spread to all the inhabitants of the province of Asia, both Jews and Greeks (Acts 19:10).

CIRCUMSTANCES: The letter was written at a time when Christians were beginning to experience sharp opposition and persecution because of their faith (1:6; 2:12, 19–21; 3:9, 13–18; 4:1, 12–16, 19). As the early decades of the church's expansion through the Roman Empire passed, it grew explosively in numbers due to the missionary zeal of the early Christians. At first, Christians were thought of as a sect of Judaism, but increasingly they became viewed as a distinct people, which opened the door to persecution. There is no evidence in the letter of empire-wide persecution by tribunals, judges, or confiscation of property. However, persecution in parts of the empire may have been sanctioned by local officials as Christians were seriously misunderstood for several reasons:

1. Their refusal to worship the Emperor and Rome's gods was viewed as a lack of patriotism
2. Their private worship meetings were viewed with suspicion, rumors and growing hostility
3. Their failure to adhere to the Mosaic Law was viewed by Judaizers as heresy

Against this background of increasing misunderstanding and cruelty by the majority of the Empire, Peter writes this pastoral letter, emphasizing that future glory outweighs present sufferings. Hence, Christian life can be summarized as a call to victory and glory through the path of suffering.

TEXT AND STYLE: The oldest and complete Greek manuscript of this letter is Papyrus 72 (housed in the Bibliotheca Bodmeriana in Geneva), which dates to the end of the third century. Peter's constructions and words are simple, forceful and to the point, yet his Greek is unsurpassed in the NT.

Proportionately, there are more OT quotes in this letter than any other NT book; therefore, it is written from a Jewish point of view. As with Paul, Peter's OT references align with the Greek Septuagint, indicating that many Jews knew Greek as well as Hebrew or Aramaic. Since the letter is written in Greek, it is not surprising that a Greek translation of the OT was employed.

This letter resembles the later letters written by Paul, especially Ephesians. One would expect similarities since Peter knew Paul and his writings (cf. Galatians 1:18; 2 Peter 3:15-16), and Silas was with both apostles. Undoubtedly, these men influenced one another. There are thirty-two teachings of Christ in this letter.

Additionally, there are parallels in the writings of James and Peter, for example:

1.	1 Peter 1:1	James 1:1
2.	1 Peter 1:6	James 1:2-3
3.	1 Peter 1:23	James 1:10-11, 18
4.	1 Peter 5:5-6	James 4:6-7, 10
5.	1 Peter 5:8	James 4:7

Peter drew from three sections of the OT—the Law, the Prophets and the Writings:

1.	1 Peter 1:16	Leviticus 19:2
2.	1 Peter 1:24-25	Isaiah 40:6-8
3.	1 Peter 2:6	Isaiah 28:16
4.	1 Peter 2:7	Psalm 118:22
5.	1 Peter 2:8	Isaiah 8:14
6.	1 Peter 2:9a	Isaiah 43:20

7.	1 Peter 2:9b	Exodus 19:6
8.	1 Peter 2:9c	Isaiah 43:21
9.	1 Peter 3:10-12	Psalm 34:12-16
10.	1 Peter 4:18	Proverbs 11:31
11.	1 Peter 5:5	Proverbs 3:34

Overall, this letter is easy to understand; except 1 Peter 3:18–22, which is one of the most difficult NT texts to translate and interpret. There are five questions that need to be answered to understand this passage.

1. Does "Spirit" refer to the Holy Spirit or to Christ's Spirit (3:18)?

2. Did Christ preach through Noah before the Flood, or did He preach in person after the crucifixion (3:19)?

3. Was the audience to this preaching composed of humans in Noah's day or demons in the abyss (3:19)?

4. Does Peter teach baptismal regeneration (salvation) or salvation by faith alone in Christ (3:20–21)?

KEY VERSES:

You rejoice in this, though now for a short time you have had to be distressed by various trials so that the genuineness of your faith—more valuable than gold, which perishes though refined by fire—may result in praise, glory, and honor at the revelation of Jesus Christ (1 Peter 1:6-7 HCSB).

But even if you should suffer for righteousness, you are blessed. Do not fear what they fear or be disturbed, but set apart the Messiah as Lord in your hearts, and always be ready to give a defense to anyone who asks you for a reason for the hope that is in you (1 Peter 3:14-15 HCSB).

Through Silvanus, whom I consider a faithful brother, I have written briefly, encouraging you and testifying that this is the true grace of God. Take your stand in it! (1 Peter 5:12 HCSB).

KEY WORDS: God (41 times); Christ (22); Suffer/ing/s (18); Glory (8); Holy (8); Grace (7); Hope (5); Brothers/hood (5); Precious (4); Salvation (4). If we understand "theological" as referring to God, then this letter is a very "theological" writing since the word "God" appears in every 43 words.

THEMATIC THEMES:

1. Obedient Children (1:14-5:9)
2. Prepare Your Minds for Action (1:17)
3. Sufficiency of God's Grace (1:2, 10, 13; 2:19-20; 3:7; 4:10; 5:5, 10, 12)
4. Christian Suffering (3:9, 14; 4:12-13, 19; 5:9)
5. Beneficial Results of Suffering (1:6-7; 2:19-20; 3:14; 4:14)
6. Stand fast in God's Grace (5:12)
7. Life of Holiness (1:15-16; 2:5, 9)

PRIMARY THEMES:

1. Doxology of salvation (1:3-12)
2. Exhortation to live a life befitting this great salvation (1:13-2:10)
3. Exhortation to submission in view of our position in the world (2:11-3:12)
4. Exhortation in light of Christian suffering (3:13-5:11)

SUBORDINATE THEMES:

1. Sufferings of Christ (1:11; 2:21, 23; 4:1) —> Example to follow (2:2)
2. Living and Sure Hope (1:3-8, 13)
3. The Future (1:6-9, 13; 2:2; 4:13; 5:10)

THEOLOGICAL THEMES:

1. Doctrine of God the Father
2. Doctrine of Christ
3. Doctrine of the Holy Spirit

155

4. Doctrine of God's Elect
5. Doctrine of Eschatology

QUESTIONS ANSWERED:

1. Do Christians need a priesthood to intercede with God for them (2:5–9)?
2. What should be the Christian's attitude to secular government and civil disobedience (2:13–17)?
3. What should be the Christian employee's attitude toward a hostile employer (2:18)?
4. How can a believing wife win her unbelieving husband to Christ (3:1–2)?
5. How should a Christian woman conduct herself (3:3–4)?

PORTRAITS OF CHRISTIANS

1. Sojourners (1:1)
2. Obedient Children (1:14)
3. Newborn Infants (2:2)
4. Living Stones (2:5)
5. Chosen Generation (2:9)
6. Royal Priesthood (2:9)
7. Holy Nation (2:9)
8. Purchased People (2:9)
9. God's People (2:10)
10. Bondservants (2:16)

STRUCTURE:

1. The Glories of Salvation in Christ (1:3-12)
2. The Personal Experiences of Christians (1:13-2:10)
3. The Position of Christians in the World (2:11-3:12)
4. The Responses of Christians to Suffering (3:13-5:11)

OUTLINE:

I. Salutation, 1:1-2
   A. Writer, 1:1
   B. Recipients, 1:2

II. The Matter of Salvation, 1:3-9
   A. A Living Hope, 1:3
   B. A Secure Inheritance, 1:4-5
   C. A Joyous Salvation, 1:6
   D. A Genuine Faith, 1:7
   E. A Glorious Joy, 1:8-9

III. The Matter of Scripture, 1:10-12
   A. An Intensive Search, 1:10-11
   B. A Personal Revelation, 1:12

IV. The Matter of Sanctification, 1:13-25
   A. Be Holy, 1:13-16
   B. Live in Reverent Fear, 1:17
   C. Know Your Position, 1:18-21
   D. Love One Another, 1:22-25

V. The Matter of Separation, 2:1-12
   A. Grow Spiritually, 2:1-3
   B. Living Stones, 2:4-8
   C. Chosen People, 2:9-10
   D. Call to Good Works, 2:11-12

VI. The Matter of Submission, 2:13-3:12
   A. Instituted Authority, 2:13-15
   B. Workplace, 2:18-20
   C. Shepherd and Overseer, 2:21-25
   D. Wives and Husbands, 3:1-7
   E. Unity in Christ, 3:8-12

VII. The Matter of Suffering, 3:13-4:19
   A. Mindset, 3:13-14
   C. Defense, 3:15-16
   D. Undeserved Suffering, 3:17
   E. Ministry of Christ, 3:18-22

EXPOSITION

Salutation (1:1-2)

This letter begins with important doctrines as Peter incorporates the Trinity and soteriological declarations into the salutation. The apostle describes in a few words the roles of the Father, Son and Spirit and the recipients in salvation.

THE RECIPIENTS (1:1-2): The recipients of this letter are identified as παρεπιδημοις, which has been translated as "sojourners," "pilgrims," "strangers," "temporary residents," "foreigners," "temporarily residing abroad" in the Dispersion or in the world, scattered throughout five provinces of the empire. "The Diaspora" originated as a negative term for Jews living outside of Palestine. Peter employed it for Christian Jews and Gentiles, implying that they are present in the world, but not at home in it— they have an inheritance in heaven (1:4).

Presently, verse 2 is hotly debated by theologians as to what God knows and when He knows it. There are several ways to understand this verse.

1. God the Father predetermined who (the elect) will be saved according to His foreknowledge—*Classic Reformed Theism.*

2. God the Father foreknew who (the elect) would have faith and thus chose them to be saved—*Classic Arminian Theism.*

3. God the Father did not foreknow who would be saved, but elects those who have faith in Christ according to His prearranged (προγνωσις *prognosis*) plan—*Neotheism.*

Peter an apostle of Jesus Christ, to elect (εκλεκτοις, chosen) sojourners (παρεπιδημοις) of the dispersion of Pontus, of Galatia, of Cappadocia, of Asia, and of Bithynia, according to prearrangement (προγνωσιν, advance determination, purpose) of God [the] Father by sanctification of [the] Spirit unto obedience and sprinkling of [the] blood of Jesus Christ: Grace and peace to you be multiplied to you (1 Peter 1:1-2 My Literal Translation).

Understanding God's Chosen People

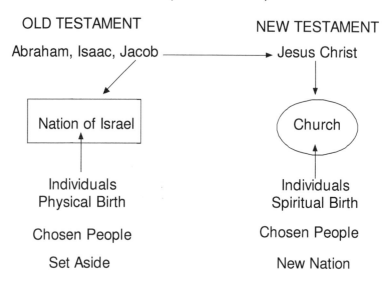

SEED (OFFSPRING)

Under the Old Covenant, God's chosen people were the physical descendants of Abraham, Isaac and Jacob, who became the nation of Israel (Deuteronomy 7:6). In the New Covenant, God's chosen people are the spiritual descendants of the Chosen One—Christ (Luke 23:35; Psalm 22:30-31; Isaiah 53:10), who are the Church.

> This is why the promise is by faith, so that it may be according to grace, to guarantee it to all the descendants—not only to those who are of the law, but also to those who are of Abraham's faith. He is the father of us all (Romans 4:16 HCSB).

At the heart of the Abrahamic Covenant is God's promise to bless all peoples of the earth through Abraham's seed—Jesus Christ (Genesis 12:3).

> Now the promises were spoken to Abraham and to his seed. He does not say "and to seeds," as though referring to many, but **and to your seed**, referring to one, who is Christ (Galatians 3:16 HCSB).

Christians are chosen because they are in Christ—Abraham's seed!

Understanding God's Foreknowledge

The term *foreknowledge* or *foreknew* does not appear in the OT. The Greek term προγνωσις (*prognosis*) occurs twice in the NT (Acts 2:23; 1 Peter 1:2) and is used by Peter both times. It should be translated "forethought" or "prearrangement" or "determined in advance" instead of "foreknowledge" as does several translations. It cannot merely mean "previous knowledge."

> By using men who don't acknowledge Moses' Teachings, you crucified Jesus, who was given over to death by a plan that God had determined in advance [προγνωσις] (Acts 2:23 GW; cf. CEV; GNB; MSG; NirV).

"Sprinkling by blood" recalls the blood of the Old Covenant that Moses sprinkled on the Israelites, who committed themselves to obey the LORD (Exodus 24:1-8). Likewise, Peter's readers need to be obedient to the Spirit (cf. Romans 1:5), who sanctified them since they are receiving sprinkling with the blood of Jesus Christ; that is the blood of the New Covenant (Hebrews 9:18-23; Hebrews 12:24). Through the work of the Trinity and their own obedience, they are sojourners in the world.

God the Father has determined in advance the means of salvation— sanctification unto obedience, which is the work of the Spirit and sprinkling by Jesus Christ's blood, which is for the forgiveness and cleansing of sin. The elect or chosen sojourners are such because of the work of the Spirit and Christ.

Hence, the individual's election is dependent upon becoming a faithful disciple (follower) of Christ, which is according to the Father's forethought or predetermined plans—past and future.

> These will make war against the Lamb, but the Lamb will conquer them because He is Lord of lords and King of kings. Those with Him are called and elect and faithful (Revelation 17:14 HCSB).

Peter has transferred to the Christian church the word "elect" or "chosen," which applied to the nation of Israel in OT (cf. Deuteronomy 14:2; Isaiah 45:4). Individuals need to be born into the community to be part of God's chosen or elect people—Israelites by natural birth and Christians by spiritual

161

birth.

The Matter of Salvation (1:3-9)

A LIVING HOPE (1:3): This verse is a beautiful outpouring of an adoring heart. "Praise [ευλογητος *eulogetos*, blessed] be to the God and Father of our Lord Jesus Christ!" is a difficult assertion, which occurs also in 2 Corinthians 1:3 and Ephesians 1:3. If Jesus Christ is God, how can the Father be His God?

The one article with the two nouns, "the God and Father," denotes a two-sided relationship of the Father to the incarnate Christ (cf. Philippians 2:5-11; 1 Corinthians 15:24-28; Psalm 2:7; Hebrews 1:5; 2 Samuel 7:14; 1 Chronicles 7:13). It is a double assertion of the subordination of the Son in His redemptive mission, where He took on the positions of Son and Servant, not only for man (Mark 10:45) but also for Yahweh (Isaiah 42:1-9; 49:1-13; 52:10-53:12).

> You have heard Me tell you, 'I am going away and I am coming to you.'
> If you loved Me, you would have rejoiced that I am going to the Father, because the Father is greater than I (John 14:28 HCSB).

Jesus stated His subordination to the Father; therefore, the Father is His God. In Gethsemane, Christ's subordination was magnified when He prayed, "Father, if you are willing, take this cup from me; yet not my will, but yours be done" (Luke 22:42).

"In his great mercy he has given us new birth into a living hope through the resurrection of Jesus Christ from the dead," is a predetermined plan, which Peter articulated in his sermons on Pentecost and at Solomon's Colonnade. "Great mercy" is consistent with God's character of mercy (ελεος *eleos*). It is a word used of God's kindness and good will in bringing in the outsider and the unworthy to salvation, especially the Gentiles (cf. Romans 11:30-32; 15:9; Ephesians 2:1-7; Titus 3:5).

"New birth" is the result of the sanctification of the Spirit and sprinkling of the blood of Jesus, which Paul explains this way:

But when the goodness and love for man appeared from God our Savior, He saved us—not by works of righteousness that we had done, but according to His mercy, through the washing of regeneration and renewal by the Holy Spirit. This Spirit He poured out on us abundantly through Jesus Christ our Savior, so that having been justified by His grace, we may become heirs with the hope of eternal life (Titus 3:4-7 HCSB).

A SECURE INHERITANCE (1:4-5): The Christian's "living hope" is grounded in the resurrection of Jesus Christ from the dead, which is an energizing principle of new birth. Living hope is an expectancy that grips the soul, standing in contrast to the false, empty, frustrating hope of the world. Christ's resurrection is the crowning point of the redemptive work of God for the present and future—realized in abundant life and eternal life.

Every Christian has a living hope, which is grounded in the living Christ and the living Word of God (1:23). Consequently, we have a secure inheritance that can never perish, spoil or fade, kept in heaven for us. It has been said these three negatives picture an inheritance that is "death-proof," "sin-proof," and "time-proof."

It is totally unlike an earthly inheritance, having no decaying elements. The Greek for "inheritance" (κληρονομια *kleronomia*) includes the idea of a fully realized possession rather than just the title to it. This inheritance is called "salvation" (1:5, 9) when Christ is revealed in the last time. As Christians, we are already heirs, yet there remains a future aspect since full enjoyment of the inheritance awaits the future (Romans 8:15-17; Ephesians 1:13-14).

The Dead Sea Scrolls and other Jewish texts speak of everything being revealed in the "last time," when the deeds of the wicked will be made known but the righteous will be "saved" and "delivered" from all who oppress them. The OT and Jewish traditions present the end as preceded by times of great testing. Therefore, Peter words are reassuring that believers "through faith are shielded by God's power until the coming of the salvation that is ready to be revealed in the last time."

The present participle "being shielded" (φρουρουμενους *phroumenos,* being guarded, protected, kept) indicates something in progress, a continuous process of protection. It is a military term, indicating that the citizens need continual protection from enemies. "Through faith" is the Christian's continual response to God's power and protection (cf. Philippians 4:7). Such is God's part and our part in salvation.

A JOYOUS SALVATION (1:6): Now, Peter introduces a thematic theme: "In this you greatly rejoice, though now for a little while you may have had to suffer grief in all kinds of trials." This theme echoes the teaching of James and Paul.

> Consider it a great joy, my brothers, whenever you experience various trials, knowing that the testing of your faith produces endurance (James 1:2-3 HCSB).

> And not only that, but we also rejoice in our afflictions, because we know that affliction produces endurance, endurance produces proven character, and proven character produces hope (Romans 5:3-4 HCSB).

"Trials" (πειρασμος *peirasmos,* "temptations" or "tests" according to context) refer to general problems rather than persecutions or tribulations. The trials are ποικιλος (*poikilos,* various, variegated, many colored). In assurance of salvation, Christians rejoice amid trials as their faith is tested and they persevere, growing in living hope.

Understanding Why People Suffer

The Bible provides many insights into why people suffer, but determining a single or multiple reasons for nations, communities or individuals is often not apparent. Hence, more than one of the following reasons or purposes may be operative in any given instance of suffering. The following insights are not comprehensive.

1. We live in a sin-cursed world, Genesis 3:14-19; Job 14:1; Romans 8:18-23.
2. We need to be disciplined because of sin, Hebrews 12:5-11;

164

Psalm 94:12-14.

3. We need to be kept from sin through humility, 2 Corinthians 12:1-10.

4. We need to learn of God's character, Job 1:8; 31:2-6.

5. We need to trust God's sovereignty, 1 Peter 4:19; Job 42:2-4.

6. We need to be a testimony, ever winning unbelievers to the Lord, John 9:11:17-45.

7. We must expect it is inevitable if we believe in Christ, Philippians 1:29.

8. We need to be purified, James 1:3; 1 Peter 1:7; 4:1-2, 5:10.

9. We need to be able to comfort others, 2 Corinthians 1:3-7.

10. We may experience it because of another's disobedience, Numbers 14:33; Jonah 1:3-6; Joshua 7:1-5ff.

11. We need to anticipate glory, 2 Corinthians 4:16-5:10; 1 Peter 5:10.

12. We need to be reminded that we are to repent, Luke 13:1-5.

13. We need to be strengthened in perseverance, character, hope and love, Romans 5:3-5.

14. We need to be turned back to the LORD, Book of Jonah.

15. We need to be brought to salvation personally or as a nation, Daniel 4:33-37; Zechariah 12.

16. We need to silence Satan by demonstrating that there are those who serve God because they love Him, not because it pays to do so, Job 1-2.

17. It promotes living for the will of God, 1 Peter 3:17; 4:1-2.

18. It refines and tests our faith as to its genuineness, Genesis 22; Job 23:10; 1 Peter 1:6-7; James 1:3-4; Romans 5:3-4.

19. It enables us to be more like Christ, 1 Peter 3:17-18.

20. It results in praise and glory and honor at Christ's coming, 1 Peter 1:7.

21. It makes us more sympathetic, 2 Corinthians 2:4; Romans 12:15.

22. It enables us to reign with Christ, 2 Timothy 2:12.

23. It enables us to honor God, Job 1:21.

24. It prepares us for greater service, Acts 9:16.

25. It teaches us dependence upon God, Many of the Psalms, e.g., Psalm

63.

26. It completes the sufferings of Christ, Colossians 1:24.

27. It reminds us of our own mortality, Ecclesiastes 7:2-4.

28. It may come from our own sinful actions, Numbers 14:34; Hosea 8:7; Galatians 6:7.

29. It may come from Satan, Book of Job; Luke 13:16; 1 Peter 5:8-9.

30. It may come from profaning the Communion Table, 1 Corinthians 11:29-30.

31. It may come from God making us that way for His purposes, Exodus 4:10-13.

32. It may come from wounded love, 2 Corinthians 2:1-4.

33. It may come from unforgiveness, 2 Corinthians 2:5-10.

34. It may come from Satan outwitting us, 2 Corinthians 2:11.

35. It may come from being a companion of a fool, Proverbs 13:20.

36. It may come from demon possession, Matthew 15:22; Mark 1:34.

37. It may come from living a godly life, 2 Timothy 3:12.

38. It happens even to the godliest people, 2 Kings 13:14.

39. It happens so we might be counted worthy of the kingdom of God, 2 Thessalonians 1:4-5; 2 Timothy 2:12.

40. It happens to wean us from the pleasures and cares of this world, Hebrews 11:24-26.

41. It is the expectation of those who stand for their faith, Daniel 3:6; Jeremiah 18:19-20; 20:7-10; John 15:20; 16:33; Acts 5:41; Acts 7:54-60; Philippians 1:29; 3:10; Hebrews 11:36-38.

42. It teaches us that the path of blessing is often through suffering, but always through obedience, Isaiah 52:12-53:12; Hebrews 5:7-9; Philippians 2:8-9.

43. It teaches us to value the future over the present, 2 Corinthians 4:17-18; cf. Matthew 6:19-21; 1 Corinthians 9:24-25.

44. It produces greater wisdom, Job 28:12-20, 23-24, 28; James 1:5.

Basic ways to deal with suffering:

1. Have a proper attitude toward suffering, 1 Peter 4:12-14.
2. Rejoice in suffering, Matthew 5:11-12; James 1:2-4.
3. Evaluate suffering. Ask God for discernment to understand the purpose and how it contributes to placing you in the center of His will, James 1:5; 1 Peter 4:15-19.
4. Embrace the attitude of entrusting yourself to God in suffering, 1 Peter 4:19.
5. Be sensitive to Philippians 4:4-13 no matter how difficult your suffering is.

A GENUINE FAITH (1:7): Times of testing test our faith. Hence, the purpose of God allowing trials is to test the genuineness of our faith, which will be revealed when Christ comes to reward His redeemed people (cf. 1 Peter 1:13; 4:13; 1 Corinthians 1:7). Christ's Second Coming is twofold—first He comes in the air—*the Rapture* (1 Thessalonians 4:13-18) and then He returns to the earth to judge and reign—*the Revelation* (Revelation 19:11-20:10). These two events are separated by at least seven years known as the Tribulation Period.

> For we must all appear before the judgment seat of Christ, so that each may be repaid for what he has done in the body, whether good or bad (2 Corinthians 5:10 HCSB; cf. 1 Corinthian 3:11-15).

Just as an assayer tests the gold to see if it is pure gold or counterfeit, so the trials of life test our faith to prove its genuineness. Genuine faith has greater worth than gold, which perishes. Too many people, who claim to be Christians, will be proved to have false faith, when Christ is revealed. Those with genuine faith will bring praise, glory and honor to Him and to themselves (cf. Matthew 25:21; 1 Corinthians 4:5; Romans 2:7; Hebrews 2:7-9).

As we have seen in Peter's sermons and speeches, his mindset was fixed on the return of Christ. If we fix our minds on what this world has to offer, we will become disappointed, discouraged and depressed.

167

A GLORIOUS JOY (1:8-9): "Though now you do not see [Him], yet believing, you rejoice" parallels the writer of Hebrew's definition of faith: "Now faith is being sure of what we hope for and certain of what we do not see" (Hebrews 11:1). Such are blessed according to Christ's beatitude: "Blessed are those who have not seen and yet have believed" (John 20:29).

The Spirit's byproduct of such faith is glorious joy. Peter gave four instructions for having glorious joy in the midst of trials.

1. Love Christ—though you have not seen him, you love him
2. Trust Christ—believe in him
3. Rejoice in Christ—filled with an inexpressible and glorious joy
4. Receive from Christ—the goal of your faith, the salvation of your souls

"Receiving" (κομιζομενοι *komizomenoi*) is a present middle participle, expressing the idea of acquiring for oneself in personal appropriation and enjoyment. If we love Christ, trust Christ, and rejoice in Christ, we will receive from Christ all that we need to turn our trials into triumphs. Such is the paradoxical nature of the Christian's experience—having been put to grief, we greatly rejoice, for our response to adversity reveals the genuineness of our faith—confirming our living hope that we are receiving the goal of our faith, the salvation of our soul. Can anything be more precious?

One must be born again to "love" (αγαπαω *agapao*) Christ because the Holy Spirit pours God's love into our heart at new birth (cf. Romans 5:5; 1 Peter 1:3; 1 John 4:7). If we love Christ, we will obey Him (John 14:15)—a theme, which Peter has introduced (1 Peter 1:2) and will develop (1:13-2:3).

Jesus asked Peter twice, "Do you *agapao* (God's love) me?" Having denied Christ three times, Peter did not measure up to God's unfailing love (1 Corinthians 13:4-8) so he answered with φιλεω (*phileo*), an affectionate word of friendship. The third time Jesus asked, "Do you love (φιλεω) me," Peter again responded with φιλεω (John 21:14-17). Peter was incapable of αγαπη (*agape,* God's love) until he was born again. Love (αγαπη) is the

168

first portion of the fruit of the Spirit (Galatians 5:22).

Joy sometimes is an emotional outburst that lasts momentarily, but Peter is speaking of an internal, deeper joy of gladness and cheerfulness that is a gift we receive from God (Psalm 16:11; John 16:24; Romans 15:13). Joy is the second portion of the fruit of the Spirit (Galatians 5:22; 1 Thessalonians 1:6; Romans 14:17). Such is inexpressible and glorious joy, which cannot be put in human terms since it connotes the presence of heavenly glory.

In verse 2, Peter conferred peace, the third portion of the fruit of the Spirit, to be multiplied or in abundance to his readers.

The fourth portion of the fruit of the Spirit is μακροθυμια (*makrothumia*, longsuffering, patience, endurance, constancy, steadfastness, perseverance), which is the ultimate purpose for his readers since it proves their genuineness of faith and living hope.

The Matter of Scripture (1:10-12)

The NT and especially Peter's teachings are full of OT texts, which was a practice of the community at Qumran, who not only preserved the OT Scriptures but also interpreted them. Of great importance is this community's interpretation of the OT, which predicts the founder of a group, the group's way of living out righteousness before God and that he would vindicate their covenant loyalty at the end of days. In all likelihood, Peter's teaching and use of Scripture would not have been unfamiliar to the Jews. Since the Scriptures were read in the synagogue every Sabbath, we may assume that the OT also would have become precious to the newborn Gentiles, who also were being taught the OT Scriptures by the apostles.

In this section, Peter looked at the OT Scriptures from the perspective of:

1. The OT Prophets, 10-11
2. The Holy Spirit, 11-12
3. The NT Apostles, 12
4. The Angels, 12

AN INTENSIVE SEARCH (1:10-11): Peter held a high view of the prophetic Scriptures, their importance to the Christian faith and employed them in his proclamations of the Gospel. He pointed out that the OT prophets studied their own writings to determine the time and circumstances of Christ (cf. Isaiah 6:11-12; Daniel 12:8-9). The prophets realized that they had predicted His sufferings and glories that would follow. We are in a greater position than the prophets were since the cross, empty tomb and ascension; we are able to differentiate the fulfilled predictions of Christ's sufferings from the glories that will follow.

Foretelling the future was not the only function of the prophets; they were deeply concerned with the application of God's truth and will for their own day.

"The grace" indicates personal grace God had in store for the readers of this letter. It embraces both the present and future aspects of salvation.

A PERSONAL REVELATION (1:12): Peter attributed the apostolic preaching, which embraced these prophetic revelations, to the Holy Spirit, who was sent from heaven. Peter asserted that these predictions were divinely inspired by the Holy Spirit and the prophets knew that their writings were intended for future generations living in the age of the Gospel and grace.

Indeed, their predictions of the future glories of Christ still remain unfulfilled and should whet the appetite of every Christian to do an intensive search of their writings to determine the time and circumstances surrounding the fulfillment of these predictions. As with the apostles, we have the Holy Spirit also to assist our intensive search.

> But as it is written: What no eye has seen and no ear has heard, and what has never come into a man's heart, is what God has prepared for those who love Him. Now God has revealed them to us by the Spirit, for the Spirit searches everything, even the deep things of God. For who among men knows the concerns of a man except the spirit of the man that is in him? In the same way, no one knows the concerns of God except the Spirit of God. Now we have not received the spirit of the world, but the Spirit who is from God, in order to know what has been

170

freely given to us by God (1 Corinthians 2:9-12 HCSB).

Peter added, "Even angels long to look into these things." "To look" (παρακυψαι *parakuphai*) is an aorist active infinitive, denoting that at some point the angels began to look and continue to look into these things. This word was used of Peter, John and Mary, who were stooping down and looking into the empty tomb (Luke 24:12: John 20:5, 11). Metaphorically, it means "to look carefully into, to inspect curiously." "Long" (επιθυμεω *epithumeo*, desire, covet) refers to a passionate desire. The righteous angels, who do not receive grace, have a passionate desire to look carefully into the prophetic Word—possibly looking for the time and circumstances when they come with Christ (Jude 1:14; Revelation 19:14).

Undeniably, the apostles, angels and Holy Spirit must be grieved by the current neglect of OT prophecy in preaching. Let us make an intensive search so we may receive a personal revelation from the Holy Spirit of what the future aspects of the grace holds for us. Assuredly, some aspects will remain perplexing, but everything we do understand will strengthen and encourage us in our living faith and hope.

The Matter of Sanctification (1:13-25)

This section deals with Peter's challenge to live differently from the world as obedient children. One of Peter's key commands is "Prepare your minds for action," and this theme permeates this letter. Christians have the mind of Christ (1 Corinthians 2:16) and Peter expects to fill it with knowledge, especially of Christ, which is a theme of his second letter.

BE HOLY (1:13-16): "Therefore" (διο *dio*, wherefore, for this reason) points back to the grace received by Peter's readers that he has outlined in the first twelve verses.

Holiness will not occur without preparation.

1. Prepared Mind, 1:13
2. Self-control, 1:13
3. Hope, 1:13
4. Unconformity, 1:14

5. Holiness, 1:16
6. Different Life, 1:16
7. Reverent Fear, 1:17
8. Purified Life, 1:22
9. Obeying Truth, 1:22
10. Sincere Love, 1:22

Such is the response to grace and new birth.

In light of the present grace, they are to prepare their minds for action in light of the future grace to be received when Christ is revealed. Christianity is lived from the mind, for example:

> Do not be conformed to this age, but be transformed by the renewing of your mind, so that you may discern what is the good, pleasing, and perfect will of God (Romans 12:2 HCSB).

> For: who has known the Lord's mind, that he may instruct Him? But we have the mind of Christ (1 Corinthians 2:16 HCSB).

The NT portrays Peter as a man of action, but not always with self-control before receiving the Holy Spirit. The transforming experience of salvation and future hope of glory should result in action, which is self-controlled (νηφω *nepho*, sober), which is the opposite of intoxication. In five instances, *nepho* means acknowledgment of the reality of revelation and discharge of the resultant ministry in worship, hope, love and conflict (1 Thessalonians 5:6, 8; 2 Timothy 4:5; 1 Peter 1:13; 4:7; 5:8).

"Obedient children" picks up the imagery of "new birth" from verse 3. Both Jewish and Roman law required children to obey their parents. As obedient children of God, believers are to do His will, becoming like Him. Hence, religion and ethics are welded together in the Scriptures.

> But just as he who called you is holy, so be holy in all you do; for it is written: "Be holy, because I am holy" (quoted from Leviticus 11:44-46; 19:2; 20:7).

Like the Israelites, Christians are called to be holy. The Gospel of the NT does not leave the OT behind; it expands upon its demands. What was humanly impossible under the Law is now possible through the Holy Spirit's enabling power under the New Covenant (cf. Ezekiel 36:25-27). Therefore, Christians are no longer to conform to the evil desires they had when they lived in ignorance. Obedient children conform to their parent's commands and character.

Here "holy" (αγιος *hagios*) has the sense of separation from evil desires to the purity of Yahweh that comes from the renewing of the mind and preparing it for action (see the chart: *The Obedient Child*).

LIVE IN REVERENT FEAR (1:17): The imagery of God as Father and Judge is continued—He impartially judges the saved and unsaved according to their work; therefore, believers are to live as sojourners on the earth in fear (φοβος *phobos*), that is dread, terror or reverence. "Fear of Yahweh" or "Fear of God" is one of two primary attributes required of man throughout the OT (e.g., Genesis 22:12; Exodus 18:21; Leviticus 19:14; Deuteronomy 10:12; 2 Chronicles 26:5; Job 28:28; Psalm 33:8; Proverbs 1:7; 9:10; Ecclesiastes 12:13; Isaiah 11:2; Jeremiah 5:24; Daniel 6:26; Malachi 3:5).

In the OT, "fear of God" is the expression for "faith." Therefore, as God's children we are to be serious about sin and holy living since He will be our Judge. After examining life from every possible angle, the Teacher wrote:

> When all has been heard, the conclusion of the matter is: fear God and keep His commands, because this is for all humanity. For God will bring every act to judgment, including every hidden thing, whether good or evil (Ecclesiastes 12:13-14 HCSB).

KNOW YOUR POSITION (1:18-21): The second primary attribute required of man in the OT is love—love of God and neighbor. Above all, Peter wants his readers to know reasons why they are to love God.

1. It was not with perishable things such as silver or gold that you were redeemed.
2. It was the precious blood of Christ, a lamb without blemish or defect, which redeemed you.
3. It was Christ, who was chosen before the creation of the world, who

173

redeemed you.

4. It is Christ, whom will be revealed in these last times for your sake.
5. It is through Christ you believe in God.
6. It is in the risen and glorified Christ that your faith and hope are in God.

Some fifty million people were slaves during this period in the Roman Empire. Hence, the word "redeemed" was precious to them—it meant having one's freedom purchased. Spiritual redemption came at an awesome price—the precious blood of Christ, a lamb without blemishes or defect. The price for redemption from Egyptian bondage was the sprinkling of the blood of Passover lambs on the doorposts (cf. Exodus 6:6; 12:21-23; 15:13; 1 Peter 1:2). Peter's use of "redemption" includes "ransom," which was used for the price for redemption of the firstborn (Exodus 30:12 LXX). Christ's redemption effectively removes the newborn child of God from an empty way of life.

> Clean out the old yeast so that you may be a new batch, since you are unleavened. For Christ our Passover has been sacrificed (1 Corinthians 5:7 HCSB).

The Greek anarthrous perfect passive participle προεγνωσμενου (*proegnosmenou*) can be translated, "He was foreknown before the foundation of the world but was manifested in these last times for your sake" (1 Peter 1:20 NET). In other words, He was previously foreknown but now revealed.

The curious phrase, "before the creation of the world," occurs in John 17:24, when Christ's speaks of the Father having loved Him in His preincarnate state (cf. Ephesians 1:14). Most likely, Peter's statement expresses Christ's deity and says nothing about the redemption of sinners being foreordained in eternity past, which is the common interpretation.

Yahweh God had redeemed the people of Israel out of slavery in Egypt, but they wanted to go back to their old way of life. Peter told his readers, "You have been redeemed from the empty way of life handed down to you from your forefathers." They thought their lives were full and happy, when they

174

really were empty and miserable.

"Through him you believe in God" for Christ is the only way to the Father (cf. John 14:6). "Raised him from the dead" is a fundamental belief for saving faith (cf. Romans 10:9-10). "Glorified Him" refers to Christ's ascension and exaltation to the right hand of the Majesty in Heaven (Hebrews 1:3). The Son returned to the glory He had with the Father before the world began (Luke 24:51-53; John 17:4-5; Acts 1:9-11; Philippians 2:9-11; Hebrews 1:1-3:29). So what does this mean to the believer according to Peter? "And so your faith and hope are in God." What God has done for Christ, He will do for us!

LOVE ONE ANOTHER (1:22-25): As obedient children, Peter's readers are to demonstrate their holiness by loving their brothers, deeply from the heart. He wants them to live by the truth of the Word of God to implement Jesus' teaching, "Love one another" (John 13:34). They have been purified by the sprinkling of the blood of Jesus Christ (1 Peter 1:2); therefore, their conduct and relationships should manifest their purity. There are two steps to obtaining purity: (1) the blood of Christ and (2) obedience to the Word of God.

Here Peter speaks of two kinds of love:

1. Sincere brotherly love (φιλαδελφιαν ανυποκριτον *philadelphian anupokriton*) out of an earnest (εκτενως *ektenos*) heart

2. Love (αγαπησατε *agapesate*), an aorist active imperative to love with God's love

It has been said, "There is plenty of *phile* fondness and affection among the saints, and too little *agape* divine love." How can the saints love with God's love? The answer is to be filled with the Spirit by letting the Word of Christ dwell richly in the hearts of the saints (cf. Ephesians 5:18; Colossians 3:16). It is the transforming power of the Word of God as it is energized by the Holy Spirit in the life of His obedient children.

Peter tells his readers that they have been born again, not of perishable seed, but of imperishable, through the living and enduring word of God. Again,

175

we see the importance of the Word of God to Peter as he appeals to the OT to substantiate his teaching.

> For All flesh is like grass, and all its glory like a flower of the grass. The grass withers, and the flower drops off, but the word of the Lord endures forever. And this is the word that was preached as the gospel to you (1 Peter 1:24-25 HCSB).

Peter quoted from Isaiah 40:6-8, omitting, "because the breath of the LORD blows on them." He uses this illustration as a contrast between temporal man and the abiding word of God, which he identified as "the living and enduring word of God" (1:23). Creation will pass away, but not God's Word (cf. Isaiah 40:8; Mark 13:31).

The Matter of Separation (2:1-12)

In this section, Peter sets forth the doctrine of progressive sanctification; his readers are a chosen people of God separated from the world. In other words, what it means to be sojourners, pilgrims or aliens on the earth, who are to grow unto salvation. He employs a number of mixed metaphors, which have one thing is common—the idea of growing to maturity or becoming what God wants His people to be in the world. It has been said, "We cannot expect God to do everything for us; He has certain things for us to do for ourselves."

GROW SPIRITUALLY (2:1-3): "Therefore" or "wherefore" relates chapter two with chapter one. Spiritual growth is the logical and natural consequence of new birth.

Mark Twain is quoted as saying, "Most people are bothered by those passages in the Bible which they cannot understand; but as for me, I always notice that the passages in the Scripture which trouble me the most are those which I do understand." His statement is a commentary of this passage. The question is, "What are we going to do about it?" Peter invites us to take one specific step and implies that several others are occurring:

1. Ridding ourselves of all kinds of evil
2. Crave pure spiritual milk

176

3. Growing up unto salvation
4. Tasted that the Lord is gracious

"Ridding ourselves" (αποθεμενοι *apothemenoi*) is a second aorist middle participle, which indicates the reader has begun and continues to take this action. The term denotes "to put off" "lay down" or "cast away" and is commonly used of putting off clothes and is used metaphorically of putting off evil; for example, the removal of the high priest's filthy clothes in Zechariah 3:3-4; or putting on garments of salvation in Isaiah 61:10. Before one's yearning for milk can be realized, there must be a definite break with all the evils that hinder spiritual growth. Peter mentions five kinds of evil preceded by the word "all."

1. All κακια *(kakia*, malignity, malice, ill-will, desire to injure, maliciousness) is the harboring of evil thoughts against another person. Malice nourishes antagonism, builds up grudges, and secretly hopes that revenge, harm, or tragedy will overtake another.

2. All δολος *(dolos*, craft, deceit, guile) is any form of dishonesty and trickery.

3. All υποκρισις *(hupokrisis,* hypocrisy) is insincerity, pretense, or sham. The hypocrite is a play-actor, pretending to be someone he is not.

4. All φθονος *(phthonos*, envy) is barefaced jealousy. Vine defines it as the feeling of displeasure produced by observing or hearing of the advantage or prosperity of others.

5. All καταλαλια *(katalalia*, backbiting, evil speaking) is malicious gossip, recrimination. Slander is the attempt to make oneself look cleaner by slinging mud at someone else.

There is a progression in these evils. Malice leads to guile, which is covered up with a false face and envy produces evil speaking. Christians should be open and above-board; their lives are to be open books, easily read. There must be a sweeping removal of all hindrances to spiritual growth!

The significance of "the Word" (1:23-25) giving birth to the believers leads naturally to the image of newborn babies being nurtured and growing by it. Every newborn infant needs a healthy appetite and proper food or it will not grow. The pure "spiritual" milk that will produce healthy Christian growth is God's own Word.

Paul and the writer of Hebrews used this metaphor in a derogatory way (1 Corinthians 3:1-4: Hebrews 5:12-14), but Peter uses it in a positive way. At all times, we should be like infants craving nourishment, whether we have been a Christian for a day or seventy years.

"Crave" (επιποθησατε *epipothesate*, to long for greatly, desire) is an aorist active imperative, which is the specific and strong command of verses 1-3, which is one sentence in the Greek. "Crave" calls for the beginning of vigorous action that continues throughout one's lifetime. The new life cannot grow without the nourishing pure spiritual milk of the Word.

The goal is to grow "unto salvation" (εις σοτεριαν *eis soterian*), which is absent from the Textus Receptus. It was probably omitted due to oversight in copying or because the idea of "growing unto salvation" was theologically unacceptable (Bruce M. Metzger, *A Textual Commentary on the Greek New Testament,* 689). Therefore, this phrase is not in the KJV but in modern translations.

"Now that [ει *ei*, if] you have tasted that the Lord is good [χρηστος *chrestos*, gracious, kind, virtuous, excellent]" assumes the reality of experience. On the other hand, the conditional construction implies an invitation for the readers to make self-examination of this matter. Peter is loosely quoting: "Taste and see that the LORD is good" (Psalm 34:8). To continue to experience the Lord, we must do it through His Word!

Before exploring the various metaphors Peter employs for believers, review the following chart, *The Obedient Child*, which illustrates the dynamics of spiritual birth and growth that we have studied thus far. I prepared this chart some forty years ago and still find it very useful. It demonstrates the importance of the Word of God from salvation unto salvation, culminating in God's command, "Be holy because I am holy."

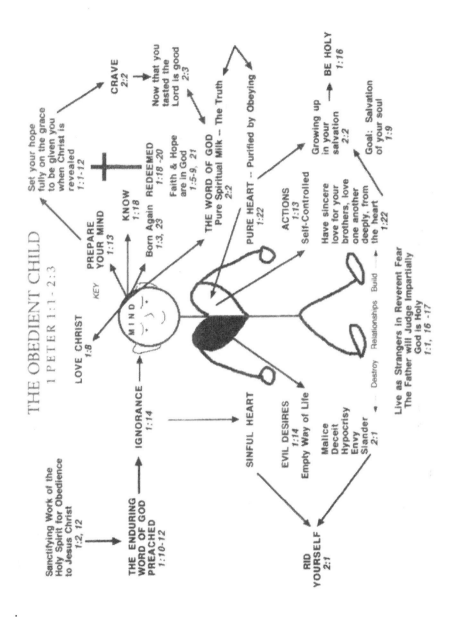

THE OBEDIENT CHILD
1 PETER 1:1 - 2:3

Sanctifying Work of the
Holy Spirit for Obedience
to Jesus Christ
1:2, 12

THE ENDURING
WORD OF GOD
PREACHED
1:10-12

LOVE CHRIST
1:8

IGNORANCE
1:14

PREPARE
YOUR MIND
1:13

KEY

KNOW
1:18

Born Again
1:3, 23

Set your hope
fully on the grace
to be given you
when Christ is
revealed
1:1-12

CRAVE
2:2

Now that you
tasted the
Lord is good
2:3

REDEEMED
1:18 -20

Faith & Hope
are in God
1:5-9, 21

THE WORD OF GOD
Pure Spiritual Milk -- The Truth
2:2

PURE HEART -- Purified by Obeying
1:22

ACTIONS
1:13
Self-Controlled

Have sincere
love for your
brothers, love
one another
deeply, from
the heart
1:22

Growing up
in your
salvation
2:2

BE HOLY
1:16

Goal: Salvation
of your soul
1:9

MIND

SINFUL HEART

EVIL DESIRES
1:14
Empty Way of Life

Malice
Deceit
Hypocrisy
Envy
Slander
2:1

Destroy   Relationships   Build

Live as Strangers in Reverent Fear
The Father will Judge Impartially
God is Holy
1:1, 16 -17

RID
YOURSELF
2:1

LIVING STONES (2:4-8): These verses offer an extended study of early Christian interpretation of the tested stone, a precious cornerstone for a sure foundation (Isaiah 28:16) and the stone the builders rejected has become the capstone (Psalm 118:22), which Jesus (Mark 12:1-2; Matthew 21:33-46) and Paul (Romans 9:31-33) used as prophetic evidence of Israel's rejection of the Messiah. In their teaching, both Jesus and Paul viewed the Church as a different entity than the nation of Israel—as does Peter.

Keeping with the theme of a living hope, Peter called Christ "the Living Stone" and compared believers in Him to "living stones" since they became aligned to the chosen and precious cornerstone—Christ. Jesus said, "Because I live, you also will live" (John 14:19).

Peter continues the metaphor by saying the believers οικοδομεισθε (*oikodomeisthe*, an inductive "are built up" or an imperative "be built up") into a spiritual house—Christians collectively. The writer of Hebrews refers to two households: (1) God's household under Moses—Israel and (2) Christ's own household—the Church.

> Now every house is built by someone, but the One who built everything is God. Moses was faithful as a servant in all God's household, as a testimony to what would be said in the future. But Christ was faithful as a Son over His household, whose household we are if we hold on to the courage and the confidence of our hope (Hebrews 3:4-6 HCSB).

"Spiritual" indicates that the living stones belong to the Holy Spirit. The living stones, who make up the spiritual house, are a holy priesthood—they are not two separate and distinct entities. The term priesthood (ιερατευμα *hierateuma*) occurs here and in verse 9 and in the Septuagint's Exodus 19:6, where Israel is called a "Holy Priesthood" and in an addition to the Hebrew in Exodus 23:22.

Since the nation of Israel rejected Christ, the Church has become not only the holy priesthood, but also "a royal priesthood," denoting that the believer belongs to the King-Priest.

Israel stumbles because they disobey the message—which is what they were destined (τιθημι *tithemi*, appointed, assigned, committed, conceived,

180

destined, etc.) for. It was because of their own stumbling—disobedience and unbelief—that they were appointed to shame because of God's judgment of their unbelief.

"Shame" is a metaphor connected to everlasting contempt—the opposite of eternal life (cf. Daniel 12:2; Isaiah 66:24; Jeremiah 20:11; Romans 9:2). Hence, those who reject Christ are destined to shame. Those who continue trusting (πιστευων *pisteuon*, believing, committing to) in Christ will never be put to shame. The present active participle signifies that saving faith must be ongoing.

CHOSEN PEOPLE (2:9-10): At Mt. Sinai, Yahweh God created the nation of Israel, saying:

> Now if you will listen to Me and carefully keep My covenant, you will be My own possession out of all the peoples, although all the earth is Mine, and you will be My kingdom of priests and My holy nation. These are the words that you are to say to the Israelites (Exodus 19:5-6 HCSB).

Since the nation of Israel had stumbled and tripped over the Cornerstone, a new nation was created in Him. After quoting Psalm 118:22-23, Jesus predicted this new nation—the Church—and the crushing of the old nation—Israel, which occurred in A.D. 70

> Therefore I tell you, the kingdom of God will be taken away from you and given to a nation producing its fruit. [Whoever falls on this stone will be broken to pieces; but on whomever it falls, it will grind him to powder!]" (Matthew 21:43-44 HCSB).

Verse 9 contrasts Christ's rejecters with the emphatic, "But you" [are]:

1. A chosen people
2. A royal priesthood
3. A holy nation
4. A people belonging to God
5. A called out people
6. The people of God

181

"Chosen" or 'elect' is applied by Peter to Christ, the cornerstone (1 Peter 2:6), to Him the Church is aligned and attached. Therefore, those in Christ are the chosen or elect people (γενος *genos*, kindred, offspring, family, generation; hence, people). The church is a corporate solidarity in Christ.

Peter considers that the privileges and responsibilities of Israel are now being transferred to the Church as the people of God in his own day. Quoting from Yahweh, he transferred Israel's obligation to those in Christ:

> For you are a holy people belonging to the LORD your God. The LORD your God has chosen you to be His own possession out of all the peoples on the face of the earth (Deuteronomy 7:6 HCSB).

> My chosen people. The people I formed for Myself will declare My praise (Isaiah 43:20b-21 HCSB).

The Church is not saved for personal gratification. This new people of God in the world are to declare the praises of Him who called them out of darkness into His wonderful light; that is, from the dominion of darkness under the sway of Satan into the kingdom of Christ (cf. Ephesians 2:1-3; Colossians 1:13-14).

Everyone is born into the dominion of darkness by natural birth and no one by natural birth belongs to God's people; one must be born again to enter the kingdom of light.

An Israelite entered the nation of Israel through natural birth; however, not all Israel is Israel. A person enters the Church by spiritual birth and not by natural birth. Once Israel was God's people, they were a chosen people, a kingdom of priests and a holy nation, but now the Church comprised of Jews and Gentiles are the people of God. There is a believing remnant of Jews (Romans 11:1-6). Therefore, Peter includes Jews and Gentiles.

> Once you were not a people, but now you are God's people; you had not received mercy, but now you have received mercy (1 Peter 2:10 HCSB).

This was predicted in Hosea 1:6–10; 2:23 and explained in Romans 9:23–26, where Paul explained that Hosea explicitly referred to the calling of a people made up of Jews and Gentiles. Obviously, the Church was part of God's plans and purposes from the time of Hosea.

Note that Peter changed the designation "a kingdom of priests" to "a royal priesthood." The Church is a royal priesthood because they are in the King-Priest, who is after the order of Melchizedek (cf. Hebrews 4:14; 7:1-28).

CALL TO GOOD WORKS (2:11-12): Peter begins his call to good works, addressing his readers as αγαπητος (*agapetos*, beloved, dearly beloved), which is the more excellent love of 1 Corinthians 13.

If the Church is to be a holy nation—aliens and strangers in the world—we must abstain from sinful desires that war against our soul, which Peter described earlier. Paul also wrote of this spiritual war (Romans 8:4-13; Galatians 5:16-17; 6:8). To grow unto salvation, one must abstain from sinful desires, which is the offering of spiritual sacrifices acceptable to God through Jesus Christ (1 Peter 2:5). This is what Jesus meant by, "If anyone would come after me, he must deny himself and take up his cross daily and follow me" (Luke 9:23).

The manner of life is to be καλος (*kalos*, good, beautiful, handsome, excellent, eminent, choice, surpassing, precious, useful, suitable, commendable, admirable) among the nations (εθνος *ethnos*) of the world. Do not expect to be treated well for doing good; expect to be accused of doing wrong.

Again, Peter focuses the mind of his readers on the Second Coming of Christ, when their good deeds will be recognized and God glorified. Judgment day is coming when everyone will fall on their knees and acknowledge Christ is Lord and what He has done through His people.

Unbelievers watch what we do, and even though we may be mocked (or apparently disregarded), the evidence of our lives will speak so loudly that, on the Day of Judgment, the unsaved will glorify God, because they will have to concede that the testimony was laid before them quite explicitly, even if they failed to heed it.

The Matter of Submission (2:13-3:12)

Logically, Peter addresses several broad areas of life where God's people are being watched. He begins with submissiveness in the public realm.

INSTITUTED AUTHORITY (2:13-15): The Roman Empire was highly organized politically from the Emperor and Senate down to proconsuls and local magistrates. In Palestine, the Romans allowed the Sanhedrin to judge matters regarding Judaism. Roman soldiers were everywhere. It was commonplace for the governors and other officials to punish the bad and honor the good.

At this time and for the same reasons, Peter and Paul (Romans 13:1-4) shared the expectation that officials would indeed administer justice.

> Submit to every human institution because of the Lord, whether to the Emperor as the supreme authority, or to governors as those sent out by him to punish those who do evil and to praise those who do good. For it is God's will that you, by doing good, silence the ignorance of foolish people (1 Peter 2:13-15 HCSB).

However, when John wrote Revelation (A.D. 95-96), Christians could expect nothing but injustice from Roman authorities. Yet, it appears after Peter wrote this letter, suffering was considered a virtue in the Roman Empire. At the end of the first century, Musonius wrote, "To commit injustice is a thing hated by the gods, but if one suffers an injustice, one enjoys the support of the gods and good men" (quoted by David A. de Silva in *The Bible Knowledge Background Commentary*, 303).

Perhaps the Christian testimony in the midst of suffering affected the thinking of many. Clearly, Jesus taught that the righteous should expect persecution.

> Blessed are those who are persecuted for righteousness, because the kingdom of heaven is theirs (Matthew 5:10 HCSB).

"Submit" (υποτασσω *hupotasso*) denotes "to arrange in military order under a commander." It is a key word in this letter, occurring six times

(2:13, 18; 3:1, 5, 22; 5:5). God's people are to live in a humble, submissive way in the midst of any hostile, godless, slandering society. Peter employed Christ as the perfect example of such submission (cf. 1 Peter 2:22-23) and continues to do so as he calls us to walk the same road as the Savior was called to walk.

Christ could have destroyed His enemies with one word, but instead of retaliating during His arrest, trial and crucifixion, He committed Himself to God and the ruling authorities. Thus, Christians are not only to be obedient children, they are to be obedient citizens also.

WORKPLACE (2:18-20): In some areas of the Roman Empire, one-half of the people were slaves, and in the provinces, one of four people was a slave. Often "professionals" such as teachers, doctors and civil servants were technically slaves. Therefore, slavery was viewed with a neutral attitude.

Here οικετης (*oiketes*) denotes "household servants," who are under the authority of the same householder or master. Many household servants saved enough money to achieve freedom. Many cooperated with their masters as members of the family. The laws viewed them as property as well as people, but some owners abused them as property and nearly all owners treated them as inferior. Paul's letter of friendly persuasion to Philemon, called for his friend Philemon to receive his runaway slave Onesimus as brother in Christ. Eventually, this letter would affect positively the prevailing attitude of inferiority.

Peter does not address the institution of slavery per se since spiritual freedom did not entitle one to personal and political freedom. In some cases, both the masters and servants were being saved and in other cases, one or the other was saved. Paul dealt with this problem in 1 Corinthians 7:20-24, Ephesians 6:5-9 and his letter to Philemon. Peter approached this circumstance from the angle of suffering and persecution.

> Household slaves, submit yourselves to your masters with all respect, not only to the good and gentle but also to the cruel. For it brings favor if, because of conscience toward God, someone endures grief from

185

suffering unjustly. For what credit is there if you endure when you sin and are beaten? But when you do good and suffer, if you endure, it brings favor with God (1 Peter 2:18-20 HCSB).

What Peter and Paul wrote applies to employer and employee relationships today. Christian employees are to be submissive, whether the employer is kind or unkind. Christians are never to take advantage of Christian employers; each should treat the other fairly and honestly. The sinful nature's tendency is to fight back—but when wronged, the Christian is to take it, even though he is not wrong. Such is the response of a Spirit-filled Christian—a spiritual sacrifice acceptable to God through Jesus Christ.

SHEPHERD AND OVERSEER (2:21-25): To nail down submitting, Peter turned to Christ's example of submission, telling his readers that they should follow in His steps. Here Peter draws from the predictions of the prophet's *Song of the Suffering Servant* (Isaiah 52:13-53:12) and of Christ's vicarious sufferings recorded in the Gospels.

> For you were called to this, because Christ also suffered for you, leaving you an example, so that you should follow in His steps. He **did not commit sin, and no deceit was found in His mouth**; when reviled, He did not revile in return; when suffering, He did not threaten, but committed Himself to the One who judges justly. He Himself bore our sins in His body on the tree, so that, having died to sins, we might live for righteousness; by **His wounding you have been healed.** For you **were like sheep going astray**, but you have now returned to the shepherd and guardian of your souls (1 Peter 2:21-25 HCSB).

If Christ could entrust Himself to God who judges justly, then all believers can do likewise. Christ's submission was not a sign of weakness but of power. Ironically, Peter opposed Christ's suffering (Matthew 16:21-23), but he has learned the lesson that suffering precedes glory.

Peter combined two metaphors, writing, "For you were like sheep going astray, but now you have returned to the Shepherd and Overseer of your souls." "Shepherd" (ποιμην *poimen*, pastor) can be a messianic title for Jesus, referring to His kingship, but here it refers to His pastoral care of His

186

flock, the Church. "Overseer" (επισκοπος *episkopos*, bishop, curator, guardian or superintendent) is the person charged with the duty of seeing that things to be done by others are done rightly. Paul combined both terms in his exhortation to the Ephesian elders.

> Be on guard for yourselves and for all the flock, among whom the Holy Spirit has appointed you as overseers, to shepherd the church of God, which He purchased with His own blood (Acts 20:28 HCSB).

Christians are to submit themselves to their leaders as the leaders submit themselves to the Shepherd and Overseer of their souls for His guidance and care. If both are in submission to Christ, there will be praise and glory to God.

WIVES AND HUSBANDS (3:1-7): This section is not popular in today's society, where men and women seek to assert their perceived rights at the expense of others. The world of Peter's day was a male dominated society, where women had fewer rights and very little public influence. Thus, the Greeks, Romans and Jews all agreed that the "ideal wife" would submit to her husband's authority rather than try to dominate him and would remain silent in public gatherings. Obviously, this view inflamed God's curse: "Your desire will be for your husband, yet he will dominate you" (Genesis 3:16 HCSB).

In light of the Gospel, how were spouses to react to each other? Society believed that a married woman should worship and recognize the gods whom her husband held dear and these alone. This was impossible for wives who became Christians of husbands who had not received the Lord, as indicated by "do not obey the word."

Of course, a saved woman was never to marry an unsaved man, and vice versa (2 Corinthians 6:14). The saved wife would not be able to submit to the Shepherd and Overseer of her soul while submitting to the gods of her unsaved husband.

Peter's answer to this dilemma was to win the unsaved husband to the Lord, without saying a word, by a sevenfold submission and behavior that would not violate her faith and hope in God.

187

1. Submission to her husband
2. Purity of life
3. Reverence of life
4. Inner beauty, not outward adornment
5. Gentle and quiet spirit
6. Do what is right
7. Do not give way to fear

The first instruction is difficult in today's society because many wives work outside the home, placing themselves under the submission of others. In Peter's day, the norm was for men to have an outdoor occupation and women to work indoors in the home. Paul grounded submission in the order of creation (1 Timothy 2:9-15). Hence, when a woman entered into marriage, she was to place herself voluntarily in submission to her husband.

> Wives, submit to your own husbands as to the Lord, for the husband is head of the wife as also Christ is head of the church. He is the Savior of the body. Now as the church submits to Christ, so wives should submit to their husbands in everything (Ephesians 5:22-24 HCSB; cf. Colossians 3:18-19).

The home, like every human institution, to operate effectively must have a head, someone who is the final authority. God assigned that position to the husband, which was illustrated by holy women of the past, who were submissive to their own husbands, like Sarah, who obeyed Abraham and called him her master (Genesis 18:12). Unfortunately, Abraham listened to Sarah's plan and he fathered Ishmael through Hagar. Later, God told Abraham to listen to his wife and he sent away Hagar and Ishmael. In both instances, Abraham made the decision, but his wife told him what he should do!

Peter is not saying that wives are inferior in intellect or in any other way to their husbands any more than servants are to their masters—it is a matter of position in the home or society. A submissive spirit runs counter to the values of today's society. However, it remains God's standard for all believers—male and female—for all time (cf. Philippians 2:3-8).

Does Peter really mean that Christian wives are not to have braided hair and wear gold jewelry? What if we say, "Yes!" Are they to look like slobs? No! So what is the right answer? Literally, wives are not to adorn themselves by "putting on of clothes (ιηαριομ *himation*, garments, apparels)" The adjective "fine" is not in the Greek, and obviously, Peter is not saying that wives are to go naked; therefore, wives can have braided hair, wear jewelry and put on clothes, but their real beauty is to be inward spirituality, not outward appearance.

Inward adornment is the biblical and evangelistic strategy that will win an unsaved husband to Christ—without a word! He should be attracted to Christ by his wife's beautiful lifestyle. "For this is the way the holy women of the past who put their hope in God used to make themselves beautiful."

"Gentle" (πραυς *praus*) can be translated "meek." In the OT, the meek are those wholly relying on God rather than their own strength to defend themselves against injustice. Gentle or meek goes along with a quiet, tranquil, peaceable spirit. These two characteristics are the strength of submissiveness.

"Do not give way to fear" denotes not being terrified or frightened by intimidation, or the subjective feelings of fear coming from external causes of hostile neighbors, or threats and intimidations of an unbelieving husband. Terrifying things should be handled like all persecutions and sufferings. Doing what is right might result in mistreatment, but more likely will be winsome. Whatever the outcome of this inward adornment, the wife is not to conform to this world, but follow Christ's example of endurance.

Here Peter has described the Spirit controlled life with seven characteristics of the holy woman, which are of great worth in God's sight. Both wife and husband are to live in the awareness that God is watching.

Whether the wife is saved or she is unsaved, the saved husband is to act in like manner.

> Husbands, in the same way, live with your wives with understanding of their weaker nature yet showing them honor as co-heirs of the grace of life, so that your prayers will not be hindered (1 Peter 3:7 HCSB).

189

"Live with your wives with understanding (γνωσις *gnosis*)," that is a general knowledge of Christian behavior. A Christ-centered marriage relationship is built on understanding, a spirit of love, and cooperation between the spouses.

"The weaker σκευος (*skeuos*, vessel, stuff, goods)," the NIV interprets as "partner" and HCSB interprets as "nature." "Vessel" was a common Greek metaphor for "body" since Greeks thought of souls living temporarily in bodies. As a metaphor, σκευος also referred to an instrument of God. Some think "weaker vessel" refers to (1) the physical differences in the sexes; (2) the vulnerable plight of first-century women; or (3) the pattern God established for the home.

Note that Peter thought both husband and wife as weak vessels or instruments used by God for His purposes (cf. Jeremiah 18:1-6; Acts 9:15; Romans 9:21-23; 2 Timothy 2:20-21). Both husband and wife are God's handiwork, designed for each other. The wife is weaker because of her role in the marriage, not because she is intellectually or in other ways inferior to the husband. Peter is not a chauvinist!

A husband's failure to treat his wife as co-heir of the grace of life will hinder his prayers reaching the throne or cut off his practice of prayer. "Co-heirs of the grace of life" is not salvation, but the oneness and unity of marriage, indicating that Peter's principles apply to a saved couple as well as a mixed marriage. Obedient children will follow the rules of marriage laid down in Scripture.

UNITY IN CHRIST (3:8-12): Does "finally" begin a new section or expand the previous section? Since there is no main verb in the Greek of verse 8, "finally" appears to be a continuation.

On the way to Gethsemane, Peter listened to Christ's High Priestly prayer, where He prayed for the oneness of all believers (John 17:20-26) and now the apostle exhorts all his readers to fulfill it. Finally, all of you,

1. Live in harmony (ομοφρων *homophron*, be of one mind) with one another
2. Be sympathetic

3. Love as brothers
4. Be compassionate and humble
5. Do not repay evil with evil or insult with insult, but with blessing because to this you were called so that you may inherit a blessing
6. Keep tongue from evil and lips from speaking deceit
7. Seek peace and pursue it

These seven virtues are essentials of Christian conduct whether in society, the workplace or the home.

Again, Peter turned to Psalm 34; this time quoting verses 13-17.

> For the one who wants to love life and to see good days must keep his tongue from evil and his lips from speaking deceit, and he must turn away from evil and do good. He must seek peace and pursue it, because the eyes of the Lord are on the righteous and His ears are open to their request. But the face of the Lord is against those who do evil (1 Peter 3:10-12 HCSB).

In the original context, the Psalmist did not forbid retaliation; however, Peter wanted his readers to rely upon the Lord for help against those who do evil. Undoubtedly, Peter quoted from this Psalm to motivate his readers to oneness in Christ. He desired the unity of Jesus' prayer.

In James 3, the tongue, though small, is shown to be a most powerful force for either good or evil. It must be kept in check if there is to be unity among believers. Nothing causes discord more than evil and deceitful speech. Evil speech mimics Satan's lies and distortions, springing from one's sinful nature, while honest and pure speech for good rises from one's new heart.

Again, Peter mentions prayer; here it is hindered where unity is destroyed by evil and deceitful evil speech. Discord causes stress and stress shortens life; hence, the legacy of unity is long life.

The Matter of Suffering (3:13-4:19)

In this section of the letter, Peter tackles the problem of suffering and persecution. In Hebrews and Revelation, the writers warn their readers of

191

the awful consequence of apostasy, even under the pressure of persecution. When Peter wrote, there was less enticement to abandon Christ since persecution was sporadic. Therefore, his emphasis is on conduct under persecution.

MINDSET (3:13-14): Since the eyes of the Lord are on the righteous, we are not "to fear their fear," which comes from the Septuagint, "Do not fear what they fear, and do not dread it" (Isaiah 8:12). Those who do not know Christ should live in fear and dread.

> Don't fear those who kill the body but are not able to kill the soul; rather, fear Him who is able to destroy both soul and body in hell (Matthew 10:28 HCSB).

The next verse from the Septuagint affirms this view.

> You are to regard only the LORD of Hosts as holy. Only He should be feared; only He should be held in awe (Isaiah 8:13 HCSB).

If we prepare our minds for action (1:13), we will be eager to do good, then who is going to harm us? The Greek "but and if you suffer" points to a rare thing. By some small chance if we suffer for what is right, we will be blessed—grace will be given to us when Jesus Christ is revealed.

DEFENSE (3:15-16): A prepared mind sanctifies the Lord "Christ" (in diverse earlier manuscripts and "God" in Textus Receptus) in the heart— Yahweh Almighty as holy (set apart, sanctified) according to Isaiah 8:13. The enthronement of Christ in our heart is a key to sanctification and overcoming fear.

A right mind and heart will always be prepared to give an answer to everyone who asks you to give the reason for the hope that you have. Do not answer with "a holier than thou" attitude!

We must synthesize what we believe and be able to express our faith and hope in a way that is gentle, respectful and in keeping with a clear conscience when questioned. If spoken maliciously against our good behavior, as Peter and John were by the Sanhedrin (Acts 4:5-22), they may be ashamed of their slander. A prepared mind is always ready to evangelize, whether to the government authorities, in the workplace or in the home.

UNDESERVED SUFFERING (3:17): We might say it is better not to suffer, but Peter says, "It is better, if it is God's will, to suffer for doing good than for doing evil." No suffering occurs outside the will of God, who can allow or prevent it. If one suffers for doing good, God intends it to be for some good reason and purpose. It has been said, "The church was built on the blood of martyrs." Like Job, it is not for us to question why, but to remain faithful to the Lord. He has an outcome in mind that we cannot perceive.

MINISTRY OF CHRIST (3:18-22): Peter's purpose for this passage is to demonstrate Christ's confidence in the face of persecution; that His suffering preceded glory. Again, Peter declares the basic truths of the Gospel. Christ did not deserve death, but He died once for all—the righteous for the unrighteous to bring us to God (cf. 2 Corinthians 5:21). "For sins" describes the reason why Christ had to die—His death was a substitutionary death. As the Righteous Servant, Christ suffered in the place of sinners (cf. Isaiah 53:5-6; Hebrews 10:12).

The apostle sets forth a statement of faith in 1 Peter 3:18 (HSCB):

> For Christ also suffered for sins once for all,
>   the righteous for the unrighteous,
>   that He might bring you to God,
>   after being put to death in the fleshly realm
>   but made alive in the spiritual realm.

The Ministry of Christ:

1. His death, 3:18
2. His propitiation, 3:18
3. His proclamation, 3:19-20
4. His resurrection, 3:21
5. His baptism, 3:21
6. His ascension, 3:22

7. His rule, 3:22

Note that the HCSB translates "flesh" as "fleshly realm" and "spirit" as "spiritual realm." In the Greek, there is no article before "flesh" or "spirit" (θανατωθεὶ" μὲν σαρκὶ ζῳοποιηθεὶ" δὲ πνεύματι UBS4). Therefore, it is most likely Christ's spirit, not "the Spirit" as translated in KJV and NIV.

In His spirit, before the resurrection of His body, Christ went to the realm where human spirits go at death and/or to the realm where fallen angels are being kept in prison, which is the interpretation of the HCSB translators.

This is one of the most difficult passages to interpret in the NT. Seven interpretations of this passage have been suggested.

1. Christ preached through Noah to the wicked generation of that time. However, this view does not relate to Christ's death and resurrection as the context in seems to imply.

2. Christ preached to the fallen angels held and chained in Tartarus because they had married human women in Noah's time (cf. Genesis 6:1-4; 2 Peter 2:4; Jude 6). Hence, Christ's message was a declaration of victory. However, this intermarriage view is uncertain.

3. Christ went to Hades and preached to the spirits of Noah's wicked generation, proclaiming the Gospel or His victory, thereby sealing their doom. However, the term "spirits" is only used of human beings when qualifying terms are added, such as "departed spirits" (cf. Isaiah 26:19).

4. Christ's preaching was done while the spirits of humans why they were alive. However, this view does not fit the context.

5. Christ's preaching refers to departed OT saints, who had not heard the Gospel while alive and are now dead, but hear it before taken to heaven from Hades since they live according to God in the Spirit.

6. Christ preached to the spiritually dead so that they will become spiritually alive. However, this view does not take into account: "And just as it is appointed for people to die once—and after this, judgment" (Hebrews 9:27 HCSB).

7. Christ preached to those who are now dead refers to those who have suffered physical abuse by the world's judgment but now enjoy life in the heavenly realm. However, this view is least probable because the preached to were in prison.

The interpretation of this passage depends on how the following questions are answered:

1. When did Christ make this proclamation?
2. Where was Christ's proclamation made?
3. Who are the "spirits" to whom Christ made a proclamation?
4. What was its content?

Most likely, this declaration was made between the hours following Christ's death, resurrection and before His ascension into heaven forty days after Passover A.D. 33.

If "spirits" refers to fallen angels, Christ's declaration of victory is made to fallen angels who co-habited with women during the days of Noah. The place is Tartarus, where they are being kept in everlasting chains in this prison until Judgment Day (2 Peter 2:4; Jude 6).

If "spirits" refers to humans, Hades is be the place of Christ's proclamation since He told the criminal crucified next to Him, "Today you shall be with me in Paradise' (Luke 23:43). Hence, His message of victory could have been to the departed "spirits" on the side of Abraham and/or to the departed "spirits" in the place of torment (cf. 1 Peter 4:6; Luke 16:19-31).

Another difficult passage seems to refer to Christ descending into Hades and subsequently taking the righteous to heaven with Him at His ascension.

This is why it says: "When he ascended on high, he led captives in his

195

train and gave gifts to men." (What does "he ascended" mean except that he also descended to the lower, earthly regions? He who descended is the very one who ascended higher than all the heavens, in order to fill the whole universe (Ephesians 4:8-10).

Based on these passages, the *Apostles' Creed* asserts that Christ descended into Hades and He rose on the third day from the dead.

Certainly, a goal of Peter is for his readers to win the lost (2:12; 3:1). Yet, it is unlikely that Christ's proclamation was to bring salvation to the departed "spirits" of the dead since "man is destined to die once, and after that to face judgment (Hebrews 9:27).

His twofold illustration of water baptism fits this interpretation of a proclamation of salvation to the righteous and judgment to the unrighteous. Water baptism (identification with) was the central rite of initiation into the Christian community. It was an outward testimony, symbolizing being born crucified—dying with Christ and rising with Him (cf. Romans 6:1-11). The flood symbolizes baptism, and water baptism symbolizes salvation. The flood was a figure of baptism in that in both instances the water that spoke of judgment (in the flood the death of the wicked, in baptism the death of Christ and the believer) is the water that saves.

The Flood and Water Baptism

The Type	The Antitype
Water of the flood	Water of baptism, Psalm 51:2
Cleansed the earth of man's wickedness/sin	Cleansed the conscience of man's wickedness/sin, Ezekiel 36:25
Separated Noah's family from the evil of their day	Separates Christ's family from the evil of our day, Acts 22:6; Titus 3:5
Noah's family saved in the Ark	Christ's family is saved in Him, Romans 6:1-7
Eight people saved, many are lost	Many are invited, few are chosen, Matthew 22:14; cf. 7:13-14

How does baptism "save?" Peter says it does not concern an external washing from filth but relates to the conscience. The conscience is stirred

196

by the proclamation of the gospel, salvation from sin and its punishment is announced through Jesus' death and resurrection.

Again, Peter emphasized that *suffering precedes glory* with the ascension of Christ to the right hand of God and with angels, authorities, and powers subjected to Him.

PREPARATION (4:1-6):   When life is easy, we tend to drift into carelessness and complacency, but that all changes when suffering comes our way.   In this passage, Peter stated three virtues of suffering, which prepare us for what lies ahead.

1.   Suffering identifies us with Christ, 4:1
2.   Suffering reminds us that life is short, 4:2-3
3.   Suffering points ahead to God's judgment, 4:4-6

Like the previous passage, verses 1 and 6 are difficult to interpret. Radically different interpretations appear in the commentaries.

Possibly, Williams has captured the meaning of the first two verses in his translation of the NT.

> So then, since Christ has suffered in our physical form, you too must arm yourselves with the same determination. For whoever suffers in his physical form has done with sin, so that he no longer can spend the rest of his earthly life in harmony with human desires but in accordance with God's will (1 Peter 4:1-2 Williams).

Peter has returned to his thematic theme of "prepare your minds for action." Here he says, "Arm yourselves with the same mind" is the imagery of soldiers arming, training or otherwise preparing themselves for battle and possible death.   Those who have died with Christ are to be ready for whatever comes, even martyrdom. So how does suffering help us to be done with sin? Sinful desires become less alluring if we arm ourselves with the same determination of Christ and depend on Him to help us through times of sufferings.

We take life for granted until we have to suffer, then our values change.

For there has already been enough time spent in doing the will of the pagans: carrying on in unrestrained behavior, evil desires, drunkenness, orgies, carousing, and lawless idolatry (1 Peter 4:3 HCSB).

Six evils are listed, headed by "debauchery" (ασελγεια *aselgeia*), which is unbridled lust, excess, licentiousness, lasciviousness, wantonness, outrageousness, shamelessness, and insolence.

The Greco-Roman world was a cesspool of immorality with the worship of false gods and spirits, which often encouraged, as part of its exercise, both drunkenness and sexual vice and carelessness. Heavy drinking and men often pursuing and lusting for slave women or boys; religious festivals were occasions for lust, drunkenness, orgies, and carousing (ποτος *potos*, drinking parties).

Social clubs, household cults, religious festivals and drinking parties were normal from the world's perspective, but were condemned as immoral by Jews and Christians. The born again Gentiles had spent enough time in the past living this lifestyle and no longer were indulging in pagan activities. Therefore, the Christians were not understood by the pagans.

> In regard to this, they are surprised that you don't plunge with them into the same flood of dissipation—and they slander you (1 Peter 4:4 HCSB.)

Since Christians did not participate in debauchery, their pagan neighbors often portrayed them as lawless and subversive because of their alleged antisocial behavior. A changed life will rub people the right way or the wrong way! They will be attracted by the Christian lifestyle or repelled by it. Consequently, persecution was around the corner when Peter wrote this letter. History repeats itself so Christians should not be surprised that the twenty-first century worldview mirrors the first century Greco-Roman worldview.

Today's Christian, just as Peter's original readers, are to take heart that Christ will come from heaven to Judge the living and the dead—another tenet of the *Apostles' Creed*.

EVENTS FOLLOWING CHRIST'S RETURN

IN HEAVEN

ANGEL WITH KEY TO THE ABYSS & GREAT CHAIN 20:1-3

SOULS OF TRIBULATION MARTYRS 20:4-6

THRONES OF THOSE GIVEN AUTHORITY TO JUDGE 20:4

The Judgment Seat of Christ
1 Corinthians 3:11-15; 4:5;
2 Corinthians 5:10

Matthew 25:31-46
THE SON OF MAN SEPARATES SHEEP & GOATS

DEVOURING FIRE

SATAN DECEIVES THE NATIONS GATHERS THEM TO THE BATTLE OF GOG & MAGOG AT JERUSALEM 20:7-9

SATAN 20:10

THE GREAT WHITE THRONE 20:11-14

THE HOLY CITY THE NEW JERUSALEM 21-22

SATAN SEIZED

RESURRECTED TO REIGN WITH CHRIST AS PRIESTS

RIGHTEOUS ENTER THE MILLENNIAL KINGDOM TO ETERNAL LIFE

ABYSS OPENED

GREAT & SMALL RESURRECTED FROM THE SEA, DEATH, HADES

THE NEW HEAVEN & NEW EARTH

THROWN INTO THE LOCKED ABYSS

SAINTS BODIES FROM GRAVES

OLD TESTAMENT SAINTS RESURRECTED AT THIS TIME OR AT THE RAPTURE OF CHURCH Daniel 12:2-3, 13

ETERNAL FIRE PREPARED FOR THE DEVIL & HIS ANGELS

THROWN INTO THE LAKE OF FIRE TO BE TORMENTED DAY AND NIGHT FOREVER

ON EARTH

THE GREAT SUPPER OF GOD ARMAGEDDON THE BEAST & FALSE PROPHET CAPTURED 19:17-21

THROWN ALIVE INTO THE FIERY LAKE OF BURNING SUFFER

Christ's Judgments after His Coming in the Book of Revelation

199

Peter's mind that there is a Judgment Day for everyone.

> They will give an account to the One who stands ready to judge the living and the dead. For this reason the gospel was also preached to those who are now dead, so that, although they might be judged by men in the fleshly realm, they might live by God in the spiritual realm (1 Peter 4:5-6 HCSB).

Though Peter speaks of the Father as Judge (1:17: 2:23), all judgment has been entrusted to Jesus Christ the Son (cf. John 5:22; Acts 10:42; 2 Timothy 4:1), who is the subject in the contexts from 3:18 forward. Presently, angels, authorities and powers are in submission to Christ (3:22) and all authority in heaven and earth has been given to Him (Matthew 28:18). Christ is "ready," that is fully qualified to judge decisively. The living will be judged by Christ when He returns to earth to reign.

> All the nations will be gathered before Him, and He will separate them one from another, just as a shepherd separates the sheep from the goats. He will put the sheep on His right, and the goats on the left (Matthew 25:32-33 HCSB).

Those on His left will go away to eternal punishment, but the righteous to eternal life, which begins with entering the Millennial Kingdom for the Tribulation saints (Matthew 25:46). Following His thousand year reign comes the Great White Throne Judgment, where Christ will judge the resurrected dead from all the ages.

> I also saw the dead, the great and the small, standing before the throne, and books were opened. Another book was opened, which is the book of life, and the dead were judged according to their works by what was written in the books. Then the sea gave up its dead, and Death and Hades gave up their dead; all were judged according to their works. Death and Hades were thrown into the lake of fire. This is the second death, the lake of fire (Revelation 20:12-14 HCSB).

Apparently, the Gospel was preached by Christ to the dead in Hades so that they would know that He has authority to judge them, not to save their souls.

This tragic outcome should be a strong motivation for the Christian to evangelize the lost.

In the midst of suffering, the realization of the coming judgment should motivate Christians to be obedient children—to be holy as He is holy!

PRACTICAL PRINCIPLES (4:7-11):   This section contains Peter's practical principles for Christian living.   He gave three motivations for living this way.

1. The end of all things is near
2. So that in all things God may be praised through Jesus Christ.
3. To him be the glory and the power for ever and ever

It has been almost two thousand years since Peter wrote, "The end is near" or "the end of all things has drawn near."   Paul (Philippians 4:5), James, (James 5:8), John (1 John 2:18) and the writer of Hebrews (Hebrews 10:13) taught that the coming of Christ was near.   Are we to think that they had misunderstood Christ's teaching, or would they be saying the same words if they were with us today?

First, Peter's word for "end" (τελος *telos*) is never used in the NT as a chronological end, as if something simply stops.   Instead, the word means a consummation, a goal achieved, a result attained, or a realization.   Second, Christ's return is "imminent," it could take place at any moment with suddenness (cf. Romans 13:12; 1 Thessalonians 1:10; James 5:7; Revelation 22:20).   We are not to become lazy dreamers or overzealous fanatics as we are watching and waiting for the consummation of God's plan of the ages.

In light of this consummation, Peter sets forth eight practical principles for Christian living:

1. Be clear minded
2. Be self-controlled so that you can pray
3. Love each other deeply, because love covers over a multitude of sins
4. Offer hospitality to one another without grumbling
5. Use whatever gift you received to serve others

6. Faithfully administer God's grace in its various forms
7. Speak the very words of God
8. Serve with the strength God provides

Primarily, Christian living begins in the mind (Romans 12:2). For that reason, Peter commanded his readers to "be clear minded" as he returns to a thematic theme, "Prepare your minds for action" (1:17).

"Love" is to be εκτενης (*ektenes*, fervent, stretched, without ceasing, deep) because "love covers a multitude of sins," which is quoted from Proverbs 10:12. Such love does not preclude the discipline of a sinning, unrepentant church member (cf. Matthew 18:15-18; 1 Corinthians 5). It means Christians should overlook sins against them if possible, and always be ready to forgive insults and unkindness.

"Gift" (χαρισμα *charisma*) refers to a spiritual endowment by the Holy Spirit to be used for the benefit of others; spiritual gifts are not for self-edification. God's grace is to be faithfully administered in its various forms (cf. 1 Corinthians 12-14). Christians are to be good stewards or managers of what God has entrusted to them.

Peter implies there are two kinds of gifts, serving and speaking, which were the distinct ministry functions of the early church (cf. Acts 6:2-4). Peter's style is to highlight what he expected his readers to know, especially Paul's explanation of spiritual gifts.

Peter's point is that cooperation, sharing, and mutual service are values to be enacted within the household of God; competition and status-seeking mark relationships of the world. All things are to be done to the praise and glory of Christ.

CHRISTIAN SUFFERING (4:12-19): Many Christians are surprised or shocked when the trials and sufferings of Christ come into their lives. The sun does not always shine upon Christians; our grass is not always green; and the temperature is not always ideal. Therefore, Peter reminded his readers that sharing in Christ's suffering is a prerequisite to sharing in His glories. He encouraged his readers to endure suffering with Christlike faith so they might be further identified with Him, receive a blessing, and trust God completely.

> Beloved, think it not strange at the fiery suffering among you that is coming to try you, as if a strange thing were happening to you (1 Peter 4:12 YLT).

> Dear friends, when the fiery ordeal arises among you to test you, don't be surprised by it, as if something unusual were happening to you (1 Peter 4:12 HCSB).

It is difficult to determine by the Greek whether the suffering is present or coming. Whatever the case, his readers are to rejoice because they are participating in the sufferings of Christ. Once more, he focuses their mind on the hope of the Second Coming of Christ, when they will be overjoyed.

Through verbal assaults, their neighbors will attempt to have them conform to the world, but they need not be ashamed for they are not suffering because of wrongdoing. If they are insulted because of the name of Christ, they are blessed, for the Spirit of the glory and of God rests on them. This kind of fiery ordeal proves that they bear the name "Christian" and they should praise God. This speaks loudly to the present age when Christians are being maligned by the media, politicians, professors, neighbors, etc.

Peter has repeated his subjects from the previous passages: (1) judgment is coming and (2) suffering occurs according to the will of God. Now the apostle asks two piercing questions with verses 17 and 18:

1. For it is time for judgment to begin with (ἀπό *apo* from) the οἶκος (*oikos*, house, household) of God and if it begins with us, what will the outcome be for those who do not obey the gospel of God?

2. If it is hard for the righteous to be saved, what will become of the ungodly and the sinner?

Some interpret "the household of God" in the first question to refer to the purging, chastening, and purifying of the church by the loving hand of God.

203

The "time" (καιρος *kairos*) referred to is the dispensation of the church, which began at Pentecost and will continue to the Rapture (cf. 1 Peter 2:5; Galatians 6:10; Ephesians 2:19; 1 Timothy 3:15; Hebrews 3:6; 10:21).

Others interpret the word "time" as referring to a specific, designated, or predicted time when something is supposed to happen. Hence, Peter is again referring to the end time, with this being an apocalyptic pronouncement of persecution, beginning with believers. When God brings great calamities, judgments and wrath upon whole nations, He generally begins with his own people (cf. Isaiah 10:12; Jeremiah 25:29; Ezekiel 9:6).

Others understand Peter to be referring to believers appearing before the Judgment Seat of Christ.

This writer believes "the household of God" refers to the nation of Israel since the Jewish Wars began in A.D. 66 and Jerusalem would be destroyed in A.D. 70, with a remnant of Jews being scattered to the provinces outside of Palestine. This is the predicted "time." Jesus lamented and predicted:

> Jerusalem, Jerusalem! The city who kills the prophets and stones those who are sent to her. How often I wanted to gather your children together, as a hen gathers her chicks under her wings, but you were not willing! See, your house is abandoned to you. And I tell you, you will not see Me until the time comes when you say, Blessed is He who comes in the name of the Lord! (Luke 13:34-35 HCSB).

The fall of the Northern Kingdom of Israel to the Assyrians in 722 B.C. was a warning to the Southern Kingdom of Judah to obey God's commands. By 586 B.C., God's judgment fell on Judah because they ignored His warning. Now, the fall of Israel would be a warning to the Gentiles to obey the gospel of God.

The second question Peter quoted from Proverbs 11:31 of the Septuagint. It is intended to bring the reader back to reality. The righteous are to endure fiery trials; they will be saved from final judgment; but not so for the ungodly and sinner, who will be cast into Hell.

So then, those who suffer according to God's will should commit themselves to their faithful Creator and continue to do good (1 Peter 4:19).

The Matter of Shepherding (5:1-7)

DUTIES OF ELDERS (5:1-4): With a right perspective of times of suffering and the Second Coming of Christ set forth, Peter made his appeal to fellow elders (πρεσβυτερος *presbuteros*, shepherds, overseers, bishops) to the noblest form of leadership.

The term "elder" might emphasize spiritual maturity, not necessarily physical age; however, elders are compared to "young men" in verses 5. Usually age and maturity go together, but not always! For the sake of worldly concepts many denominations and churches are casting aside the most experienced and prepared shepherds, preferring a "younger" pastor to an "older" pastor. Often older men are discarded when it comes to lay leadership in the church.

Some think the plural "elders" suggests a plurality of pastors for a local church; however, "among you" refers to the sojourners of the five provinces mentioned in the first verse of this letter. Therefore, Peter did not indicate that a church should have multiple pastors.

Peter's principles for elders, who have a mind prepared for action:

1. The Ministry: Be shepherds of God's flock that is under your care.
2. The Motive: Serve as overseers not because you must, but because you are willing, as God wants you to be.
3. The Satisfaction: Not to be greedy for money, but eager to serve.
4. The Manner: Not κατακυριευω (*katakurieuo*, holding in subjection, exercising lordship over) those entrusted to you, but being examples to the flock.
5. The Expectation: To receive the crown of glory that will never fade away.

"Not to be greedy for money" is a telling sign of a wrong motive for ministry

205

(cf. 1 Timothy 3:3, 8; Titus 1:7). However, this does not mean that a pastor is not to be paid well. Jesus instructed His disciples that a "worker deserves his wages" (Luke 10:7), which Paul reiterated, "In the same way, the Lord has commanded that those who preach the gospel should receive their living from the gospel" (1 Corinthians 9:14). In addition, Paul wrote concerning wages, "The elders who direct the affairs of the church well are worthy of double honor, especially those whose work is preaching and teaching" (1 Timothy 5:17). The mindset makes all the difference—does the pastor see himself as a willing servant or a paid servant?

Peter's appeal to the elders is sandwiched between "who will share in the glory to be revealed" and "when the Chief Shepherd appears, you will receive the crown of glory that will never fade away." The Chief Shepherd is Christ (cf. Isaiah 40:11; Zechariah 13:7; John 10:2, 11-12, 16; Hebrews 13:20-21). He will evaluate the ministry of pastors at the Judgment Seat (cf. 1 Corinthians 3:9-15; 4:5; 2 Corinthians 5:9-10).

Believers are promised crowns of life (James 1:12), righteousness (2 Timothy 4:8), and rejoicing (1 Thessalonians 2:19) and pastors are promised the crown of unfading glory. The pastor is not to seek glory in this life. The pastor, who carries out Peter's principles, will receive glory as reward when Christ is revealed. Glory does not have a color, shape or size, but it is something wonderful since glory is intrinsic to God (cf. Psalm 19:1). After His own suffering, Christ was "crowned with glory and honor" (Hebrews 2:9).

SUBMISSION TO ELDERS AND GOD (5:5-7): "Likewise, you younger men, be subject to the elders" is another area where Christians are to be submissive—someone must have the final say! That does not mean the elders are free to do as they please according to Peter's principles for elders, or vice versa for the younger men. The young men's mindset is to parallel the mindset of the elders. It has been suggested that "young" refers to both age and spiritual maturity, but it does not refer to younger pastors since history does not support that interpretation.

Note how quickly Peter brings everyone into his principles—"and all of you clothe yourselves with ταπεινοφροσυνη (tapeinophrosune, humility, lowliness of mind) toward one another." Again, he quotes from the OT, "Because God resists the proud, but gives grace to the humble" (Proverbs 3:34). The pride of life is evidence of worldliness (see 1 John 2:16).

All believers (elder or subordinate) are to think and act with lowliness of mind toward each other; all believers are to submit to God!

> Humble yourselves therefore under the mighty hand of God, so that He may exalt you in due time, casting all your care upon Him, because He cares about you (1 Peter 5:6-7 HCSB).

Jesus is a perfect example of this mindset of humility—from Heaven to Gethsemane to the Cross to the Tomb to Heaven (cf. Philippians 2:5-8). Why did the Creator take on a human nature? Did He do it to have everyone serve Him and exercise His lordship over those around Him? No! "For even the Son of Man did not come to be served, but to serve, and to give his life as a ransom for many" (Mark 10:45). He demonstrated the mindset of humility when He washed the feet of His disciples (John 13:3-15). Such is the mind prepared for action.

"The mighty hand of God" reminds us that we are weak and He is strong. He is sovereign and we are His subjects. Therefore, we are to humble ourselves—submit to His lordship as Christ did in Gethsemane—"Father, if you are willing, take this cup from me; yet not my will, but yours be done" (Luke 22:42).

Again, Peter inserted the theme of prayer into this letter. With a right attitude toward others and God, you are free to cast all your care upon Him, because He cares about you.

"Casting" (επιρριπτω *epirrhipto*, throwing upon, placing upon, handing over) is a decisive act of ridding oneself of the (μεριμνα *merimna*, care, anxiety, worry) by giving it to God (cf. Matthew 5:25-34).

Is this a guarantee that all requests will be answered to our satisfaction? No! The answer is that He may exalt you in due time. When you pray, keep in mind that suffering precedes glory! It is important that we realize that God works *in* us as well as *for* us. His will for us is often different from ours.

207

He has an eternal perspective, while we tend to have an earthly one, as David discovered during a time of complaining and groaning due to persecution.

Cast your burden on the LORD, and He will support you; He will never allow the righteous to be shaken. You, God, will bring them down to the pit of destruction; men of bloodshed and treachery will not live out half their days. But I will trust in You (Psalms 55:22-23 HCSB).

In this passage, Peter offers four more principles of a mind prepared for action:

1. God and others can help solve difficulties if we humble ourselves.
2. God really cares about us.
3. God is able to meet our needs.
4. God works on His own time schedule.

The Matter of Satan (5:8-11)

SELF-CONTROLLED AND ALERT (5:8): Having commanded his readers to hand worry over to God, Peter commands watchfulness—"Be self-controlled (νηφω *nepho*, calm, collected, sober) and alert (γρηγορεω *gregoreuo*, cautious, vigilant, give strict attention to, watch)."

Jesus made Peter aware that Satan was after him (Matthew 13:25, 39; Luke 22:31), now the apostle tells his readers, "Your enemy the Devil prowls around like a roaring lion looking for someone to devour." The word "Devil" means "slanderer," Satan accuses the saints before God (cf. Job 1-2; Zechariah 3:1-5; Revelation 12:10) and he uses the lips of people to accuse the righteous whether deserved or falsely (1 Peter 2:12; 3:16; 4:4, 14). He comes as a serpent to deceive (Genesis 3) or a lion to devour. He is a liar and a murderer (John 8:44).

In Christ's letters to the seven churches in Asia Minor, the Devil (Satan) is mentioned in four of them (Revelation 2-3).

1. Satan is not mentioned at Ephesus, where the church has left its first love—Christ

2. Satan' synagogue is at Smyrna, where he is at work persecuting the suffering church
3. Satan's throne is at Pergamum, where compromise and indulgence have overcome the church
4. Satan is not mentioned at Sardis, where the church is dead
5. Satan's depths have permeated at Thyatira, where Jezebel's teaching is tolerated
6. Satan is overcome at Philadelphia
7. Satan is not mentioned at Laodicea, where the church is lukewarm

Throughout history, many churches were not sober and vigilant—the roaring lion devoured them!

The Devil and his demonic forces are always active, looking for opportunities to overwhelm the believer with temptation, persecution and discouragement (cf. Psalm 22:13; 104:21; Ezekiel 22:25). The Devil is a sower of discord and does all he can to drag the Christian out of fellowship with Christ and out of Christian service (cf. Job 1: Luke 22:3; John 13:27; 2 Corinthians 4:3-4; Revelation 12).

Is Satan behind many, some, or all of the "tests" that Peter wrote about? Yes! Therefore the believer should be aware of the character, schemes, wiles and tactics of Satan, the Devil, for example:

1. He rules the dominion of darkness, Colossians, 1:13; Matthew 12:26
2. He is the prince of demons, Mark 3:22; Matthew 12;24
3. He is the god of this age, Matthew 4:8-9; 2 Corinthians 4:4
4. He is a liar and murderer, John 8:44
5. He holds the power of death, Hebrews 2:14
6. He disguises himself as an angel of light, 2 Corinthians 11:13-15
7. He works in those who are disobedient, 2 Corinthians 2:11
8. He persecutes and kills Christians, Revelation 2:10, 13
9. He deceives the church with so-called deep secrets, Revelation 2:24
10. He works through demons, who are depraved, invisible, spiritual beings with intelligence and strength, which they apply to oppose God with their attacks on humans.

a. They can oppose and subject the human mind, 1 Timothy 4:1
b. They can oppress the body, Job 1:12, 16, 19; 2:7; Matthew 9:32-33; 12:22; Luke 13:11-17
c. They can alienate people from God, 1 Peter 5:8

Through demonic forces, Satan achieves his major objectives to destroy peace and harmony and to introduce as much anguish, grief, misfortune, suspicion, anxiety and confusion as possible into the world and human life.

There is good news for the Christian in the battle against Satan the Devil. Christ is the Victor!

He disarmed the rulers and authorities and disgraced them publicly; He triumphed over them by Him (Colossians 2:15 HCSB).

Consequently, if the Christian puts on the whole armor or God and pray, they can withstand the Devil's schemes (Ephesians 6:10-18).

The Devil prowls, roars and devours; there is a progression in his actions. Believers disagree about whether the Devil can destroy our salvation or only our Christian joy and fruitfulness. The NT repeatedly warns about the power of the Devil (2 Corinthians 11:14; Ephesians 6:11; 1 Timothy 4:1). The Christian is able to resist the Devil, but it is too late when he devours!

The Bible is clear that the adversary is powerless to do damage in the spiritual life of those who resist him.

RESIST THE DEVIL (5:9): The climate of the Roman Empire was becoming antagonistic toward Christians. They would face public ridicule, beating, imprisonment and even seizure of their property. Consequently, perseverance under persecution and suffering would mark an overcomer of the world, the flesh and the Devil. Peter's advice for overcoming the Devil is straightforward.

Resist him, standing firm in the faith, because you know that your brothers throughout the world are undergoing the same kind of sufferings (1 Peter 5:19).

"Resist" (ανθιστημι *anthistemi,* withstand, oppose) calls to mind an army united against a common enemy. If Christians break ranks, the Devil has an opportunity to attack and devour the church.

How does an individual Christian resist the Devil? "Submit yourselves, then, to God. Resist the Devil, and he will flee from you" (James 4:7). In the wilderness, the Devil tempted Christ and He used Scripture, each time quoting from the book of Deuteronomy. (Matthew 4:1-11; Luke 4:1-13). A prepared mind, conscience, and commonsense warn us to avoid compromising situations, false teachers and philosophers with worldly wisdom, etc.

EXPECTATION AND ASSURANCE (5:10-11): Before closing his letter, Peter summarized his overall theme of suffering precedes glory. The knowledge that other Christians, their brothers throughout the world, were suffering, would strengthen their resolve to continue to stand firm. From all that Peter has written, his readers should expect suffering for a little while, but they can rest assured of being called to His eternal glory in Christ Jesus.

In the midst of suffering or having suffered briefly, one tends to feel weak, shaky and unsteady, so Peter assured his readers that the God of all grace would personally:

1. Restore you—equipped, complete and perfect
2. Make you strong—confirmed and constant
3. Make you firm—in spiritual knowledge and power
4. Make you steadfast—stable and grounded

Pondering the power and dominion of God's grace, in the four previous verbs, caused Peter to burst into a doxology, "To him be the power [κρατος *kratos*, dominion] for ever and ever. Amen." This doxology is evidence of a mind prepared for action that has pondered the depths of God's grace. His expression of praise is appropriate for time and eternity.

The Closing Greetings (5:12-14)

Silas and Mark are with Peter at the writing of this letter. Both men were known by Peter's readers so he includes their names in the closing greetings.

PURPOSE (5:12): See the writer's introduction to his letter, regarding Silas (Silvanus). Peter identifies Silas as "our faithful brother," who was instrumental in composing, transcribing or bearing the letter to the provinces. During Paul's second missionary journey, Silas would have encountered some of the readers in the five provinces (cf. Acts 14:40-15:6).

Peter says, "I have written to you briefly, encouraging you and testifying that this is the true grace of God. Stand fast in it" (Peter 5:12).

The indicative "in which you stand (εστηκατε *estekate*, to make firm, fix establish)" in the Textus Receptus, but the best manuscripts have the aorist active imperative "stand (στητε) fast in it"—"the true grace of God," which no Christian earns or merits but which all Christians are obligated to abide in. Continuance and perseverance in this doctrine of God's grace presented by Peter is the firm ground and foundation of Christian strength and encouragement.

FAREWELL (5:13-14): She [the Church] who is in Babylon [Rome], chosen [people of God in Christ] together with you, sends you her greetings, and so does my [spiritual] son [John] Mark. See remarks in the introduction.

This letter ends with a command and a blessing. The command is "Greet one another with a kiss of love (αγαπη *agape*)." The practice of a kiss was customary in the ancient East and was continued by the early church.

The blessing is "Peace to all of you who are in Christ." Peace is abundantly available to all in Christ, who is the Prince of Peace!

"Peace" reflects the common Hebrew blessing of "Shalom." Appropriately, Peter's first letter, filled with anticipation of suffering and persecution, would begin and end with a strong desire for God's grace and "peace (ειρηνη *eirene*, rest, quietness, tranquility) for his readers. Prepare your mind for action with perfect—suffering precedes glory!

Second Peter: Growing in Grace and Knowledge

INTRODUCTION

WRITER AND DATE: The letter plainly indicates that Simon Peter is the writer. Interesting, the best manuscripts have "Simeon," the Hebrew word for his name. He may have wanted to appeal to both Jews and Gentiles since "Peter" is Greek. He identifies himself as a servant and apostle of Jesus Christ, and there is no mention of the assistance of Silas. Church tradition ascribes the letter to Simon Peter, with no other name linked to it. However, a vast number of contemporary "liberal" scholars deny that Peter wrote it, making it one of the most disputed books of the NT. This writer believes this letter was written by Peter near the end of his life, and according to tradition, from Rome about 67-68 A.D.

RECIPIENTS: "To those who through the righteousness of our God and Savior Jesus Christ have received a faith as precious as ours." He also wrote, "Dear friends, this is now my second letter to you" (3:1), which might indicate it was written to the sojourners in the five provinces of his first letter. Whatever the case, this is a circular letter to be read by all Christians.

CIRCUMSTANCES: This letter reveals the danger of apostasy and an outbreak of heresy among the churches. Clearly there was an invasion of false teachers (2:1: 3:3), who were influencing Christians in moral and doctrinal errors (2:12, 17-18; 3:5, 16). His description of the false teachers is somewhat generic—they deny Christ, twist the Scriptures and bring true faith into dispute. Peter describes the immoral character of these teachers in more detail than he describes their doctrines. Therefore, his warnings are applicable throughout the church age.

Epicureanism, Stoicism and Platonism taught that people should not expect the gods to be involved in, or concerned about, human affairs. Notions of future judgment or rewards and punishments after death were considered superstitions. Therefore, the worldview of Peter's day was to indulge oneself in pleasure since there is no future accountability. Contrary to earlier commentators, Gnosticism did not appear until after Peter's death and Gnosticism is dealt with by the apostle John in his first letter and Gospel.

A favorite subject of Peter in his sermons, speeches and first letter was the return of Christ. Mark 9:1 and 13:30 appeared to indicate that the apostles would see the return of Christ, but His return had not occurred, which led to scoffers who denied His return. This letter combats this skepticism. Consequently, Peter wrote this letter as a reminder to stimulate his readers to accurate thinking from the Scriptures about the Day of the Lord (3:1-13). For the periods covered by Peter, see the chart *God's Timetable* at the end of this introduction.

Herein Peter instructed Christians in how to defend themselves against these false teachers and their deceptive lies. Thus, the keyword of this letter is "knowledge," occurring sixteen times in various forms.

Modern writers consider this a comparatively mediocre writing and not worthy of much attention. However, this letter has many important things to say to the church and the making of a well-informed disciple. For instance, it sets forth the important place the OT Scriptures occupy in a Christian's knowledge and its divine origin (1:20-21; 3:15-16).

TEXT AND STYLE: Papyrus 72, which dates to the third century, is the oldest manuscript of this letter and it contains the entire text. It is housed in the Bibliotheca Bodmeriana in Geneva. However, there are fewer copies of this text and they are in poorer condition than the first letter. Reasonable solutions for most of the variants in the manuscripts have been made.

The most important argument for Peter not writing this book is its similarity with Jude. No less than nineteen of the twenty-five verses of Jude are included in 2 Peter. However, seventy percent of the words differ in these inclusions. Neither writer can be said to be more concise than the other (Carson, Moo and Morris, *An Introduction to the New Testament*, 435). Possibly, Peter or Jude used the other as a resource or they collaborated in writing their letters. We can be certain that the danger of false teachers is very great since the Holy Spirit used both writers to warn us of them.

Warnings (3:17) and exhortations (3:18) run throughout the whole letter and give it unity and coherence. There is no Epistorial ending as with Peter's first letter.

KEY VERSES:

Therefore, brothers, make every effort to confirm your calling and election, because if you do these things you will never stumble (2 Peter 1:10 HCSB).

Therefore I will always remind you about these things, even though you know them and are established in the truth you have (2 Peter 1:12 HCSB).

Therefore, dear friends, since you have been forewarned, be on your guard, so that you are not led away by the error of the immoral and fall from your own stability. But grow in the grace and knowledge of our Lord and Savior Jesus Christ. To Him be the glory both now and to the day of eternity. Amen (2 Peter 3:17-18 HCSB).

KEY WORDS: Know/ledge (16); Lord (15); Christ (8); Prophet/Prophesy (7); Savior (5); Judgment (3)

THEMATIC THEMES:

1. Make your calling and election sure (1:10 cf. 1:5; 3:11-14, 17).

2. Steady growth will assure an abundant entrance into the eternal kingdom (1:11).

3. Knowledge that springs out of a living faith in Christ and the promises of God (1:2-4) is characterized by growth and development (1:5-11), and is anchored in the certainty of the apostolic testimony and divine inspiration of prophetic revelation (1:16-21).

   Full Knowledge (the Word of God) is the safeguard against Satan and error. A balanced life is to learn and live the Word of God. It is not enough to abide, stand fast; there must be growth. Believers must increase in their knowledge of Jesus Christ (1:2-4, 8; 2:20; 3:18).

PRIMARY THEMES:

Re-emphasize certain basic matters:

Remind (1:12)		
Refresh (1:13)	Contrasted	Forgotten (1:9)
Remember (1:15)	with	Forget (3:5, 8)
Reminder (3:1)		

Some of Peter's many warnings against false teachers:

1. They deny the Lord who bought them (2:1)
2. They are daring and irreverent (2:10b, 12)
3. They scoff at the promise of the Lord's Return (3:3-4)
4. They live immoral lives (2:13)
5. They seduce unstable souls (2:14, 18)
6. They cause the way of truth to be evil spoken of (2:2)
7. They make great promises of liberty to their followers but are themselves slaves to sin (2:19)
8. They are insubordinate to established authority (1:10c, 12)

SUBORDINATE THEMES:

Three worlds in light of God's judgment:

1. Antediluvian (3:5-6)
2. Present Cosmic System (3:7)
3. New Heavens and a New Earth (3:13)

STRUCTURE:

1. Exhortation to Grow Spiritually (1:1-21)
2. Instructions to Oppose False Teachers (2:1-22)
3. Teachings to Prepare for the End (3:1-18)

THE OUTLINE:

I. The Salutation (1:1-2)

II. To Stimulate Christian Growth (1:3-21)

    A. The Maturity of Believers, 1:3-11

    B. The Testimony of an Apostle, 1:12-18

    C. The Authority of Scripture, 1:19-21

III. To Combat False Teachers (2:1-22)

    A. Their Methods, 2:1-3a

    B. Their Judgment, 2:3b-13

    C. Their Character, 2:14-22

IV. To Encourage Watchfulness (3:1-17)

    A. The Purpose of the Letter, 3:1-2

    B. The Scriptural Answers, 3:3-13

    C. The Stability of Effort, 3:14-17

V. To Encourage Christian Growth (3:18)

God's Timetable

ETERNITY ———————— H I S T O R Y ——————— ETERNITY

CREATION ——————————————————— RECREATION
Heavens & Earth   New Heaven & New Earth

ANTEDILUVIAN AGE———THIS PRESENT AGE————THE AGE TO COME

The Flood   *Tribulation*

Day of Salvation ——————————— *Millennial Kingdom*

Old Covenant	New Covenant Blessings	New Covenant Fulfilled
Grace, Law & Israel	Grace, Spirit & Church	Israel & Saved Nations

Times of the Gentiles ——————]   *All Israel Saved*

Babylon, Medo-Persia, Greece, Rome   *Everlasting Kingdom*

Fall of		Fall of	Second Advent
Jerusalem		Babylon	of Christ &
586 B.C.		the Great	Israel Restored

69 Sevens (*Church Age*)	70th Seven
	End Times

444 B.C.   A.D. 33   A.D. ?

Restoration of Jerusalem	*The Last Days*	*The Day of the Lord*	*Millen-nium*	*The Day of God*
	Messiah &	The Lamb	Christ	The Son
	Israel	Opens the	Reigns	hands the
	Cut Off	Seven Seals	on Earth	Kingdom
				over to
				the
				Father

The above chart should prove helpful in understanding the terminology of the past and future periods covered by the apostle in Second Peter.

EXPOSITION

The Salutation (1:1-2)

THE WRITER, RECIPIENTS AND BLESSING: To identify himself, the writer combined his birth name "Simon" with "Peter," the name Jesus gave him. He adds δουλος (*doulos*, slave, servant or bondservant) to apostle of Jesus Christ—a balance of humility and dignity. In the OT, Moses (Joshua 14:7), David (Psalm 89:3) and Elijah (2 Kings 10:10) were "servants (or slaves) of Yahweh. Hence, bondservant refers to a free person voluntarily serving one he considers his master. Obviously, Peter had a clear understanding of who he is and who his Master is.

The letter is addressed, "To those who have obtained a faith of equal privilege with ours" or "the same kind of faith as ours." In other words, a faith of equal worth, rank, position and honor with "ours"—the apostles or the Jewish believers. This shared privilege comes, literally, "in (εν *en*) the righteousness of our God and Savior, Jesus Christ," which is imputed righteousness (cf. Romans 3:26; 4:5; 2 Corinthians 5:21; Philippians 3:8-9). Prepositions mark direction and relative position. The preposition εν (*en*) primarily denotes (fixed) position (in place, time or state), and (by implication) instrumentality. Peter used δια (*dia*) with the genitive, the usual preposition for "through" in this letter (cf. 1:3, 4; 2:2). Hence, Peter is speaking of position, not means.

The Greek indicates that Peter referred to one Person of the Trinity, not two—it is a clear declaration of Christ's divinity. However, when he gave the blessing, he referred to two Persons of the Trinity—"of God and of Jesus our Lord." See other comments above on the recipients of this letter.

Another addition to the first letter is made, this time to the blessing, "Grace and peace be yours in abundance through the knowledge of God and of Jesus our Lord." "Knowledge" (επιγνωσις *epignosis*) does not mean a mere intellectual understanding of some truth, though that is included. It denotes a living participation "in" (εν *en*) the knowledge, in the sense that our Lord used it, "Now this is eternal life: that they may know [γινωσκω *ginosko*] you, the only true God, and Jesus Christ, whom you have sent" (John 17:3).

The addition of επι refers to a fuller, deeper, complete, intimate spiritual knowledge. Such knowledge multiplies God and Jesus' grace and peace in the reader, which is the very nature of the Christian's transformed life.

In the salutation and the next section, we find Peter's principles for spiritual well-being.

Full Knowledge x Grace + Peace = Participation in the Divine Nature

Full Knowledge + Promises of God = Growing in Living Faith

Divine Power + Seven Virtues – World's Corruption = Godly Life

To Stimulate Christian Growth (1:3-21)

The best defense is a strong offense, which Peter illustrated by calling his readers to a life of maturity as the best safeguard against the inroads of apostasy.

THE MATURITY OF BELIEVERS (1:3-11): Peter opens with a positive declaration of what God has done and the great privileges of his readers. Divine power and full knowledge is everything for life and godliness.

The datives (ιδια δοξε και αρετε, *idia doxē kai aretē*) are either instrumental ("*by* [means of] his own glory and excellence") or advantageous ("*for* [the benefit of] his own glory and excellence").

As in his first letter, Peter expected godly living of his readers. By Christ's glory and excellence, the believer participates in the divine nature and escapes corruption in the world caused by evil desires; this is His very great and precious promise. Hence, Christ is the believer's sufficiency for life and godliness.

To be godly is to live reverently, loyally, and obediently toward God. Nothing else is needed to sustain growth, strength and perseverance because every spiritual resource is provided to escape the corruption in the world caused by evil desires. In his first letter, Peter warned of the Devil prowling, roaring and devouring; here he focuses on the world and the flesh (sinful nature). "Escaped" depicts a successful flight from danger. Having the divine nature, Christians should desire to grow spiritually by adding (επιχορηγεω *epichoregeo*, providing, supplying) the following seven characteristics to faith in verses 5-7:

1. To your faith goodness (αρετη *arête*, virtue, excellence)
2. To goodness, knowledge (γνωσις *gnosis*, practical knowledge)
3. To knowledge, self-control (εγκρατεια *egkrateia*, temperance, mastery over desires and passion)
4. To self-control, perseverance (υπομονη *hupomone*, patience, endurance)
5. To perseverance, godliness (ευσεβεια *eusebeia*, reverence, respect, piety towards God)
6. To godliness, brotherly kindness (φιλαδελφια *philadelphia*, brotherly love)
7. To brotherly kindness, love (αγαπη *agape*, sacrificial love of God)

We get our word "chorus" from the word for add. Interestingly, this chorus begins with faith and ends with love. Though we come to know Christ through faith, we need to grow in God's love, which the Holy Spirit poured into our heart at conversion (cf. Romans 5:5). According to Peter, sanctification is an ongoing progression in the full knowledge that brings practical results.

> For if these qualities are yours and are increasing, they will keep you from being useless or unfruitful in the knowledge [επιγνωσις *epignosis*] of our Lord Jesus Christ (2 Peter 1:8 HCSB).

In this letter, "full knowledge" comes from the Word of God, which is "precious faith" and "the precious promises" of God, so that we might live godly lives. Unfortunately, not all were progressing in salvation by adding to their faith. Therefore, Peter describes a person who has fallen since he did not add those seven characteristics to faith.

> The person who lacks these things is blind and shortsighted, and has forgotten the cleansing from his past sins (2 Peter 1:9 HCSB).

221

Forgetfulness is detrimental to one's spiritual life since it shuts out of one's thinking the past cleansing from past sins through the Word of God (cf. Ephesians 5:25-26).

The NIV has the reverse of the Greek, which has blind (τυφλος *tuphlos*, blind, mentally blind) and nearsighted (μυωπαζω *muopazo*, to see dimly, see only what is near). A blind person is like a person who squints, who closes his eyes to the spiritual virtues. A nearsighted person is one who looks only at earthly and material values—what is close at hand—and does not see the eternal spiritual realities. This person has lost sight of the distant future and has returned to his former sinful life. It is not possible to sing, "Blessed Assurance, Jesus is Mine," and forget the cleansing from past sins!

Be all the more eager [σπουδαζω *spoudazo*, to exert one's self, endeavor, give diligence] to make your calling and election sure. "Calling and election" refer to one's standing with God and they are stated in the proper order.

One is called (κλησις *klesis*, invited) by God to embrace salvation and one becomes elect or chosen when His invitation is accepted. Once saved, diligence and effort must follow by adding Peter's seven characteristics to faith (1:5-7); otherwise, a person will fall (πατιω *patio*, stumble, trip)— become blind and nearsighted. Some think Peter is not talking about salvation, but failure in Christian living; however, the two go hand in hand. It is contradictory to claim Christ and live according to the corruption that is in the world because of evil desires. Salvation is escaping this corruption (cf. 2 Peter 1:4).

Since doing these things is a rich welcome into the eternal kingdom of our Lord and Savior Jesus Christ, Peter does not hold the doctrine of "the eternal security of the believer." In other words, faith without action is dead (cf. James 2:14-26).

> So then, my dear friends, just as you have always obeyed, not only in my presence, but now even more in my absence, work out your own salvation with fear and trembling (Philippians 2:12 HCSB).

According to 2 Timothy 2:12-13, in order to reign with Christ, we must endure in our faith since Christ must be true to Himself in dealing with people.

> If we endure,
>> we will also reign with him.
> If we disown him,
>> he will also disown us;
> if we are faithless,
>> he will remain faithful,
>> for he cannot disown himself

The Apostle Paul's doctrine is that a believer must remain steadfast in faith.

> But now He has reconciled you by His physical body through His death, to present you holy, faultless, and blameless before Him—if indeed you remain grounded and steadfast in the faith, and are not shifted away from the hope of the gospel that you heard (Colossians 1:22 HCSB).

According to 2 Peter 1:10-11, the believer's actions cause him to stand or be established since "never" is emphatic; he will receive ((επιχορηγεω *epichoregeo*, add, provide, supply) a "rich welcome," which is the climax of living a godly life. Jesus preached that the kingdom of heaven/God was at hand. Peter identified this kingdom as the eternal kingdom of our Lord and Savior Jesus Christ.

The term translated "eternal" (αιωνιος *aionios*) describes duration, either undefined but not endless, as "for long ages" in Romans 16:25 and "before time began" in 2 Timothy 1:9; Titus 1:2; or undefined because endless as "eternal" in Romans 16:26 and most other places in the NT.

What is "the eternal kingdom?" It cannot refer to a place called "heaven" since Peter wrote about the heavens being destroyed and new heavens and a new earth, where the righteous will dwell (2 Peter 3:10-13 HCSB).

The Bible presents the Kingdom as always existing (Psalm 145:13; Jeremiah 10:10); yet in other places it seems to have a definite historical beginning among men (Psalm 10:16; Daniel 2:44). It is universal in its scope, outside of which there is no created thing; yet again the Kingdom is revealed as a local rule established on earth (Psalm 103:19; Isaiah 24:23). Sometimes the Kingdom appears as the rule of God directly, with no intermediary standing between God and man; yet it is also pictured as the rule of God through a mediator who serves as the channel between God and man (Ezekiel 37:21-28). The Kingdom is set forth as an unconditional rule arising out of the sovereign God; yet it sometimes appears as a Kingdom based on a covenant made by God with man (Daniel 4:34-35; Psalm 89:27-29).

Therefore, the Kingdom of God/Heaven is a present reality (Matthew 12:28), and yet future in its blessing (1 Corinthians 15:50). It is an inner spiritual redemptive blessing (Romans 14:17), which can be experienced only through new birth (John 3:3), and yet it will have to do with the government of the nations of the world (Revelation 11:15). The Kingdom is a realm into which men enter now (Matthew 21:31) and yet is a realm into which they will enter tomorrow (Matthew 8:11). It is at the same time a gift of God which will be bestowed by Him in the future (Luke 12:32) and yet which must be received in the present (Mark 10:15). This now/yet tension of the Kingdom is apparent in Luke 17:20-25. The present order in heaven and earth will end.

> Then comes the end, when He hands over the kingdom to God the Father, when He abolishes all rule and all authority and power (1 Corinthians 15:24 HCSB).

Interestingly, Peter is the only NT writer to combine the titles "Lord and Savior" for Jesus Christ (cf. 2 Peter 1:11; 2:20; 3:2, 18). Theologians disagree whether Jesus must be Lord to be Savior of one's life. In verse 1, he called Jesus "God and Savior" to emphasize His divinity and here he emphasizes His twofold position in the believer's life.

THE TESTIMONY OF AN APOSTLE (1:12-18): Peter informed his readers that he will "soon" (ταχινος *tachinos*, shortly, quickly) die, making this letter his last contribution to the expanding and growing church in the Empire. He will not be negligent in reminding his readers of these things, that is what he wrote in verses 3-11. He adds, "even though you know them and are firmly established in the truth you now have." Consequently, he is concerned that they will be led astray by the coming onslaught of false teachers. Therefore, his plan is to refresh their memory as long as he is alive. Though they had a basic knowledge of faith and godliness, the apostle knew the importance of refreshing their memory by rehearsing these truths. He does so pastorally and tactfully.

Like Paul, Peter employed the metaphor of a "tent" for the physical body (2 Corinthians 5:1-8). He referred to Christ's prediction as to the manner and time of his death, which must have been widely known by the church (John 21:18-19).

Peter's ministry lasted about forty years, beginning with Christ in A.D. 29 and ending with his death in A.D. 69. Interestingly, the length of Moses' service for Yahweh God was forty years.

"And I will make every effort to see that after my departure you will always be able to remember these things" probably refers to this letter or Mark's Gospel of the life of Christ.

With the thoughts of death and the glory ahead in his head, he wrote of his experience on the Mount of Transfiguration, where Christ unveiled His glory to James, John and himself (Matthew 17:1-9; Mark 9:2-10; Luke 9:28-36).

> For we did not follow cleverly contrived myths when we made known to you the power and coming of our Lord Jesus Christ; instead, we were eyewitnesses of His majesty. For when He received honor and glory from God the Father, a voice came to Him from the Majestic Glory: This is My beloved Son. I take delight in Him! And we heard this voice when it came from heaven while we were with Him on the holy mountain (2 Peter 1:16-18 HCSB).

Here is internal proof of the authorship of Second Peter. The writer of this letter witnessed the transfiguration of Christ and heard the voice of God the Father—James is dead and it is not John's style; that leaves Peter as the writer. Otherwise, this letter is not inspired by the Holy Spirit and it is not Scripture for the writer would be a liar.

225

Peter changed the pronouns from the singular to the plural, indicating he shared this experience with the apostles James and John. He utilized this experience to combat the false prophets and false teachers among the people, who denied Christ.

The apostles' testimony as eyewitness of Christ's majesty, honor and glory is reliable—what they saw and heard! The revelation they received from God on the mountain made it holy. God the Father's voice gave honor to His Son, and glory shone as light from Christ's being. Hence, Peter was able to certify "the power and coming of our Lord Jesus Christ," which undergirds all of his sermons, speeches and writings.

THE AUTHORITY OF SCRIPTURE (1:19-21): Clearly, Peter was more impressed by what he heard on the sacred mountain than what he saw, which goes along with his next declaration. Not only is the truth established by the eyewitnesses of the apostles, it is also established by prophetic Scriptures.

> And we have the word of the prophets made more certain, and you will do well to pay attention to it, as to a light shining in a dark place, until the day dawns and the morning star rises in your hearts. Above all, you must understand that no prophecy of Scripture came about by the prophet's own interpretation. For prophecy never had its origin in the will of man, but men spoke from God as they were carried along by the Holy Spirit (2 Peter 1:19-21).

God the Father's voice and the Son's transfiguration confirmed the Messianic prophecies and made clear the deity of Jesus Christ as God's Beloved Son. Others take Peter to mean that the word of prophecy is a more sure confirmation of Christ's deity than the Transfiguration.

Peter ranks the prophetic word over experience by giving emphasis to the prophetic word:

Its trustworthiness:	It is the certain Word
Its Illumination:	It is the shining Word
Its Inspiration:	It is the Spirit-given Word

226

Thus, Peter ranks Scripture over the greatest experience one might have since Peter proved his points from the prophetic Scriptures and the word order in the Greek text supports this view.

Only Christ's inner circle experienced this magnificent event, but all have available the word of the prophets made certain. Henceforth, every experience is to be tested against the Word of God. Over the centuries, many false doctrines have arisen in the Church as a result of so-called spiritual experiences. If the experience does not align with the Scriptures, it is to be rejected, and even if it does, wisdom and discernment must be applied to determine its worth.

In the truest sense, all writers of the OT were prophets, speaking forth the word of God as well as predicting the future. Therefore, "the word of the prophets" refers to the entire OT, not just the Major and Minor Prophets. If there is anything on earth that is certain, it is the Word of God.

> For I assure you: Until heaven and earth pass away, not the smallest letter or one stroke of a letter will pass from the law until all things are accomplished (Matthew 5:18 HCSB).

> The instruction of the LORD is perfect, reviving the soul; the testimony of the LORD is trustworthy, making the inexperienced wise (Psalms 19:7 HCSB).

> LORD, Your testimonies are completely reliable; holiness is the beauty of Your house for all the days to come (Psalms 93:5 HCSB).

> The works of His hands are truth and justice; all His instructions are trustworthy (Psalms 111:7 HCSB).

> Sanctify them by the truth; Your word is truth (John 17:17 HCSB).

It has been said, "The world grows darker, but the prophetic light shines brighter" (Warren Wiersbe, *Be Alert*, 35). The place it is shines the brightest is in the human heart. Prior to describing the nature of the prophetic word, Peter employed a type—"the Morning Star."

The Morning Star

Jesus revealed His glory to Peter, James and John on the Mount of Transfiguration when "His face shone like the sun, and his clothes became as white as light" (Matthew 17:2). Consequently, Peter applied the Transfiguration of Christ to salvation (1 Peter 2:9; 2 Peter 1:16-21; cf. 2 Corinthians 4:4-6). Christ's transfiguration is also noticeable in John's theology of light and glory (John 1:9, 14; 1 John 1:5-10; 2:7-11).

The first prophetic revelation of "the Star" was made by Balaam, Yahweh God's prophet, who later sold out for a profit.

> The oracle of one who hears the sayings of God and has knowledge from the Most High, who sees a vision from the Almighty, who falls into a trance with his eyes uncovered: I see him, but not now; I perceive him, but not near. A star will come from Jacob, and a scepter will arise from Israel. He will smash the forehead of Moab and strike down all the Shethites (Numbers 24:16-17 HCSB).

This prediction delivered by Balaam appeared to be fulfilled during the reign of King David, who crushed the nations of Moab and Edom (2 Samuel 8:2, 14). However, it looked beyond David to the Messiah.

The theme of Balaam's prophecy is that Israel has a coming deliverer. The early church and early Judaism believed that Balaam's prediction speaks unmistakably of the coming of the Messiah. The setting for the text is "in days to come" (24:14), indicating the last days.

"Star" (כּוֹכָב kowkab) denotes the coming Messiah's glory and brightness, while "scepter" denotes His power and authority. His crushing the foreheads and skulls denotes that Christ shall be King, not only of Jacob and Israel, but also of the entire world. Ultimately, this prophecy concerns the end days, when Christ will be victorious over the enemies of God's people and He reigns during the Millennial Kingdom.

> I, Jesus, have sent My angel to attest these things to you for the churches. I am the Root and the Offspring of David, the Bright Morning Star (Revelation 22:16 HCSB).

228

The Bright and Morning Star means that for the Christian, Jesus is the comforting light in a dark world until the dawn of His return (Revelation 2:28).

The Bright and Morning Star appears in the sky before the sun rises. Christ will first come to the church as the Bright and Morning Star at the Rapture. Afterwards, He will come to reign over the world when it is the darkest upon the earth—following the seven years of Tribulation. When Jesus comes, He will be the brightest star who will shatter the darkness of man's night and herald the dawn of His glorious reign.

> But for you who fear My name, the sun of righteousness will rise with healing in its wings, and you will go out and playfully jump like calves from the stall (Malachi 4:2 HCSB).

Malachi might be referring to both advents of the Messiah since the early church connected the star the Magi saw in the east as signifying the birth of the Messiah.

> After Jesus was born in Bethlehem of Judea in the days of King Herod, wise men from the east arrived unexpectedly in Jerusalem, saying, "Where is He who has been born King of the Jews? For we saw His star in the east and have come to worship Him" (Matthew 2:1-2 HCSB).

> To give his people the knowledge of salvation through the forgiveness of their sins, because of the tender mercy of our God, by which the rising sun [ανατολη *anatole*, "star"] will come to us from heaven to shine on those living in darkness and in the shadow of death, to guide our feet into the path of peace (Luke 1:77-79).

During His earthly ministry, Jesus had said, "I am the light of the world; he who follows me will not walk in darkness, but will have the light of life" (John 8:12). When the Risen Christ said that He is the morning star, He claimed again to be the light of the world and the vanquisher of the world's darkness.

Thus, Peter gave one of the most wonderful descriptions of salvation based on the prophetic word.

And you will do well to pay attention to it, as to a light shining in a dark place, until the day dawns and the morning star rises in your hearts (2 Peter 1:19b).

"The dark place" is the depraved human heart; "until the day dawns" is salvation; and "the morning star rises in your hearts" is the darkness displaced by the Light of the World—Jesus!

The Nature of Scripture

In the NT, the term "Scripture" refers to the Old Testament books. Peter wants his readers to understand that Scripture is not simply the product of the human mind.

Above all, you must understand that no prophecy of Scripture came about by the prophet's own interpretation. For prophecy never had its origin in the will of man, but men spoke from God as they were carried along by the Holy Spirit (2 Peter 1:20-21).

Επιλυσις (*epilusis*, loosening, unloosing) is a metaphor for "interpretation," which conveys the idea that no prophet "untied' or "loosed" the truth; it originated from God.

Peter's point is not so much about how to interpret Scripture, but rather Scripture originated not in the will of men, but from the prophets who were carried along (φερω *phero*, moved, brought forth) by the Holy Spirit as they spoke. Theologically, this is called the inspiration of the Scripture, which Paul described also.

All Scripture is God-breathed and is useful for teaching, rebuking, correcting and training in righteousness, so that the man of God may be thoroughly equipped for every good work (2 Timothy 3:16-17).

There are seven major views on the writing of Scripture, including the New Testament:

1. NATURAL: There is nothing supernatural about the Bible, the writers wrote from their own insight.

2. CONCEPTUAL: The concepts or ideas of the biblical writers are inspired but not the words of Scripture.

3. DYNAMIC: The Holy Spirit motivated the writers of Scripture, but they had freedom in writing, allowing for the possibility of errors.

4. PARTIAL: Parts of the Bible are inspired, but not necessarily all the Bible. Revelatory matters pertaining to faith and practice are inspired, but non-revelatory matters such as history and science may be in error.

5. DICTATED: The Holy Spirit used humans as secretaries to whom He dictated the words of Scripture.

6. SUPERINTENDED: The Holy Spirit superintended the writers of Scriptures so that they produced the written word of God using their own styles and personalities.

7. VERBAL PLENARY: The inspiration of Scripture extends to the actual words (verbal) and to every part of the entire (plenary) Bible; hence, the Scriptures are inerrant.

In one way or another, views one through four deny the Bible is the Word of God. This writer believes the combined *superintended* and *verbal plenary* views express the inspiration of Scripture and give an accurate view of what Peter and Paul are saying. In a number of instances, portions of the OT were dictated word for word by Yahweh God to it writers.

To Combat False Teachers (2:1-22)

The first eighteen verses of chapter two parallel the letter of Jude, denouncing and describing false prophets; referring to Israel's righteousness; mentioning of fallen angels, Sodom and Gomorrah, and denouncing Balaam's apostasy. The most obvious parallels between Second Peter and Jude are:

| 2 Peter 1:2 | Jude 2 | 2 Peter 2:11 | Jude 9 |
| 2 Peter 2:1 | Jude 4 | 2 Peter 2:12 | Jude 10 |

2 Peter 1:12	Jude 5	2 Peter 2:13	Jude 12
2 Peter 2:4, 9	Jude 6	2 Peter 2:17	Jude 13
2 Peter 2:6, 10	Jude 7	2 Peter 3:2	Jude 17
2 Peter 2:10	Jude 8	2 Peter 3:3	Jude 18

THEIR METHODS (2:1-3a): History is repeating itself in the Church as it did in the nation of Israel; false prophets and false teachers are dangerous to the spiritual well-being of God's people. A false teacher distorts the Word of God by maligning the way of truth and denying Christ. A false prophet claimed to speak for God, but actually spoke for himself or Satan.

In actuality, there are not true prophets today. When the Apostle John died around A.D. 100, God's prophets ceased with the Bible being completed and with the foundation of the church laid on Christ.

> So then you are no longer foreigners and strangers, but fellow citizens with the saints, and members of God's household, built on the foundation of the apostles and prophets, with Christ Jesus Himself as the cornerstone. The whole building is being fitted together in Him and is growing into a holy sanctuary in the Lord, in whom you also are being built together for God's dwelling in the Spirit (Ephesians 2:19-22 HCSB).

Therefore, anyone who claims to be a prophet of God is a deceiver and false teacher.

Peter described seven negative characteristics of the false teachers in the first three verses:

1. They will secretly introduce destructive heresies.
2. They even deny the sovereign Lord who bought them.
3. They are bringing swift destruction on themselves.
4. They lead others to follow their shameful (lascivious) ways.
5. They bring the way of truth into disrepute.
6. They are greedy.
7. They exploit with stories they have made up.

232

Clearly, the false teachers were not Gnostics since they would never attack "conceived myths" for they had too many of their own. The false teachers Peter describes are in the church as the false prophets were among the people of Israel; they once were saved, but they have apostatized because of greediness.

The churches of the twenty-first century are plagued with false teachers in positions of high authority, who have led others to follow their shameful ways. They continuously bring the way of truth into dispute, resulting in biblical ethics and morality being eroded under their unbridled sensuality and slick-talk. Some postulate the power of positive thinking or a wealth and health gospel. They deny the sovereign lordship of Christ Jesus, not submitting to the rule of Christ in one's life. False teachers permeate some Christian colleges and seminaries, denying the virgin birth, deity, and bodily resurrection and second coming of Christ.

Anyone who succumbs to false teaching is worse off than the false teacher according to Jesus.

> Woe to you, teachers of the law and Pharisees, you hypocrites! You travel over land and sea to win a single convert, and when he becomes one, you make him twice as much a son of hell as you are (Matthew 23:15).

Therefore, it is of upmost importance that every disciple of Christ be a good "Berean."

> Now the Bereans were of more noble character than the Thessalonians, for they received the message with great eagerness and examined the Scriptures every day to see if what Paul said was true (Acts 17:11)

THEIR JUDGMENT (2:3b-13): In his sermons, speeches and writings, Peter pointed to the Judgment Day as he does here. "Their condemnation has long been hanging over them, and their destruction (απωλεια *apoleia*, damnation, perdition) has not been sleeping." In this letter, Peter speaks of final damnation six times (2:1–3; 3:7, 16). Those who make a virtue out of the toleration of unscriptural teachings and ideas in the name of love and unity deserve damnation (see 2 Thessalonians 3:14; 1 Timothy 4:1–5; Titus

233

3:9–11).

We live in an age of tolerance—if you don't tolerate error, you're not loving! Today, everyone and everything is tolerated but Christians and truth.

The world denies the existence of God, or if God once existed, He is dead, or He does not intervene is human affairs, or He is asleep. They are dead wrong according to Peter. "Has not been sleeping" refers to final judgment—God does not slumber or sleep (Psalm 121:4). In other words, their damnation is certain. The world mocks and scoffs at the gospel of Jesus Christ because people do not follow faithfully the Lord they claim and when they do, the world hates them.

The parallel passage for the first three verses by Jude reads:

> For certain men, who were designated for this judgment long ago, have come in by stealth; they are ungodly, turning the grace of our God into promiscuity and denying our only Master and Lord, Jesus Christ (Jude 1:4 HCSB).

In one long sentence, Peter uses three examples of God's judgment from the book of Genesis. God's judgment was disputed by the false teachers, and even possibly his three examples of what happens to the ungodly in 2 Peter 2:4-6:

1. Angels thrown into dark Tartarus and chained until judgment
2. Ancient world of Noah that perished
3. Cities of Sodom and Gomorrah reduced to ashes

In 2 Peter 2:7-10, Peter has good news for God rescues the righteous as He did with Lot but bad news for the unrighteous whom He will judge.

Jude employed two of Peter's examples, angels and Sodom and Gomorrah, but he began with a different example.

> Now I want to remind you, though you know all these things: the Lord, having first of all saved a people out of Egypt, later destroyed those who

did not believe (Jude 1:5 HCSB).

Who are the angels who sinned, who did not keep their own position but deserted their proper dwelling? One of the most prominent themes of ancient Jewish tradition was the idea that the "sons of God" in Genesis 6:1-3 were fallen angels who mated with women, corrupting the human race. If so, this was Satan's attempt to stop the birth of the woman's seed—the Messiah—who would crush his head (Genesis 3:15).

"Tartarus" is not a place for holding the unrighteous dead, which is Sheol/Hades, but a place where fallen angels are imprisoned until the final judgment, when they will be cast into Hell. The Greek word for "Hell" is γεεννα (*Gehenna*). This was originally the valley of Hinnom, south of Jerusalem, where the filth and dead animals of the city were cast out and burned—it is a fitting symbol of the wicked and their future destruction.

These fallen angels are confined in chains in the gloomy dungeons of Tartarus. Other fallen angels (demons) are confined in the Abyss and will be released during the Tribulation Period, while the remaining demons are still free to plague humankind (cf. Luke 8:30-31; Revelation 9:1-11). If fallen angels are judged, certainly ungodly people will be judged!

Peter's second example is the Flood, which he referred to in his first letter (1 Peter 3:18-22) and does so again in the 2 Peter 3:5-6. The family of eight (Noah, his wife, three sons and three daughters-in law) were protected in the Ark when God wiped out the ungodly antediluvian civilization. Noah was a preacher of righteousness contrary to the false teachers who were coming into the churches.

The third example of Peter is "righteous Lot." Jewish tradition was divided on whether Lot was righteous; most rabbis and some others held that he was not righteous. Genesis seems to portray Lot as personally righteous, but not as wise as Abraham (cf. 13:10-11; 18:25; 19:1-16; 19:29, 32-35). Peter states that Lot was distressed and tormented in his righteous soul by what he saw and heard of the filthy lives of lawless men and their deeds—homosexuality.

Before they went to bed, the men of the city of Sodom, both young and old, the whole population, surrounded the house. They called out to Lot and said, "Where are the men who came to you tonight? Send them out to us so we can have sex with them!" (Genesis 19:4-5 HCSB).

Homosexuality should distress and torment the souls of the church leaders and people embracing it. They need to wake up and recognize that the Lord's judgment is sure—He will hold the unrighteous for the Day of Judgment, while continuing their punishment, which refers to torment in Hades. He adds, "This is especially true of those who follow the corrupt desire of the sinful nature and despise authority."

Peter's good news is "the Lord knows how to rescue the godly from trials"—as shown with Noah's family and Lot.

Peter is not finished with the apostate false teachers.

1. They are bold, arrogant people.
2. They do not tremble when they blaspheme the glorious ones.
3. They are like irrational animals—creatures of instinct born to be caught and destroyed.
4. They speak blasphemies about things they do not understand.
5. They are unrighteousness.
6. They consider it a pleasure to carouse (τρυφη *truphe*, luxurious, sensual living) in the daytime.
7. They are blots and blemishes, delighting in their deceptions as they feast with you.

Peter points out that the apostate false teachers are presumptuous self-willed men, who build themselves up while tearing others down. They disparage godly angels but the angels do not dare to belittle them. They lack knowledge, but speak as though they know what they are talking about while delighting in their deceptions. They are in the church—"feasting with you," which could refer to "love feasts," "communion," or participation in their sensual living.

THEIR CHARACTER (2:14-22): The believer meets the threat of error by recognizing false teachers and understanding their motives and methods.

Jesus taught in the Sermon on the Mount:

> Beware of false prophets who come to you in sheep's clothing but inwardly are ravaging wolves. You'll recognize them by their fruit. Are grapes gathered from thornbushes or figs from thistles? In the same way, every good tree produces good fruit, but a bad tree produces bad fruit. A good tree can't produce bad fruit; neither can a bad tree produce good fruit. Every tree that doesn't produce good fruit is cut down and thrown into the fire. So you'll recognize them by their fruit (Matthew 7:15-20 HCSB).

False doctrine and sensual living are fruit of these apostates.

Peter sets forth twelve more characteristics of the apostate false teachers:

1. They have eyes full of adultery
2. They never stop sinning
3. They seduce the unstable
4. They are experts in greed—an accursed brood!
5. They have left the straight way
6. They have wandered off to follow the way of Balaam son of Beor, who loved the wages of wickedness.
7. The are springs without water
8. They are mists driven by a storm.
9. They mouth empty, boastful words
10. They appeal to the lustful desires of sinful human nature.
11. They entice people who are just escaping from those who live in error.
12. They promise them freedom, while they themselves are slaves of depravity—for a man is a slave to whatever has mastered him.

Peter employed Balaam, who had been a true prophet of God, as a classic example of an apostate prophet. Israel's infidelity and God's fidelity take center stage in the account of the prophet Balaam (Numbers 22:1-25:5). Balaam knew the true God and was able to predict the future of Israel. He listened to and saw God's Word in four visions, received a revelation from the Holy Spirit, and he faithfully proclaimed the future. Yet for wealth,

237

Balaam turned right around and led Israel into sin and judgment and he died with Israel's enemies (Numbers 31:16).

According to Peter, Balaam was rebuked for his wrongdoing by a donkey—a beast without speech—who spoke with a man's voice and restrained the prophet's madness. In the OT account, Yahweh God told Balaam to go, but He became angry with the prophet. After the encounter with his talking donkey, Balaam was permitted to go and bless the nation of Israel. It appears Peter condensed the account to make a point that the prophet Balaam listened to his donkey, but these apostates are not that smart! Significantly, Yahweh compared apostate Israel to a donkey.

> The ox knows its owner, and the donkey its master's feeding-trough, but Israel does not know; My people do not understand (Isaiah 1:3 HCSB).

The blackest darkness is reserved for apostate false teachers. James, the brother of Jesus, warned, "Not many of you should presume to be teachers, my brothers, because you know that we who teach will be judged more strictly" (James 3:1).

Jesus spoke of darkness, where there will be weeping and gnashing of teeth (Matthew 8:12; 22:13; 23:30). "Blackest darkness" might signify a greater degree of punishment in Hell, especially for those who lead others astray; for Jesus taught concerning His disciples:

> But whoever causes the downfall of one of these little ones who believe in Me—it would be better for him if a heavy millstone were hung around his neck and he were thrown into the sea (Mark 9:42 HCSB; cf. Matthew 18:6; Luke 17:2).

It is easy to see why Peter called them, "Accursed children!" (2:14), which is a Hebraism denoting those who certainly will be destroyed, that is damned, which Peter makes absolutely clear.

> For if, having escaped the world's impurity through the knowledge of our Lord and Savior Jesus Christ, they are again entangled in these things and defeated, the last state is worse for them than the first. For it would have been better for them not to have known the way of

righteousness than, after knowing it, to turn back from the holy commandment delivered to them. It has happened to them according to the true proverb: A dog returns to its own vomit, and, "a sow, after washing itself, wallows in the mud" (2 Peter 2:20-22 HCSB).

It appears the apostle based his point on a third proverb.

In the way of righteousness there is life; along that path is immortality" (Proverbs 12:28).

Reformed commentators tend to hold that these false teachers were never genuinely converted to Christ—that they only had a "head knowledge" of Christ. However, the word "if" (ει *ei*) is a first class condition in the Greek, which indicates an assumed fact; hence, this particle can be translated "since." "For since they have escaped the corruption of the world in full knowledge (εν επιγνωσει) of our Lord and Savior Jesus Christ" is the very thing Peter said of his readers in 2 Peter 1:4.

Words like "escaped," "knowing" "again entangled," "overcome," worse off," "to have known," "not to have known," "turn their backs" indicate the false teachers were once saved, but now are apostate! As a result, "they are worse off at the end than they were at the beginning." This concept probably is taken from Jesus' words in Matthew 12:45 and repeated in one of five warning passages to Christians in the book of Hebrews.

For if we deliberately sin after receiving the knowledge of the truth, there no longer remains a sacrifice for sins, but a terrifying expectation of judgment, and the fury of a fire about to consume the adversaries. If anyone disregards Moses' law, he dies without mercy, based on the testimony of two or three witnesses. How much worse punishment, do you think one will deserve who has trampled on the Son of God, regarded as profane the blood of the covenant by which he was sanctified, and insulted the Spirit of grace? For we know the One who has said, Vengeance belongs to Me, I will repay, and again, The Lord will judge His people. It is a terrifying thing to fall into the hands of the living God! (Hebrews 10:26-31 HCSB).

Peter's assessment of the condition of the teachers and their followers is reminiscent of Hebrews 6:4–6. Upon coming to Jesus Christ, they escaped the corruption of the world but through their false teaching, they are again entangled in the corruption of the world caused by evil desires.

Knowledge without obedience is dangerous. Jesus said of Judas that it would have been better for him not to be born than to have turned from the truth he had known (Matthew 26:24). Knowing Christ and rejecting Him is far worse!

Jesus and the Jews considered dogs and pigs among the lowest of animals (Matthew 7:6), so Peter chose these animals to describe people who have known the truth but have turned away from it. The first proverb is found in Proverbs 26:11; the second is from the Syrian story of Ahikar, known to Peter and his readers.

By vomiting, the dog relieves itself of internal impurities; the sow, when washed, is cleansed from external mud. Nevertheless, both animals return to filth! As a pig enjoys wallowing in the mud, so the apostates take pleasure in revelry and immorality. Thus, the meaning of the proverbs is that these teachers once cleansed internally and externally have returned to their former lifestyle. Peter applied this disastrous outcome from Jesus' teaching.

> When an unclean spirit comes out of a man, it roams through waterless places looking for rest but doesn't find any. Then it says, "I'll go back to my house that I came from." And when it arrives, it finds the house vacant, swept, and put in order. Then off it goes and brings with it seven other spirits more evil than itself, and they enter and settle down there. As a result, that man's last condition is worse than the first. That's how it will also be with this evil generation (Matthew 12:43-45 HCSB).

To Encourage Watchfulness (3:1-17)

The last words from Peter cover what appears to be his favorite subject, and certainly his living hope—the Second Coming of Christ. A famous philosopher said, "Not ignorance, but ignorance of ignorance, is the death of knowledge." Peter disapproves of the willingly ignorant in this chapter for their willing rejection of the truth that Jesus is coming again. He wants his readers to have wholesome thinking so he reminds them God's Word is true (3:1-4), His work is consistent (3:5-7) and His will is merciful (3:8-10). Therefore, they are to be watchful and diligent (3:11-17).

THE PURPOSE OF THE LETTER (3:1-2): For the second time, Peter told his readers that he is writing to remind them of certain things, especially that they know and are established in the truth (2 Peter 1:12). This should be the primary goal of every pastor and teacher of God's Word. It was the commission given to Peter by Christ—to feed His sheep and care for them.

"Dear friends" (αγαπετοι *agapetoi*, beloved, dearly beloved, dear, well loved) is repeated in verse 8, 14, and 17 in this chapter. He also used this term of endearment in 1 Peter 2:11 and 4:12.

"This is now my second letter to you." Does this refer to 1 Peter? Most commentators answer the affirmative, but it could refer to a letter not preserved if the recipients are different from the first letter.

The reminder is for his readers to recognize, accept, and obey only the true word of God as found in the OT (the holy prophets) and in the preaching of the apostles (himself and the others). This is parallel to 1:16–21, demonstrating that there is continuity between the OT Scriptures and the promise and fulfillment themes of the apostolic preaching.

THE SCRIPTURAL ANSWERS (3:3-13): The apostles taught the imminence of the Second Coming of Christ. As time passed, there would be some who first doubted and then an onslaught of scoffing at the whole idea, especially in the last days. The reason for scoffing is attached to "following their own evil desires." Ultimately, this is why Christ is rejected. The Sadducees are perfect examples in Judaism, of people who rejected God's future judgment, so they could "go for the gusto" without fearing a day of reckoning in the future. Diverse philosophies permeated the Roman world of the first century.

Like the Deists of the eighteenth century, Epicureans denied that God acted in the world; they also believed that matter was indestructible and that the universe was infinite. The Stoics believed that fire was eternal and that the universe would periodically be reduced into the primeval fire and that

241

eternity was a cycle of ages.

The idea of matter being created out of preexisting substance comes from the Reconstruction (Gap) Theory, which has been rejected for many reasons by current commentators.

The first century historian Josephus knew of a tradition that spoke of Adam predicting two destructions of the world: "that the world was to be destroyed at one time by the force of fire, and at another time by violence and quantity of water (*Antiquities* 1.2.3.70).

"In the last days" refers to the time from Christ's ascension until "the end times," commencing with the signs of His coming. "The day of the Lord" starts when Christ opens the first seal of the seven-sealed scroll and it continues through the millennial kingdom until the new creation, when Christ turns the kingdom over to God the Father, which inaugurates 'the day of God" (see the chart, *God's Timetable*, to differentiate these periods).

Peter's first reply to the scoffers is that the world we live in has not always existed, and has not proved consistently stable.

What is the doctrine of the last day scoffers? We are bombarded by it today. Creationism and God's judgment are rejected by those who do not have a biblical worldview. Uniformitarianism and evolution are the only doctrines taught in public schools and most secular colleges and universities in the United States. Uniformitarianism is a geological doctrine that existing processes acting in the same manner as at present are sufficient to account for all geological changes—"everything goes on as it has since the beginning of creation." Today, God the Creator is also rejected!

The doctrine of uniformitarianism arose out of the evolutionary theory of Charles Robert Darwin (1809-1882), a British scientist. He laid the foundation of modern evolutionary theory with his concept of the development of all forms of life through the slow-working process of natural selection. His work was a major influence on the life and earth sciences and on modern thought in general. Atheism and the denial of Christ's return are offspring of Darwin.

Darwin was a scoffer trained as a minister in a seminary; he deliberately forgot that long ago by God's word, the heavens existed and that God intervenes in judgment, causing changes on the earth to take place.

"And the earth was formed out of water and by water. By these waters also the world of that time was deluged and destroyed" is deliberately forgotten by uniformitarianism. This assertion by Peter is proved in *The Genesis Flood: The Biblical Record and Its Scientific Implications* (1961) by John C. Whitcomb and Henry M. Morris. This book has been reprinted some thirty times and remains a classic apologetic for Biblical creationism and the universality of the Flood described in the book of Genesis. Of course, there are many other books with additional evidences for the worldwide Flood in Noah's day. Atheistic scientists tend to explain away what they find in the earth's geological formations with catastrophes like a giant meteor striking the earth, an ice age, etc.

Almost certainly, Peter had in mind when he wrote, "the earth was formed out of water and by water"—the dividing of the waters, which produced the dry land by God's spoken word (cf. Genesis 1:6-10).

After the Flood, God promised Noah that He would not destroy the earth by water again (Genesis 9:15), but God through the prophet Isaiah predicted a future fiery destruction and new creation.

> Behold, I will create new heavens and a new earth. The former things will not be remembered, nor will they come to mind (Isaiah 65:17).

> "As the new heavens and the new earth that I make will endure before me," declares the LORD, "so will your name and descendants endure" (Isaiah 66:22).

In 95-96 A.D., a vision of the new creation was revealed to the Apostle John.

> Then I saw a new heaven and a new earth, for the first heaven and the first earth had passed away, and there was no longer any sea. I saw the Holy City, the new Jerusalem, coming down out of heaven from God, prepared as a bride beautifully dressed for her husband (Revelation 21:1-2).

243

Hence, Peter's revelation of a new creation is neither new nor complete, telling his readers: "by the same word the present heavens and earth are reserved for fire, being kept for the day of judgment and destruction of ungodly men" (verse 7). Before describing the destruction in verse 10, he reminds his readers of the way time passes for the Lord and why He delays.

> But do not forget this one thing, dear friends: With the Lord a day is like a thousand years, and a thousand years are like a day. The Lord is not slow in keeping his promise, as some understand slowness. He is patient with you, not wanting [βουλομαι *boulomai*, willing deliberately, purposing, ordaining] anyone to perish, but everyone to come to repentance (2 Peter 3:8-9).

Again, Peter draws from the OT: "For a thousand years in your sight are like a day that has just gone by, or like a watch in the night" (Psalms 90:4). Like the psalmist, he tells us that God understands time much differently from man. From man's viewpoint, Christ's coming seems like a long time away. From God's viewpoint, it will not be long.

The Lord's delay is for the salvation of souls—we might say, "He is filling His house" (cf. Matthew 22:1-14; Romans 11:25). Consequently, this delay does not invalidate Christ's return, which in the Father's perspective has been about two days since His Son returned to heaven. Nevertheless, the Lord's patience will end.

What Peter predicts next is like the OT prophets who were unable to determine the time and circumstances of Christ's sufferings and glory. He appears to have run together the coming of Christ in the air (the Rapture) with the climax of history for this current creation. On the other hand, "But the day of the Lord will come like a thief" might refer to the time of the Battle of Gog and Magog, when fire will come out of heaven and destroy the nations deceived by the Devil (Revelation 20:7-9). Definitely, as a thief in the night comes, the rebels of the last day of the earth will be surprised and overtaken. Whatever the case:

> The heavens will disappear [παρερχομαι *parerchomai*, pass away, perish] with a roar; the elements will be destroyed [λυω *luo*, loosed,

unlossed] by fire, and the earth and everything in it will be laid bare [κατακαιω *katakaio*, burned up, consumed by fire] (2 Peter 3:10b).

Presently, Christ is "sustaining all things by His powerful word and in Him all things hold together" (Hebrews 1:3: Colossians 1:17). When Christ says, "be unloosed" all the elements within the universe will be unloosed as atoms are split and everything will perish by fire and disappear. All Christians should be looking forward to this day and to their new home in the Holy City, the New Jerusalem on the new earth (Revelation 21:1-22:6) and it should make a tremendous difference how we live today.

Since all these things are to be destroyed in this way, it is clear what sort of people you should be in holy conduct and godliness as you wait for and earnestly desire the coming of the day of God, because of which the heavens will be on fire and be dissolved, and the elements will melt with the heat. But based on His promise, we wait for new heavens and a new earth, where righteousness will dwell (2 Peter 3:11-13 HCSB).

"The home of the righteous" is described mostly in symbolic terms in chapters 21-22 of Revelation. The Holy City, the New Jerusalem was the hope of the Patriarchs.

These all died in faith without having received the promises, but they saw them from a distance, greeted them, and confessed that they were foreigners and temporary residents on the earth. Now those who say such things make it clear that they are seeking a homeland. If they had been remembering that land they came from, they would have had opportunity to return. But they now aspire to a better land—a heavenly one. Therefore God is not ashamed to be called their God, for He has prepared a city for them (Hebrews 11:13-16 HCSB).

Jesus encouraged His disciples by telling them of this place.

Your heart must not be troubled. Believe in God; believe also in Me. In My Father's house are many dwelling places; if not, I would have told you. I am going away to prepare a place for you. If I go away and prepare a place for you, I will come back and receive you to Myself, so that where I am you may be also (John 14:1-3 HCSB).

It is clear from Peter and John that only the righteous will occupy the New Heaven and Earth. Because of this hope (assurance) of the future, Christians are motivated to remain faithful, and not to be swayed by false teachers.

> The faith and love that spring from the hope that is stored up for you in heaven and that you have already heard about in the word of truth, the gospel (Colossians 1:5).

In light of Peter's first letter, suffering precedes glory. The Christian may be ridiculed during his lifetime by the scoffers, who malign truth, but the Christian will receive a rich welcome into the eternal kingdom but the scoffers will find the darkest blackness to be their home forever.

THE STABILITY OF EFFORT (3:14-17): Now Peter begins to make his final exhortations to Christians. Though we are escaping the corruption that is in the world because of evil desires, every effort is still necessary to be found spotless and blameless before Him if we are to keep looking forward to the eternal kingdom, the home of the righteous (cf. 1:4-11; 3:14). The idea in the Greek is "strive to be found spotless and blameless before him (or in his presence)."

In the 1950's, the Gospel became distorted by what is called "easy believism." Neither Peter nor Paul taught a Gospel where continuance in holiness is not required.

> But now He has reconciled you by His physical body through His death, to present you holy, faultless, and blameless before Him—if indeed you remain grounded and steadfast in the faith, and are not shifted away from the hope of the gospel that you heard. This gospel has been proclaimed in all creation under heaven, and I, Paul, have become a minister of it (Colossians 1:22-23 HCSB).

"Without blemish and free from accusation" means one is spotless and blameless. The unblemished and spotless Lamb of God took away our sin and we became righteous—positionally (justification) with God and practically (sanctification) in our life.

> God made him who had no sin to be sin for us, so that in him we might

become the righteousness of God (2 Corinthians 5:21).

He was delivered over to death for our sins and was raised to life for our justification (Romans 4:25).

Christ loved the church and gave himself up for her to make her holy, cleansing her by the washing with water through the word, and to present her to himself as a radiant church, without stain or wrinkle or any other blemish, but holy and blameless (Ephesians 5:25-27).

Christ will present His Church before God the Father as holy; therefore, we need to be holy as He is holy.

Ironically, Peter wrote that Paul's letters are hard to understand.

Bear in mind that our Lord's patience means salvation, just as our dear brother Paul also wrote you with the wisdom that God gave him. He writes the same way in all his letters, speaking in them of these matters. His letters contain some things that are hard to understand, which ignorant and unstable people distort, as they do the other Scriptures, to their own destruction (2 Peter 3:15-16).

Paul wrote in the same way in all his letters, speaking of these matters. In other words, Peter and Paul's theology mesh! Possibly, with the exception of Second Timothy, Paul had written all his letters by the time Peter wrote this letter.

Although Peter states that some of Paul's letters contain things hard to understand, they are not impossible to understand. The word of God is infinite, inexhaustible and difficult! In studying it, we must always be willing to give God credit for knowing things that we know through the illumination of the Spirit and for the things that we can never fully fathom.

In their ignorance and instability, the false teachers twisted the difficult things to their own destruction. Note that Peter attributes Paul's letters to God's wisdom—they are divinely inspired Scripture!

Therefore, dear friends, since you already know this, be on your guard so that you may not be carried away by the error of lawless men and fall

247

from your secure position (2 Peter 3:17).

Persevering in Our Secure Position

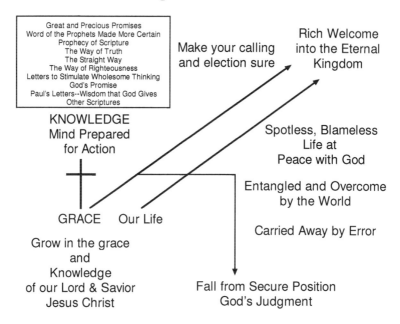

"Carried away (συναπαγω *sunapago*, led away) by error" refers to being led away from truth and salvation, which is to apostatize (cf. 2 Timothy 2:14–18; Titus 1:10–16). The best defense against error is to be grounded in the knowledge of truth. Paul wrote to the Galatians, who were led astray by the Judaizers, who were teaching them they had to be circumcised to be a Christian.

> You who are trying to be justified by law have been alienated from Christ; you have fallen away from grace (Galatians 5:4).

"Fall from your secure position" is a paradoxical statement by Peter. If we have a comprehensive knowledge of Scripture and apply it to our life, we will be secure in Christ.

The following chart illustrates Peter's teaching on perserving in our secure position and securing our rich welcome into the eternal kingdom.

To Encourage Christian Growth (3:18)

But grow in the grace and knowledge of our Lord and Savior Jesus Christ. To him be glory both now and forever! Amen (2 Peter 3:18).

Peter has been building up to his climax:

1. Remember what you know
2. Be mindful of the words spoken by the prophets
3. Be mindful of the commandments of the apostles
4. Be on your guard against false teachers
5. Beware lest you fall from steadfastness
6. Make every effort to be spotless and blameless before Christ
7. Grow in the grace and knowledge of our Lord and Savior Jesus Christ

Grace is the sweet music of the Gospel's salvation message. It is the free gift of God, which cannot be earned and it is not deserved (Ephesians 2:8-9). Grace and wrath flow from God's righteousness because He is holy. Consequently, a few are saved and many are lost.

For God did not send his Son into the world to condemn the world, but to save the world through him. Whoever believes in him is not condemned, but whoever does not believe stands condemned already because he has not believed in the name of God's one and only Son (John 3:17-18).

In Adam, everyone comes into the world standing condemned in sin before God. (Romans 5:12-19). In Christ, the believer stands righteous before God. As a result of Christ's death and resurrection, God the Father imputes and imparts His righteousness by the Holy Spirit to all who believe in His Son for them to be holy before Him.

But when the kindness and love of God our Savior appeared, he saved us, not because of righteous things we had done, but because of his mercy. He saved us through the washing of rebirth and renewal by the

249

Holy Spirit, whom he poured out on us generously through Jesus Christ our Savior, so that, having been justified by his grace, we might become heirs having the hope of eternal life (Titus 3:4-7).

The following chart illustrates salvation by grace and condemnation by rejection of Christ.

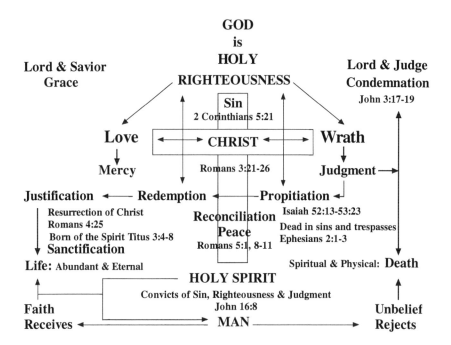

SALVATION

As illustrated by the chart, grace is the gift of God and it can be defined as follows:

God's
Righteousness
At
Christ's
Expense

250

In his first letter, Peter gave the answer to what we should do to grow in knowledge of our Lord and Savior Jesus Christ when he wrote, "Like newborn babies, crave pure spiritual milk, so that by it you may grow up in your salvation" (1 Peter 2:2).

We need to prepare our minds for action. Christian growth does not take place without a prepared mind. We will grow in grace and knowledge when we apply God's Word to our life and obey it. A full knowledge of our Lord and Savior Jesus Christ is critical to our growth and stability.

Grace flows in and through Christ and the more we grow in His grace, the more we should become like Him—and the more we become like Him, the more we grow in Him, and the more His grace flows from our lives to others.

Growth begins in the mind, moves to the heart, and comes out in actions!

Only Peter uses the designation "Our Lord and Savior Jesus Christ" in the NT (2 Peter 1:11; 2:20; 3:18), which shows how precious He had become to this rough, old fisherman who became a shepherd of Christ's sheep and lambs.

The key to the kingdom of heaven had been turned for the last time, there was only one thing left for Simon Peter to write; fittingly, his final words are a doxology:

To him be glory both now and forever! Amen.

Principles of Discipleship

1. Disciples are born, not made.
2. Disciples represent Christ in the world.
3. Disciples reproduce themselves.
4. Disciples carry the burdens of others.
5. Disciples are servants of God and others.
6. Disciples grow in the grace and knowledge of Jesus Christ.
7. Disciples commit to loving and caring relationships.
8. Disciples are committed to the Lordship of Jesus Christ.
9. Disciples renew their minds.
10. Disciples follow commands and precepts of Christ.
11. Disciples are students of the Bible.
12. Disciples help to spread the message of Christ.
13. Disciples are evangelists.
14. Disciples are the light of the world.
15. Disciples are the salt of the earth.
16. Disciples rely on the power of the Holy Spirit.
17. Disciples are guided by the Holy Spirit.
18. Disciples cannot be made with a disciple-maker.
19. Disciples are to baptize people and teach them.
20. Disciples produce disciples.
21. Disciples are learners and followers.
22. Disciples are partners with other disciples in spreading the Gospel.
23. Disciples are devoted to equipping and building the saved.
24. Disciple-making requires a strategy.
25. Disciples cannot be made without the power of the Holy Spirit.
26. Disciple-making is not accomplish through impersonal and non-relational means.
27. Disciple-making is the responsibility of individuals and the church.
28. Disciple-making begins with mass, family or individual evangelism.
29. Disciple-making is not just a way of fulfilling the Great Commission it is the Great Commission.
30. Disciple-makers are fishers of men, not fish!

Gone Fishing

I tried and tried to catch fish all night
I should know how to do this—right?

Oh well, enough for today, I'll try tomorrow
If it gets real bad, I'll just have to borrow

What! Throw my net to the right side and I'll find some
    What do you think I am, dumb?
Well, it won't take long and then I'm done
    Wow! All these fish, what's going on

I've tried and tried to bring people to Christ
    I should know how to do this, right?
Maybe I just need to keep throwing out the net.
    And let the results up to Jesus as to how many I get.

Be a disciple of Christ—a fisher of men!

BIBLIOGRAPHY

Barker, Kenneth L., General Editor. NOTES FROM NET BIBLE FOOTNOTES. Biblical Studies Press L.L.C., 1996-2006.

Barker, William P. EVERYONE IN THE BIBLE. Westwood, New Jersey: Fleming H. Revell Company, 1966.

Barnes, Albert. ALBERT BARNES' NOTES ON THE BIBLE. Albert Barnes (1798-1870).

Browning, Ronald. WHO'S WHO IN THE NEW TESTAMENT. New York: Oxford University Press, 1993.

Bruce, F. F., general editor. THE INTERNATIONAL BIBLE COMMENTARY. Grand Rapids: Zondervan Publishing House, 1986.

Carson, D.A., Douglas J. Moo & Leon Morris. AN INTRODUCTION TO THE NEW TESTAMENT. Grand Rapids: Zondervan, 1992.

Clarke, Adam. ADAM CLARKE'S COMMENTARY ON THE BIBLE. Adam Clarke (1715-1832).

Dehann, M. R. SIMON PETER: SINNER AND SAINT. Grand Rapids: Zondervan Publishing House, 1954.

Elwell, Water A., Editor. EVANGELICAL COMMENTARY OF THE BIBLE. Grand Rapids: Baker Book House, 1995.

Evans, Craig A. JOHN'S GOSPEL, HEBREWS-REVELATION IN THE BIBLE KNOWLEDGE COMMENTARY. Colorado Springs: Cook Communication Ministries, 2005.

Fickett, Harold L., Jr. PETER'S PRINCIPLES. Glendale, California: G/L Publications, 1974.

Gaebelein, Frank E. THE EXPOSITOR'S BIBLE COMMENTARY: JOHN-ACTS. Volume 9. Grand Rapids: Zondervan Publishing House, 1981.

Gaebelein, Frank E. THE EXPOSITOR'S BIBLE COMMENTARY: 1 & 2 PETER. Volume 12. Grand Rapids: Zondervan Publishing House, 1981.

Green, Michael. THE SECOND EPISTLE GENERAL OF PETER AND THE EPISTLE GENERAL OF JUDE. Grand Rapids: Wm. B. Eerdmans Publishing Company, 1968.

Gromacki, Robert C. NEW TESTAMENT SURVEY. Grand Rapids: Baker Book House, 1974.

Heibert, D. Edmond. AN INTRODUCTION TO THE NEW TESTAMENT: THE NON-PAULINE EPISTLES AND REVELATION. Volume 3. Chicago: Moody Press, 1977.

Heibert, D. Edmond. FIRST PETER: AN EXPOSITIONAL COMMENTARY. Chicago: Moody Press, 1984.

Hindson, Edward E., Woodrow Michael Kroll, Editors. KJV BIBLE COMMENTARY. Nashville: Thomas Nelson, Inc. 1994.

Jensen, Irving. JENSEN'S SURVEY OF THE NEW TESTAMENT. Chicago: Moody Press, 1981.

Keener, Craig S. THE IVP BIBLE BACKGROUND COMMENTARY: NEW TESTAMENT. Downers Grove, Illinois: InterVaristy Press, 1993.

Kent, Homer A., Jr. JERUSALEM TO ROME: STUDIES IN ACTS. Winona Lake, Indiana: BMH Books, 1972.

Kistemaker, Simon J. EXPOSITION OF THE EPISTLES OF PETER AND OF THE EPISTLE OF JUDE. Grand Rapids: Baker Book House, 1987.

Lenski, R. C. H. THE INTERPRETATION OF THE ACTS OF THE APOSTLES. Minneapolis: Augsburg Publishing House, 1934.

Lenski, R. C. H. THE INTERPRETATION OF I & II EPISTLES OF PETER, THE THREE EPISTLES OF JOHN AND EPISTLE OF JUDE. Minneapolis: Augsburg Publishing House, 1966.

255

MacArthur, John. THE MACARTHUR BIBLE COMMENTARY. Nashville: Thomas Nelson, Inc., 2005.

Metzger, Bruce M. THE NEW TESTAMENT: ITS BACKGROUND, GROWTH AND CONTENT. Nashville: Abington Press, 1965.

Robertson, Archibald Thomas. WORD PICTURES IN THE NEW TESTAMENT.

Stibbs, Alan M. THE FIRST EPISTLE GENERAL OF PETER. Grand Rapids: Wm. B. Eerdmans Publishing Company, 1959.

Wiersbe, Warren W. BE ALERT. Wheaton, Illinois: SP Publications, 1984.

Wiersbe, Warren W. BE DYNAMIC. Wheaton, Illinois: SP Publications, 1987.

Wiersbe, Warren W. BE HOPEFUL. Wheaton, Illinois: SP Publications, 1982.

Willimington, Harold L. WILLIMINGTON'S BIBLE HANDBOOK. Wheaton, Illionis: Tyndale House Publishers, Inc., 1997.

Wuest, Kenneth S. WUEST'S WORD STUDIES: FIRST PETER IN THE GREEK NEW TESTAMENT. Grand Rapids: Wm. B. Eerdmans Publishing Company, 1942.

ABOUT THE AUTHOR

Robert P. Conway holds a Master of Divinity Degree from Grace Theological Seminary, Winona Lake, Indiana. He has studied on four occasions with Jerusalem University College in the land of Israel and he is a graduate of the York Bible Training Institute.

Bob is an ordained minister in the Church of the United Brethren in Christ. He retired as a senior pastor in 2004.

Before entering into the pastoral ministry for seventeen years, Bob was a vice president in the senior management of a bank's trust division. He graduated from American Institute of Banking, National Graduate Trust School of Northwestern University and was a Certified Financial Services Counselor of the American Bankers Association.

He has been teaching Bible, Theology and Biblical Hebrew for the past eight years at Regent College of the Caribbean, Mandeville, Jamaica WI.

Bob has taught many courses for continuing education credits for pastors, spoken at conferences and taught at various Bible institutes.

Bob and his wife Lois will celebrate their fiftieth wedding anniversary in 2014. They have worked side by side in various ministries, especially enjoying the pastorate along with teaching at youth and children's camps for some forty years.

Bob has been an avid student of the Bible, which he has been teaching for almost fifty years. He has self-published thirty books. Eight of his books can be read online at www.decodingdaniel.com.

Bob's *Decoding Daniel* and *Yahweh God of the Pentateuch: Theological Handbook* are available in paperback books and eBooks at Amazon.com.

Made in the USA
San Bernardino, CA
20 September 2015